Culture and Activism

MW00861574

'In this lovely comparison of French and American animal rights movements, Cherry helps us understand why the French have so resisted vegetarianism, among other differences. She also shows how culture and strategy are deeply entwined, an important lesson for scholars as well as activists.'

James M. Jasper, Graduate Center of the
City University of New York, USA

This book offers a comparison of the animal rights movements in the US and France, drawing on ethnographic and interview material gathered amongst activists in both countries. Investigating the ways in which culture affects the outcomes of the two movements, the author examines its role as a constraining and enabling structure in both contexts, showing how cultural beliefs, values, and practices at the international, national, and organizational levels shape the strategic and tactical choices available to activists, and shedding light on the reasons for which activists make the choices that they do.

With attention to the different emphases placed by the respective movements on ideological purity and pragmatism, this volume provides an account of why their achievements differ in spite of their shared ultimate goals, offering policy recommendations and suggestions for activists working in a variety of cultures. Informed by the work of Giddens and Bourdieu, *Culture and Activism: Animal Rights in France and the United States* constitutes an empirically grounded, comparative study of activism that will appeal to scholars of sociology, anthropology, political science, and cultural geography with interests in social movements and social problems.

Elizabeth Cherry is Associate Professor in the Department of Sociology and Anthropology at Manhattanville College, USA.

Solving Social Problems

Series editor:

Bonnie Berry, Director of the Social Problems Research Group, USA

Solving Social Problems provides a forum for the description and measurement of social problems, with a keen focus on the concrete remedies proposed for their solution. The series takes an international perspective, exploring social problems in various parts of the world, with the central concern being always their possible remedy. As such, work is welcomed on subjects as diverse as environmental damage, terrorism, economic disparities and economic devastation, poverty, inequalities, domestic assaults and sexual abuse, health care, natural disasters, labour inequality, animal abuse, crime, and mental illness and its treatment. In addition to recommending solutions to social problems, the books in this series are theoretically sophisticated, exploring previous discussions of the issues in question, examining other attempts to resolve them, and adopting and discussing methodologies that are commonly used to measure social problems. Proposed solutions may be framed as changes in policy, practice, or more broadly, social change and social movement. Solutions may be reflective of ideology, but are always pragmatic and detailed, explaining the means by which the suggested solutions might be achieved.

Also in the series

Preventing Human Trafficking Education and NGOS in Thailand
Robert W. Spires

Service Sociology and Academic Engagement in Social Problems
Edited by A. Javier Treviño and Karen M. McCormack

Women, Incarceration, and Human Rights Violations
Feminist Criminology and Corrections
Alana Van Gundy and Amy Baumann-Grau

Regulating Alcohol around the World Policy Cocktails
Tiffany Bergin

Culture and Activism

Animal Rights in France and
the United States

Elizabeth Cherry

Routledge
Taylor & Francis Group

LONDON AND NEW YORK

First published 2016
by Routledge
2 Park Square, Milton Park, Abingdon, Oxon OX14 4RN

and by Routledge
711 Third Avenue, New York, NY 10017

First issued in paperback 2018

Routledge is an imprint of the Taylor & Francis Group, an informa business

British Library Cataloguing in Publication Data
A catalogue record for this book is available from the British Library

Library of Congress Cataloging in Publication Data
A catalog record for this book has been requested

ISBN 13: 978-1-138-59547-7 (pbk)
ISBN 13: 978-1-4724-7674-6 (hbk)

Typeset in Times New Roman
by Swales & Willis Ltd, Exeter, Devon, UK

Printed in the United Kingdom
by Henry Ling Limited

Contents

List of Figures   vii
Acknowledgements   viii

PART I
Comparing Movements   **1**

1   Investigating Movement Success   3
2   A History of Animal Rights in France and the United States   12

PART II
Cultural Resources   **25**

3   Environment and Religion   27
4   Health   43
5   Food   58
6   Media and Terrorism   75

PART III
Strategic Choices   **103**

7   American Pragmatism   105
8   French Consistency and Cross-Cultural Choices   123

PART IV
Movement Outcomes 143

9   Explaining Movement Success 145

Appendix: List of Participants 154
References 158
Index 170

Figures

5.1 New food products labeled "vegetarian," "vegan," and
    "no animal products" in France and the United States,
    1990–2014   69
5.2 New food products labeled "vegetarian," "vegan," and
    "no animal products" per 1 million people in France and the
    United States, 1990–2014   69
6.1 Pamela Anderson's vegetarian ad for PETA   79

Acknowledgements

This book grew out of a desire to contribute to academic knowledge on social movements, culture, and human–animal relations, while at the same time contributing to activists' understandings of their own work. This research never would have happened without the participation of all of the activists I met in the United States and in France. I am thankful for their generosity of time and attention to this project, and I am humbled by their dedication to working on behalf of non-human animals. Thank you to the U.S. activists from the Humane Society of the United States, People for the Ethical Treatment of Animals, Vegan Outreach, and Speak Out for Species, and activists in other organizations, who shared their stories with me. Thank you to the French activists from the Collectif Antispéciste de Paris, Association Végétarienne de France, Welfarm, Stop Gavage, the Cahiers Antispécistes, Veggie Pride, Les Estivales de la Question Animale, Animale Amnistie, l'Association Végétarienne & Végétalienne d'InformationS, PETA France, and activists in other organizations, for their time and patience with me. I would especially like to thank Eric Griffith and Wendy Moore from Speak Out for Species for their helpful participation and feedback throughout the project.

Throughout the inception, data collection, analysis, and writing of this project, I was incredibly lucky to have supportive friends and colleagues. At the University of Georgia, I would like to thank David Smilde, Patricia Richards, Linda Grant, and Jim Dowd for their extensive feedback, and Erin Winter-Shirey, Chudamani Basnet, Adam Henne, and Meredith Welch-Devine for their empathy and encouragement. At Manhattanville College, I would like to thank my colleagues for their support, including Patrick Redding, David Gutman, Caralyn Bialo, Meghan Freeman, Beth Williford, Hephzibah Strmic-Pawl, Megan Cifarelli, Lisa Rafanelli, Colin Morris, and Greg Swedberg. I'm also especially thankful to have a wonderful mentor down the road in Lisa Jean Moore. I would like to thank everyone who provided feedback on sections of this book, including Ross Haenfler, Heather Macpherson Parrott, Jeff Larson, and Erin Evans.

Special thanks goes to Michael Ramirez for all of our time laughing in the dog park, and to Heather Macpherson Parrott for her feedback and friendship. My family's support has endured; thank you to Ann, Hank, and Henry Cherry. I definitely would not be here without them. Thank you to Nicolas Marie for all of his help during my fieldwork in France, to Nicolas Trempcourt for his transcription help, and to both of them for their friendship. And of course, thank you to my husband Anthony Saunders for his support for this project and for my wellbeing in completing it. I look forward to many more books together.

Completion of this project was enabled by generous funding from the University of Georgia, Manhattanville College, the French Embassy of the United States, and the Animals and Society Institute. In France, Louis Quéré and Christine Colpin welcomed me to the Centre d'Études des Mouvements Sociaux at the École des Hautes Études en Sciences Sociales, and I am very grateful for the opportunity to spend time there. I would especially like to thank Neil Jordan from Routledge and Bonnie Berry, Director of the Social Problems Research Group, whose feedback helped me immensely in completing this book.

Finally, and more generally, I would like to thank my colleagues in the Animals and Society section of the American Sociological Association and the Animals and Society Institute. It is wonderful to have professional organizations devoted to the study of animals and society, and I look forward to reading more and more books in this area. Onwards!

Part I
Comparing Movements

1 Investigating Movement Success

Animal rights activists oppose animal exploitation in all its forms. Activists fight to end human use of nonhuman animals for food and clothing, in experiments, and as entertainment.[1] Many activists also work to protect wildlife from extinction and from hunters or fishers. The first wave of modern animal rights activism began in Britain in the 1970s and publicized visually disturbing practices, such as medical and cosmetic testing on animals, and the most frivolous uses of animals, such as fur. Similar movements developed in the United States and in France in the late 1970s and early 1980s.

A significant shift in the animal rights movement occurred in the mid-1980s, when activists began turning their efforts to farmed animals, or animals used for food. While activists continued to combat all other forms of animal use and abuse, this shift reflected the fact that farmed animals accounted for the vast majority of animals killed for human purposes. Since the 1960s, farmed animal production has greatly increased: milk production has doubled, meat production has tripled, and egg production has quadrupled (Delgado 2003, Pew Commission on Farm Animal Production 2009). By the 1980s, farmed animals comprised fully 99 percent of all animals killed by humans each year; the other 1 percent includes all animals used for fur or leather, in experiments or entertainment, and in hunting or trapping, as well as those raised as companion animals or euthanized in animal shelters (HSUS 2015). Given this information, most animal rights activists are vegan and heavily promote veganism in their work (Herzog 1993, Gaarder 2011). Vegans avoid animal products and by-products in food, clothing, and other products, and avoid using products tested on animals. They also avoid animal entertainment, such as circuses, rodeos, zoos, or aquariums.

With this shift to the second wave of animal rights activism, which focuses on farmed animals and vegan outreach, the animal rights movement in the United States began to flourish, and the movement in France began to weaken. Some might think this divergence would be obvious, because France's rich culinary history would preclude a movement devoted to promoting vegetarianism and

---

1 For the sake of clarity, throughout the book I use the terms "human" and "animal" to denote "human animals" and "nonhuman animals."

veganism. But food is only one part of the picture, and other aspects of France's history show it to be an ideal country for an animal rights movement. In fact, it is surprising that its animal rights movement has stagnated in such a way.

France was an early adopter of animal protection measures, alongside the United States and the United Kingdom. Societies against cruelty to animals emerged in all three countries around the same time in the mid-nineteenth century. France, like the U.S., experienced a resurgence of interest in animal protection in the 1970s, when activists began to fight to protect wildlife from extinction, and companion animals from mistreatment. The actress Brigitte Bardot, one of the nation's most famous animal activists, founded her own animal protection organization at this time, focusing on companion animals, farmed animals, and wildlife. Now, France is known for its love of animals, and it has the highest rate of pet ownership in the European Union (FEDIAF 2012). The doted-upon dogs of the country can go anywhere and do anything, accompanying their guardians in restaurants and on public transportation, including trains, metros, and even airplanes.

France also has a rich history of political activism, from its Revolution, to its Communes, May 1968, and general strikes. But it is not only political activism that flourishes in France. Other new social movements commonly associated with animal rights have emerged in France in recent years, and they have enjoyed widespread support throughout the country. The environmental movement took off in France in the 1980s and 1990s, especially after Nicolas Hulot hosted an environmental-themed television show from 1987 to 1995 and founded his own environmental organization in 1990. And ever since José Bové rammed his tractor into a McDonald's in the small town of Millau in 2000, the movement to protect small farmers from losing their livelihoods to globalization and big business has thrived. Added to this is a strong anti-GMO movement, where French opposition to genetically modified foods has steadily risen from 46 percent opposition in 1996 to 65 percent opposition in 1999 (Schurman 2004: 255). The Confédération Paysanne, a union of small farmers, continues to lead anti-GMO crusades against *la malbouffe*, or bad food (Heller 2007). It would seem that France is moving away from industrialized agriculture and towards a society that would be more welcoming to animal rights.

The stage is set for a strong animal rights movement in France. They already enjoy the successes of European activists who demanded strong animal protection laws at the European Union level. These laws are even stronger than U.S. animal protection laws. However, despite all of these indicators, the animal rights movement is weak compared to other new social movements in France, and compared to the animal rights movement in the United States. The French government actively opposes these E.U.-wide animal protection laws. They have created laws protecting French *patrimoine culturel* ("cultural heritage"), such as bullfighting and forced-feeding foie gras production, from E.U. legislation. The anti-industrial agriculture movement, which would seem to provide an opening for animal issues, actively promotes animal agriculture and opposes animal rights. Bové, a sheep farmer, prefers his *produits du terroir* (traditional local foods) to tofu, even if the soybeans are not genetically modified. And Hulot, whom one might think would be vegetarian for environmental reasons, continues to eat meat.

Even France's culinary prowess, which some might think would cause French chefs to jump at the opportunity to become a leader in vegetarian foods, causes more problems than solutions for vegetarians in France. When renowned chef Alain Passard changed his restaurant *l'Arpège* to feature mainly vegetable dishes, it was met with great resistance despite the fact that it still served meat. It is still extremely difficult to find vegetarian food in France. In typical French *brasseries*, vegetarian choices are limited to a salad and fries. Finding a strictly vegetarian restaurant is also difficult: There are 2.3 times more vegetarian restaurants and stores per capita in the United States than in France (Happy Cow 2015).

The animal rights movement itself has also lagged behind. It has attracted fewer adherents and constituents than in the U.S., and it has stayed largely at the animal protection phase, rather than moving to emphasize veganism and farmed animal issues as has the U.S. movement. The Société Protectrice des Animaux, the oldest French animal protection organization, founded in 1845, counts 146,000 donors, 21,000 members, 3,000 volunteers, and 600 staff members across the country. The Fondation Brigitte Bardot, the animal protection organization founded in 1986 by the actress, claims 70,000 donors. Thus both members and one-time donors of these largest of the animal protection organizations combined comprise less than 1 percent of the French population. The largest animal rights, welfare, and vegetarian organizations barely touch this, with One Voice's 20,000 members, the 11,000 members of Welfarm (formerly Protection Mondiale des Animaux de Ferme), and the 2,600 adherents of the Association Végétarienne de France.

In the United States, in contrast, animal protection organizations attract much higher memberships. The ASPCA (American Society for Prevention of Cruelty to Animals) claims one million members, and the Humane Society of the United States (HSUS) counts more than 11 million members and constituents, equaling one out of every 28 people, or 3.6 percent of the entire U.S. population. People for the Ethical Treatment of Animals (PETA), the largest animal rights organization in the U.S., also claims to be the largest animal rights organization in the world with more than 3 million members.

Such numeric differences would not matter as much if the French movement led as many successful campaigns as the U.S. movement, but this is not the case. Scholars argue reaching an organization's overall goal to be the highest level of success (Gamson 1990, Einwohner 1999), but no one animal rights organization can claim to have achieved that. Instead, they have achieved concessional change, if not desired change (Einwohner 1999), meaning that institutions change their behavior or fully comply with what protesters want. PETA, for example, convinced over 500 companies, including Gillette, Avon, Revlon, and Estée Lauder, to stop testing their products on animals. HSUS passed a bill in Congress to make dog fighting and cockfighting federal felonies, and banned cockfighting in all 50 states.

Meanwhile, the few French organizations that attempt such legislative or organizational changes see much less success. Their efforts fall at the lower end of the spectrum for success, scarcely achieving what scholars call contact or acknowledgement by their targets (Einwohner 1999). There is little to no direct communication between protesters and their targets, nor do the targets acknowledge protesters as playing a relevant role on the issue. For example, One Voice in France collected 350,000 signatures against testing on dogs and cats, and, according to a One Voice survey, 72 percent of French people oppose testing on dogs and cats. Nonetheless, the Minister of Research dismissed One Voice's claims, and France remains the number one European Union country for testing on dogs (One Voice 2014).

Logical, and normally useful, explanations cannot account for why the animal rights movement is weaker in France than in the United States. France is not opposed to new social movements, in principle—France's environmental, antinuclear, and anti-GMO movements are widely popular and easy to join. France does, however, have a lower participation in such movements. Sociologists Evan Schofer and Marion Fourcade-Gourinchas (2001) consider the U.S. a "nation of joiners" compared to France, since 70 percent of U.S. Americans, in contrast to only 26.5 percent of the French, participate in voluntary associations. This may explain why the animal rights movement is smaller in France as compared to the U.S., but it cannot explain why French participation in animal rights activism lags behind participation in other new social movements or even traditional social movements in France.

The type of activism also cannot explain the differences between the two countries. Both the French and U.S. animal rights activists share similar long-term goals, as well as tactics and strategies to achieve those objectives. Finally, though the French government opposes much animal rights legislation and activism, the situation is not such that it is simply easier to be an activist in the U.S. than in France—the 2006 Animal Enterprise Terrorism Act poses a significant challenge to the U.S. movement.

Part of the reason these explanations cannot account for the variable successes of animal rights in France and the United States is that, as sociologists Douglas McAdam (1994) and Mary Bernstein (2003) note, most studies of movement success discuss political outcomes, and not cultural ones. This problem is compounded by the traditional view of culture as opposed to social and political structures, and as conflated with agency (Archer 1988). As culture, structure, and agency are intertwined, so are culture, strategies, and outcomes. Thus, to understand why the U.S. movement is stronger than the French movement, we must understand the myriad cultural structures in each country as well as their effects on activism and the public reception of activists' claims.

Understanding Social Movement Success

Why has the U.S. movement encountered more success than the French movement? Or more broadly, why do movements with similar goals, tactics, and challenges encounter varying degrees of success? I seek to examine these questions by investigating the relationship between culture, tactics, and strategic decision-making in each country. I investigate how culture affects the tactics available to the movements, as well as how activists choose among those tactics. In doing so, I aim to show which tactics are more or less successful, and under which circumstances different resources are more or less effective.

First, I break down the specific similarities and differences between the French and U.S. movements, with a view towards understanding how culture influences not just political but also cultural opportunities and constraints. Just as culture orients individual people, as sociologist Wendy Griswold (1983) argues, culture shapes the actions of groups—in this case, groups of activists. But how does this occur? My main research question in this section asks how the different contexts in which activists worked affected their options for activism. I seek to explain how the dominant culture in each country shaped the movements' strategic and tactical repertoires. I also examine which cultural opportunities and constraints French and U.S. activists share, and which ones differ. By analyzing a number of cultural resources, I show which arguments resonate in which country, and why. This will show how cultural resources available at the macro level help or hinder the movement in each country.

Then, I examine the strategic and tactical choices of the French and U.S. movements. Having shown which paths may be more or less fruitful for activists to take, I seek to understand how activists actually decide the paths they take. Why do activists make the strategic and tactical choices they do? To answer this question, I take a meso-level approach to understand how social movement organizations make such choices within their social movement field.

These questions have not been adequately addressed not because they are uninteresting to scholars and activists—indeed, activists have been some of the few people to address these issues (Lakey 1992, Stallwood 2002), and sociologists have called for more studies in the area of culture, strategies, and outcomes for decades now (McAdam 1994, Giugni 1998). In addition to the need for more empirical research in this area, this work will also address key theoretical issues in the sociology of culture and social movements.

Culture, Structure, and Agency

I address my research questions by taking a theoretical approach to the relationship between structure and agency informed by practice theory. I follow Pierre Bourdieu (1977) and Anthony Giddens (1984) in recognizing the duality of structure and the agency of individuals and groups in challenging structures, but I favor more contemporary theorists such as Sharon Hays, who critiques the dichotomy of culture and structure, and who argues that culture itself is structured:

> Culture is a social, durable, layered pattern of cognitive and normative systems that are at once material and ideal, objective and subjective, embodied in artifacts and embedded in behavior, passed about in interaction, internalized in personalities, and externalized in institutions. Culture is both the product of human interaction and the producer of certain forms of human interaction. Culture is both constraining and enabling. Culture is a social structure with an underlying logic of its own. (Hays 1994: 65)

Dominant culture typically provides challenges to activists as they work towards their long-term goals. Culture can constrain actors by "blocking out certain possibilities for action" or by "preventing certain arguments from being articulated in public discourse or, once articulated, from being favorably interpreted by others or even understood" (Emirbayer and Goodwin 1994: 1440). But culture can also enable actors "by ordering their understandings of the social world and of themselves, by constructing their identities, goals, and aspirations, and by rendering certain issues significant or salient and others not" (Emirbayer and Goodwin 1994: 1441). Thus at the same time that dominant culture provides roadblocks to activists' work, it also provides building blocks for their arguments (Sewell 1992, Williams 2002, Polletta 2004).

Structures are systems of power, meaning, and norms that are sustained and altered by human agency (Bourdieu 1977, Giddens 1984, Emirbayer and Mische 1998). While structures affect human action, I do not wish to solely place causality on social structures, as cautioned against by Emirbayer (1997). Thus in this book I focus on multiple levels of structure—rather than only looking to external social or cultural structures, I also demonstrate how the culture of a social movement may also act as a structure, and how activists' and groups' actions recreate or challenge these structures.

Not all social movement scholars are moving in this direction when studying culture and social movements. James Jasper (2006a) in particular has critiqued taking such a structural approach. To Jasper, structure misleadingly implies fixed entities. Formulating opportunities as structures makes them seem relatively permanent, rather than constantly or potentially in flux. With his colleague Jeff Goodwin (Goodwin and Jasper 1999), he critiques that most political opportunities would be better analyzed as strategic rather than structural. Other social movement scholars echo this point of view and go further, claiming that agency is the heart of strategy (Ganz 2004).

I consider agency and strategy to be connected, but not coterminous. My approach views strategy as too influenced by culture to be as powerful a concept as agency. But, to Goodwin and Jasper (1999), taking such a structural approach conflates structures and strategies. I believe that taking such a culturalist route runs the risk of conflating culture and agency. By seeing culture as structured and structuring, constraining and enabling, I avoid conflating not only structure and strategy, but also culture, agency, and strategy.

Research Methods

To investigate the animal rights movement in each country, I used in-depth interviews and participant observation. Participant observation allowed me to see the decision-making processes of animal rights activists, as they chose and implemented their strategies and tactics. I learned things that participants might not have wanted to discuss in an interview, and I was able to arrive at a more holistic, comprehensive understanding than I could have through second-hand accounts alone (Patton 2002: 263–264).

My level of participation depended upon the group and the type of event. Rarely was I ever only an observer. More often, I engaged in medium to full participation. Full participation was an option for me since I am a vegan animal rights activist and supporter myself. In each case, I made clear the fact that I was conducting my research on the animal rights movement. With Speak out for Species (SOS), the group with which I worked the most in the United States, I was clearly a full participant. I volunteered with the group before beginning my research, and was invited to join their Leadership Council shortly after my project began. I attended meetings and events, and often moderated film showings and guest lectures. I probably would have done the same even if I were not conducting research on the animal rights movement—especially since I was one of the few members who actually liked public speaking.

In France, I was welcomed by every group with whom I worked, and I attended meetings and participated in group actions. As I was in each town for only three to four months at a time, I did not have the opportunity to develop a specific role in each group. I began working with each group at a moderate participation level, which often developed into full participation shortly thereafter. That is, with each group, I attended public events as an activist. But with only about half of them did I move on to also attend meetings and participate in the planning of future events.

The U.S. fieldwork included participant observation over a two-year period, primarily with SOS, a student-run grassroots organization in Athens, Georgia. I also conducted participant observation for ten months in France. I spent four months in Paris, working with the Collectif Antispéciste de Paris, the Association Végétarienne de France, and International Campaigns. In Lyon, where I spent three months, I worked with an autonomous collective of antispeciesist activists, as well as Le Glaive. I also spent three months in Toulouse, where I worked with AVIS (l'Association Végétarienne & Végétalienne d'InformationS) and Animale Amnistie. Such participation was invaluable to this project, especially as concerns the planning and execution of events. In social movement studies there is a lack of participant observation at the planning level, which is just one of the causes of the dearth of studies on strategy in social movements.

All of this is not to say that interviewing was not important. Interviews still constituted the majority of my data, as I did not have the opportunity to observe all of the participants at tabling events, protests, or other events that lend themselves to observation. Interviews benefited this project in that they allowed me to access a broader range of animal rights activists, and they allowed participants to reflect upon the ways in which they created and implemented various strategies in their activism. As a complement to seeing what they do in their activism through observation, interviewing allowed me to "enter into the other person's perspective" (Patton 2002: 341).

I conducted a total of 72 formal, in-depth interviews, including 35 with U.S. activists from ten different organizations, and 37 with French activists from 13 organizations. The Appendix includes tables of all participants and their organizational affiliations. I used the same interview guide in both countries, making moderate adjustments as necessitated by the progress of my fieldwork. The interviews ranged from one to four hours in length. I conducted and transcribed all of the French interviews in French, with the exception of those with four native English speakers. All translations are my own. Activists could choose between public or confidential participation.

Finally, I analyzed existing artifacts from the movement in both countries. These included documents created by activists as well as artifacts created outside the movement. Activist-generated documents included flyers, films, websites, and even t-shirts, buttons, and other such materials. Documents created outside the movement largely included newspaper accounts of animal rights activism, or televised reports or debates on animal rights. These documents helped to provide a background of the milieu within which these movements exist, and served as artifacts of the movements' relations in that culture.

I analyzed the transcribed interviews and field notes with the qualitative analysis software program ATLAS.ti, using Ragin's (1987) comparative method. This comparative method was necessary for such an approach because this was a case-oriented study, best suited for addressing particular historical outcomes. Case-oriented methods are holistic, treating cases as whole entities, and understanding the relations between the parts within the context of the whole. I maintained such attention to the whole of each case by analyzing how each social movement worked within the extant culture of the country, as well as how each social movement organization functioned together within the larger social movement field. Once I understood each part of the French and U.S. social movements as a whole, I then made comparisons between the two movements. Using this analytic method also helped me explicate the macro–micro link, one often ignored in international comparative research, where macro-level investigations predominate. If international comparative research privileges the macro, ethnographies are charged with being too micro-oriented and ahistorical (Burawoy 2000). Thus I examined how the cultural logics of each social movement shaped activists' choices.

Overview of the Book

Following a historical overview of animal rights in France and the United States in Chapter 2, this book's argument follows my theoretical perspective from the macro-level to the meso-level. In the section called Cultural Resources I examine the extant culture—the cultural structures in France and the United States—to see how the cultural context affects activists' strategic and tactical options. Chapters 3, 4, 5, and 6 investigate how cultural resources found in the extant culture of both countries variably act as opportunities or constraints, in ways that largely benefit the U.S. movement. Both movements capitalized upon the increased attention to environmental issues. Additionally, U.S. animal rights activists advanced their objectives with claims about health, religion, and food through the use of celebrities and the media. These cultural resources lacked legitimacy in France and effectively worked against the French movement. However, movement opponents in the U.S. successfully painted a portrait of animal rights activists as terrorists, forming a cultural belief that hurt the U.S. movement. French activists were able to use such images to recruit young militant activists, though, making terrorism a cultural tool that worked in their favor. By placing social movements in their cultural contexts, this work demonstrates the duality of culture in constraining and enabling different strategic and tactical repertoires, as well as the variability of cultural resources.

While this approach shows which paths may be more (or less) fruitful for activists to take, it does not explain *why* activists make the strategic and tactical choices they do. I do this in the section called Strategic Choices, in which I investigate how individuals and groups create and choose the activities they implement in their activism. I argue that rather than an individual- or societal-level analysis, we need to use a meso-level analysis to understand how social movement organizations (SMOs) make such choices within a social movement field. I show how the animal rights movements in each country developed different institutional logics that they used to guide their strategic and tactical decisions.

Within Part 2: Strategic Choices, Chapter 7 explores theories of strategic decision-making and the U.S. movement's institutional logic of pragmatism. Chapter 8 explains the French movement's institutional logic of consistency. These respective logics meant that French activists did not always choose strategies or tactics that would help them successfully attain short-term goals. U.S. activists, in contrast, sacrificed philosophical consistency in order to win small, achievable goals. Combining organizational, cultural, and social movement theory, I show how and why these different logics developed in different countries within the same broad social movement.

In the final section, called Movement Outcomes, Chapter 9 explains my two particular cases and my broader theory of movement success. While activists in both countries shared long-term goals of total animal liberation, those goals are precisely that—long-term. In the shorter term, the dominant culture in each country affected the cultural resources available to activists, thus expanding the strategic and tactical repertoire of the U.S. movement, while contracting that of the French movement. Given these varying repertoires, U.S. activists chose from within them based upon a logic of pragmatism and practicality, which favored success over ideological consistency. In France, activists chose their strategies and tactics based upon a logic of consistency, favoring ideological purity over short-term practicality. Threaded together with the concept of repertoires, or toolkits, all of these aspects explain the differential success of the U.S. movement in comparison to the French movement.

2 A History of Animal Rights in France and the United States

The contemporary French and U.S. animal rights movements I investigate in this book owe their existence to the animal protection and vegetarian movements that emerged in both countries in the nineteenth century. In fact, their histories are virtually identical up to the very recent present. In the 1980s, the U.S. movement shifted to focus on factory farming and veganism. In the 1990s, a much smaller shift occurred in France, but to a large extent the French movement continues to focus its efforts on companion animal protection.

Modernity and Animal Protection

With the Industrial Revolution and the move towards Modernity, the bourgeoisie underwent a "civilizing process" (Elias 1978). Previously common practices towards animals were not considered to be social problems until this period of modernization. In the growing cities, the newly emerging sensibilities of the bourgeoisie clashed with those of the working classes, especially concerning the treatment of animals. Cruelty towards animals pervaded pre-industrial France and the United States. In France, in addition to the vilified cart-horse drivers who mercilessly lashed their horses, there was widespread institutionalized violence, especially in regional spectacle-games: cockfighting in the north, bullfighting in the south, and bull-baiting in Paris. The United States also saw such mistreatment by cart-horse drivers, and specialized in cockfights and bull-baiting—a practice in which humans pitted bulls and dogs against each other in fights, from which the bulldog got his name.

The slaughter of farmed animals took place in the streets of Paris until 1810, when the government and animal protectionists created abattoirs (slaughter-houses) to house this practice. The government wanted to create abattoirs out of concern for public safety, to guard against animals escaping and harming passersby. Animal protectionists interested themselves in the abattoir system as well because, although they were not vegetarian, they wanted the animals to die without suffering unnecessarily (Agulhon 1981: 85). The animal protection movements in both countries thus grew out of this social space for a number of reasons.

First, companion animals became the doted-upon "pets" we know today when they became popular among the middle and upper classes of the nineteenth century.

During this time, people favored dogs because they saw dogs as loyal. Cats were considered too independent, favored only by intellectuals and artists until the twentieth century, when they surpassed dogs to become the most popular pet. This increased affection for pets extended to other domestic animals such as horses, and the well-to-do who witnessed the daily beatings of cart horses in the city streets demanded such animals be protected from unnecessary cruelty.

Second, the rise of modern medicine, and especially the practice of vivisection, created another dilemma for pet lovers. Vivisection literally means the cutting open of live animals, and this description was not far from the truth as concerns these medical experiments. That beloved dogs were the animal most commonly used in vivisection only exacerbated the problem for animal protection advocates. While some protectionists believed vivisection was necessary for the advancement of medicine, others called for an all-out abolition of animal experimentation, a debate that continues today.

Third, and finally, as the rich grew richer during industrialization, there was an increasing call in both countries for them to work towards the betterment of society. French countesses, for example, underwrote many of France's first animal protection organizations. After a January 1866 *The New York Times* editorial called on the wealthy and idle to form societies for the prevention of cruelty, many of the upper class joined the animal protection movement (Finsen and Finsen 1994: 45). This betterment of society often meant "protection" in a broad sense, and the same women who worked to end child labor in both countries also began to work to protect animals from cruelty. Women comprised the majority of anticruelty activists, though it was men who often founded and ran most of the organizations. These myriad aspects of the industrialization of the nineteenth century all worked together to set the stage for the burgeoning animal protection movement.

Humane societies began cropping up in the United States in the mid-nineteenth century. Several anticruelty societies were formed after Henry Bergh, who spent time in London with the RSPCA (Royal Society for the Prevention of Cruelty to Animals), returned to the States to form the ASPCA (American Society for the Prevention of Cruelty to Animals) in 1866. Anticruelty advocates joined the fight against vivisection, especially after Caroline Earle White founded AAVS (American Anti-Vivisection Society) in 1883.

The abolitionist stance taken by many antivivisectionists engendered a backlash from opponents and other protectionists alike. The U.S. antivivisection movement faced legislative defeats after attacks from the biomedical community, and it was disowned by the more conservative "humane movement" (Finsen and Finsen 1994: 50). An international conference of humane organizations met in 1900 and formally expelled all antivivisectionist organizations. Similarly, after Bergh's death in 1888, the ASPCA became more conservative, halting its legislative battles to instead focus on taking care of stray dogs and cats. This humane movement withdrew from the fight against institutionalized cruelties in farming, vivisection, and the exploitation of wildlife. Both the ASPCA and the American Humane Association—which had originally been formed in order to deal with the cruelty involved in livestock transport—attracted support from rich and powerful patrons, which tended to thwart criticism of such institutionalized cruelty (Finsen and Finsen 1994: 51).

After World War II the institutionalized exploitation of animals increased in the U.S. because of the vast expansion of animal research and the advent of factory farming. These abuses were hidden from the public, and the humane societies also took little notice. The ASPCA even cooperated in the sale of pound animals to research laboratories in the 1950s (Finsen and Finsen 1994: 53). In response, activists created new animal protection organizations that saw more significant legislative changes than in the past.

In 1954, the Humane Society of the United States (HSUS) was founded, then called the National Humane Society. HSUS wanted to expand the humane movement beyond a local scope, attacking cruelty at the national and regional level (Unti 2004). Four years later, in 1958, Congress passed the Humane Methods of Slaughter Act, which decreed that livestock be slaughtered in a humane manner, without unnecessary suffering. Author and animal advocate Cleveland Amory founded the Fund for Animals in 1967, which launched campaigns against hunting and trapping, and which encouraged a revitalization of the ASPCA in New York. For all this renewal, the animal protection movement had not yet gelled into the contemporary animal rights movement. This sea change would occur in the 1970s.

The first major animal protection association in France emerged from this same modernizing period characterized by intense and institutionalized animal cruelty. In fact, Étienne Pariset founded the SPA (Société Protectrice des Animaux) fully 20 years before Bergh founded the ASPCA. These French activists promoted animal protection by engaging a narrative of modernity (Kete 1994). Using an economic argument, protectionists claimed that horses were a form of capital, and that their mistreatment and massacre was a waste. Treating horses better, they argued, would make them work more and worth more.

They also cited a concern for public health. The veal calves brought to Paris from Normandy were transported in horrible conditions, tied up with dozens of other calves without water or food, and thus protectionists argued that they could catch illnesses and produce tainted meat. Finally, there was a concern for the moral pedagogy of the public. Protectionists claimed these barbaric practices would offend a decent public, and that witnessing all of the violence toward animals would incite humans to violence. French historian Maurice Agulhon (1981: 85) described how animal protectionists proposed their first anticruelty law. They cited the story of a young boy who was so affected by seeing the slaughter of pigs in the streets of Paris that he decided to play a game, took a knife, and used his sister in the place of the pig.

Thus a paradox of modernity was created. While the civilizing process created anticruelty values, new techniques in science and medicine were more cruel than ever. If the cart-horse drivers with their vicious lashings epitomized animal cruelty in the early nineteenth century, the vivisector became the primary offender of the late nineteenth century. Historian Kathleen Kete (1994) argues that vivisectors became an even bigger threat to bourgeois values, as they represented modernity, unlike the cart-horse driver. Dogs were the favored animals of vivisectors, as they were cheap, docile, and easily obtained. This galvanized the SPA against this unnecessary use of dogs in experiments. However, in 1860, when the SPA organized a group to examine vivisection, they ruled in favor of the practice, so long as the vivisection was absolutely necessary (Kete 1994). The humanists of the time, as anticruelty as they were, did not oppose vivisection because they saw it as indispensable for the progression of science (Agulhon 1981).

Claude Bernard, the father of vivisection, felt this tension concerning cruelty to animals in his own family. His wife loved dogs and cats, and gave her annual dues to the SPA (Agulhon 1981). (They later divorced.) His daughter also set up animal shelters, a practice popular in the 1880s among women protectionists. In the 1880s as well, antivivisectionist societies were fashionable, as the Société Française contre la Vivisection was founded in 1882 with support from the Comtesse de Noailles (Kete 1994).

A turning point concerning early animal protection efforts came in the mid-nineteenth century, with La Loi Grammont (the Grammont Law). Jacques-Philippe Demas de Grammont was elected representative to the National Assembly in 1849. A former cavalry officer, he loved horses and reminded the Assembly that military law punished those who mistreated their horses. The Right opposed Grammont because of their religious views on human dominion over animals, but Grammont was pleasantly surprised by support from the Left. Agulhon (1981) argued that the Assembly passed the law in 1850 because they dared not contradict a cavalry officer on how to treat horses. The law covered the public mistreatment of domestic animals, including pets and working animals. Punishment included fines and prison time of up to one month, but only in the case of recidivism.

Early Vegetarian Movements

Vegetarian societies grew in the United States in the 1800s and early 1900s, especially with the newfound interest in natural diets. Sylvester Graham, a temperance lecturer, promoted vegetarianism as part of his broader-based health reform movement (Maurer 2002: 25, Shprintzen 2013). Historian Adam Shprintzen (2013: 60–61) describes the first gathering of the American Vegetarian Society in 1850 in New York City, which included a variety of dietary reformers who promoted meatless diets, including physicians, social reformers, water curists, Grahamites, and Bible Christians, the first proto-vegetarian group in the United States. John Harvey Kellogg continued Graham's work into the early twentieth century at the Battle Creek Sanitarium, as depicted in the 1994 film *The Road to Wellville*.

During the world wars, U.S. vegetarian and animal protection societies suffered. Food rationing forced citizens to be partially vegetarian, yet the nutritional value of the food offered was not good enough to nourish adequately (Spencer 1995: 318). A diet without meat represented austerity and bleakness. No one wanted to be reminded of the wars, and eating meat was a prime way to return to nutritional prosperity.

In November 1944, the world's first vegan society was founded in Leicester, England. The Vegan Society claims that as early as 1909 the ethics of consuming dairy products was hotly debated within the vegetarian movement, yet it was not until August 1944 that Elsie Shrigley and Donald Watson commenced coordinating "non-dairy vegetarians" for a new group. Watson took the word "vegan" from the first three and the last two letters of "vegetarian" (Spencer 1995: 317).

The nineteenth century vegetarian movement in France was not promoted by temperance advocates, but by anarchists. These naturist-anarchists practiced vegetarianism, veganism, and even raw-foodism for health as well as animal protection reasons (Méry 2002: 282). With about 50 vegetarian restaurants in Paris between the world wars, the vegetarian movement was stronger in the early twentieth century than it is now (Méry 2002: 284). Further strengthening this early vegetarian movement was the 1953 founding of the Association Végétarienne de France (AVF) by Jacques Colin Demarquette, a naturalist, who served as president of AVF until his death in 1969.

Animal Rights Philosophies

The contemporary animal rights movement coalesced in the 1970s, when academic philosophers developed ethical arguments for animal rights. Their philosophical contributions were so important to the birth of this contemporary movement that sociologists James Jasper and Dorothy Nelkin (1992: 90) called them the "midwives of the animal rights movement." Central to this change was the 1975 publication of Peter Singer's book *Animal Liberation*. Singer, a professor of philosophy, brought the controversial discussion of animal rights to the universities, combining arguments for animal equality with a demand for people to become vegetarian. By equality, Singer does not mean that all beings should be treated identically, nor that dogs should be given the right to vote. Rather, he means that since all sentient beings can feel pleasure and pain, they deserve equal consideration. Singer's utilitarian approach is based on the principle of minimizing suffering. Since animals are sentient beings and can suffer just like humans, they have a right to avoid unnecessary suffering at humans' hands. With graphic photos in his book from factory farms and from pharmaceutical testing on animals, Singer showed that humans' individual lifestyle choices could save animals from these horrible ends.

Around the same time, philosopher Tom Regan was writing his first article on animals, "The Moral Basis of Vegetarianism" (1975), which, along with his influential animal rights book, *The Case for Animal Rights* (1983), brought dialogue over the moral status of animals to the realm of academic philosophy. Rather than basing the value of a life on rationality as did Kant, Regan pointed out that humans ascribe inherent value to many humans that lack such rationality, such as babies or people with severe mental disabilities. Regan's central concept was that animals, like humans, are "subjects of a life," meaning that they have consciousness, needs, desires, and a sense of the future. We all have inherent value and thus moral rights, if we consistently ascribe inherent value to individuals. These moral rights include the right to be treated with respect, which entails the right to not be harmed. Regan's deontological critique of instrumentalism cemented the idea that animals are inherently worthy as living creatures, and should never be used as resources.

Legal scholar Gary Francione contributed to these philosophical arguments with his abolitionist approach. Focusing on the property status of animals in his book *Animals, Property, and the Law*, Francione (1995) critiqued that laws encouraging "humane" treatment do little to actually protect animals so long as humans consider animals to be commodities. Francione believes that the most important thing humans can do for animals is not to pass welfare laws, but to become vegans, thus living abolition in their everyday lives.

Ecofeminist scholar Carol J. Adams developed a feminist approach to animal rights in her 1990 book *The Sexual Politics of Meat: A Feminist-Vegetarian Critical Theory*. Her work links the oppression of women and the oppression of animals, arguing that both are "absent referents" in a violent, racist, patriarchal society. Adams's scholarship also informs the development of antispeciesism as a movement.

The term "speciesism" was coined by British philosopher Richard Ryder in an animal rights pamphlet published in 1970 (Waldau 2001), and was first popularly used by Peter Singer in *Animal Liberation* in 1975, but the application of the concept to the animal rights movement primarily occurs in France. David Olivier, one of the founders of the antispeciesist movement, defined speciesism in a 1992 article as follows: "Speciesism is to species what racism is to race, and what sexism is to sex: a discrimination based on species, almost always in favor of members of the human species" (Olivier 1992).

The First Wave Animal Rights Movement in the U.S. and France

Despite philosophers' calls for veganism to be an integral part of animal rights, in both countries what I call the "first wave" of contemporary animal rights activists largely focused on fur, hunting, and animal testing. Activists attacked these issues because they considered them the most egregious and unnecessary forms of animal exploitation. Celebrities jumped on PETA's (People for the Ethical Treatment of Animals) "I'd rather go naked than wear fur" campaign, and hundreds of activists protested the annual pigeon shoot in Hegins, Pennsylvania. Vivisection, and direct actions against it, characterized this first wave of animal rights activism.

French activists employed direct action against animal testing even before U.S. activists. As France is a center for medical and cosmetic research on animals, early activist efforts focused on vivisection. In 1979, a group called Commando Lynx liberated 57 dogs from a breeder who supplied animals to laboratories. Shortly thereafter, the Brigades Vertes (Green Brigade) destroyed the breeding facilities of another laboratory animal supplier in Lewarde, who suffered minor injuries. This same group was suspected to have planted a bomb at another laboratory animal supplier's house, which injured a police officer.

While previous direct action efforts focused on the suppliers of animals, one group sought to liberate animals from a research laboratory. In April 1985, Operation Greystoke rescued 17 baboons from a laboratory run by the CNRS (Centre Nationale de la Recherche Scientifique) in Gif-sur-Yvette, where they were being used for experiments on epilepsy. Two of the baboons died, but activists sent the remaining 15 baboons to a sanctuary. One year later, seven activists involved in the raid were arrested and fined a combined sum of 55,000 Euros. The activists agreed to pay under the condition that their money go towards alternative research methods. The CNRS rejected the proposal, and the activists refused to pay. Years later the government began garnishing wages from the activists' paychecks, and contemporary activists continue to campaign for the activists' amnesty.

In the United States, PETA, now known for its wide-reaching campaigns on all animal issues, catapulted onto the activist scene for its direct action against vivisection with the 1981 Silver Spring monkeys case. Alex Pacheco, who co-founded PETA in 1981 with Ingrid Newkirk, volunteered as a researcher with an animal research facility in Silver Spring, Maryland, in order to bring first-hand information to the movement. Jasper and Nelkin (1992: 30) wrote, "Pacheco claims to have chosen the lab from a list of research facilities simply because it was near his home, although it had also been the subject of humane society investigations and allegations several years before."

The laboratory conducted neurological research in which they severed nerves in monkeys' limbs. In the lab, Pacheco found the animals, 16 macaques and one rhesus monkey, crammed in cages encrusted in their own feces and urine. Pacheco documented the case and brought his findings to some influential and sympathetic people, and on September 11, 1981, the police raided a scientific laboratory for the first time in the United States. The monkeys and the files were confiscated, and PETA pressed charges against researcher Edward Taub of 17 counts of cruelty to animals—one for each monkey. Taub was found guilty of six counts of cruelty, but the case was later overturned because the state anticruelty statute on which Taub was arrested did not cover federally funded research. The National Institutes of Health (NIH) did, however, discontinue Taub's funding.

The radical flank of the animal rights movement also emerged in the early 1980s. The Animal Liberation Front (ALF), which specializes in direct action, presented their film *Unnecessary Fuss* in 1984, showing footage from the University of Pennsylvania Head Injury Lab, where researchers used a device which could deliver precisely measured blows to the heads of baboons. As ALF members broke into the lab, rather than liberate any animals or disturb the laboratory, they simply stole videos of the experiments, filmed by the experimenters themselves. After the ALF showed the tape in a press release, an inspection of the lab revealed 74 violations of the Laboratory Animal Welfare Act (Finsen and Finsen 1994: 68). *Unnecessary Fuss* brought great attention to the cause of animal liberation, as well as publicity for the ALF, an underground organization which generally contacts the public and the media through PETA or other spokespeople. Contrary to popular misconceptions, the ALF does not harm any living creatures, including humans. They do, however, sometimes engage in property destruction, according to the "ALF Credo":

> The Animal Liberation Front (ALF) carries out direct action against animal abuse in the form of rescuing animals and causing financial loss to animal exploiters, usually through the damage and destruction of property. The ALF's short-term aim is to save as many animals as possible and directly

disrupt the practice of animal abuse. Their long term aim is to end all animal suffering by forcing animal abuse companies out of business. It is a nonviolent campaign, activists taking all precautions not to harm any animal (human or otherwise). (Animal Liberation Front 2015)

PETA and the ALF promote veganism, but this first wave of animal rights activism in France and the United States focused on hunting, fur, and especially animal testing, rather than primarily promoting veganism. In the second wave of activism, especially in the United States, activists centered more of their efforts on vegan outreach, and on the regulation of industrialized animal agriculture.

Second Wave Animal Rights Activism in the United States

In the United States, what I call the "second wave" of contemporary animal rights activism distinguished itself from the animal protection movement in that this new wave of activists not only promoted legislation protecting animals, but they also encouraged humans to make changes in their own lifestyles to reduce animal suffering through vegetarianism and veganism. For the first time, vegetarianism, veganism, and animal protection merged into one movement. This newfound focus was due, in part, to the ever-expanding industrialized animal agriculture, called "factory farms."

U.S. activists took a pragmatic approach, figuring that since farm animals comprised about 98 percent of all animals killed for human purposes, they would focus on promoting veganism. Many of these activists had been active in animal rights for years, and had decided that an "all or nothing" approach would do more to alienate than attract new adherents. Thus many of them focused on promoting incremental dietary changes towards veganism.

The Farm Animal Rights Movement (FARM) was actually ahead of the curve on this issue. Having formed in 1981, FARM explicitly focused on farm animals and vegetarianism in their work when most other animal rights organizations still centered on animal testing, hunting, and fur issues. FARM created many of the annual campaigns that populate many activists' calendars, such as the Great American Meatout and World Farm Animals Day. FARM also created and continues to organize the "Animal Rights National Conference," the largest and longest-running animal rights conference in the nation.

The newer spate of vegan- and farm animal-focused organizations is better represented by groups such as Vegan Outreach (VO), Compassion Over Killing (COK), and Mercy for Animals, founded in 1995, 1995, and 1999, respectively. These groups also created a newfound interest in one of the oldest tactics in activism—leafleting. These activists figured that getting cold, hard facts into their targets' hands would bring more people to the movement than would yelling at them.

Jack Norris and Matt Ball, the co-founders of VO, started their work by holding large banners on busy street corners that read "Stop Eating Animals." After enduring vitriolic responses from passersby, they began to think that leafleting would be a more productive use of their time, as they could reach more people per hour worked. VO's specialty is leafleting, and they have created numerous pamphlets with rigorous documentation from government and industry sources. Further refining their strategy and tactics, VO decided to focus on college students, as young adults are the group most likely to go vegetarian or vegan, and thus they created the Adopt a College program. In this campaign, activists "adopt" a college and leaflet there at least once a year. When the program began in 2003, activists across the U.S. distributed over 22,000 flyers in the fall semester. It has grown exponentially since, and activists now distribute over one million leaflets per semester.

The founders of Compassion Over Killing also used their previous activist experiences to inform their more pragmatic outlook on activism. Paul Shapiro founded COK in 1995 as a high school club, and many of their first actions focused on fur and involved yelling matches with furriers and passersby. After volunteering with other organizations and completing his degree in Peace Studies, Shapiro noticed that passersby tended to avoid his group during protests, sometimes even crossing the street rather than walking past them, and he wondered if they were taking the most effective route to inform people about animal suffering and veganism. COK took a shift similar to VO, and began focusing on information outreach, most notably leafleting and advertising.

COK also focused their attention even more on chickens, as those comprise nearly 90 percent of all farm animals killed for human purposes. These groups engage in "open rescues," where activists enter chicken farms and take animals in need of veterinary attention. In 2003, COK found egregious neglect at a Cecilton, Maryland farm, which labeled their products "Animal Care Certified." In subsequent investigations, COK found that two of Maryland's three largest egg-laying facilities used the "Animal Care Certified" label, though hens in all of these farms were kept in similar conditions—numerous hens crammed into "battery cages" the size of a sheet of paper, covered in their own filth, and with their beaks cut off without anesthesia to avoid the hens pecking each other to death in such crowded conditions. COK engaged in a legal battle against United Egg Producers, the originators of the label, arguing that this was false advertising and that the label was simply capitalizing upon the public's caring tendencies. After two years of taking their case to the Better Business Bureau, lobbying federal agencies, and producing media exposés, the Federal Trade Commission announced the "Animal Care Certified" label would no longer be used on egg cartons by March 2006. Despite these groups' primary focus on farmed animals (specifically chickens), they, and most of these second wave U.S. organizations, engage multiple animal rights issues. The beginning of the divergence between the U.S. and French movements can be seen in the philosophical thrust of French activists, especially antispeciesist activists.

French Antispeciesism

The second wave of French animal rights activism emerged in September 1991 with the creation of the animal rights journal *Cahiers Antispécistes Lyonnais*. In May 1989, Yves Bonnardel and David Olivier, along with three other activists, reacted to the lack of discussion of vegetarianism in the French animal protection movement by writing and publishing a tract called "Nous ne mangeons pas de viande pour ne pas tuer des animaux" (we don't eat meat in order to not kill animals). Shortly thereafter, Bonnardel and Olivier contacted Paola Cavalieri, an Italian activist, and discussed creating a larger publication. From these efforts they founded the *Cahiers Antispécistes Lyonnais*. The publication had a decidedly philosophical theme, publishing works from all types of philosophers, but it is especially associated with the work of Peter Singer. The original idea behind the journal was to have similar reviews in many cities throughout France. When this did not happen, they dropped the subtitle "Lyonnais" in September 1994. The *Cahiers Antispécistes* publishes two to four editions per year, and continues its work today.

The *Cahiers* is closely associated with the publishing group Tahin Party. Founded in 1998, Tahin Party has published translations of short books by Peter Singer and Joan Dunayer. It also publishes original French essays on naturism, humanism, and speciesism by French activist-philosophers like Bonnardel, Olivier, and Estiva Reus.

The interest in the theoretical side of animal rights is also reflected in the theme of the only annual animal rights conference in France, "Les Estivales de la Question Animale." The Estivales began in 2002, and typically runs one week long as a sort of animal rights-themed vacation (*estival* means "of or relating to summer"). Often held in rural settings, participants set up camp at the conference location, and they take their meals together at the site. The conference is informed by anarchist organizing tactics, and it typically starts with a discussion to establish ground rules for debating, cooking, cleaning, and other chores. Much more laid-back than U.S. conferences, there might be two or three presentations per day, with a heavy focus on discussion.

While highly theoretical, French antispeciesist activism was not solely theoretical. The mid-1990s also saw a growth of grassroots antispeciesist organizations and collectives. CLAP, the Collectif de Libération à Paris, emerged during this time period, out of which grew a magazine, *Pour l'égalite Animale*, another collective called LEA, and finally the Collectif Antispéciste de Paris (CAP). Founded in 1999, CAP was very active until about 2012, and they primarily worked through education and outreach in the Paris metropolitan area. With a dozen or so other organizations that focus on factory farming and vegan outreach, a small but strong second wave activist core exists in France. But despite these activists' and activist-philosophers' heavy focus on vegetarianism and veganism, the majority of second wave French animal rights activism has largely stayed at the level of animal protection. It has not developed the same central focus on factory farming and vegan outreach that the U.S. movement has.

Second Wave Animal Rights in France

The contemporary French animal rights movement emerged around the same time as the U.S. movement. Like in the U.S., first wave animal rights efforts in France centered on fur, wildlife, hunting, and vivisection. But unlike the animal rights movement in the U.S., the majority of French animal activism continues to revolve around companion animal protection. The SPA has continued to grow, and it investigates cruelty complaints and runs refuges and adoption centers for companion animals.

Perhaps the most famous of the new animal protection organizations is the Fondation Brigitte Bardot, founded by the actress in 1986. Bardot became interested in animal protection in the 1960s. In 1962, she spoke out against the transportation of and methods of killing farm animals. In 1977, she participated in the worldwide campaign against the hunting of baby seals in Canada for their fur. Upon the creation of her foundation, she hosted a television show from 1989 to 1992, called *SOS Animaux*. Her foundation has expanded their efforts beyond companion animals to protecting wildlife, circus animals, and even farm animals from cruelty, but it does not promote vegetarianism, and Bardot herself is not vegetarian.

Other organizations that focus on farmed animals still take a welfarist stance and promote legal reforms more than promoting vegetarianism or veganism. One such organization is Welfarm, the new name as of June 2015 for the organization Protection Mondiale des Animaux de Ferme (PMAF, translated as Worldwide Protection of Animal Farms), the French branch of the international organization Compassion in World Farming (CIWF). CIWF was created in England in 1967 by Peter Roberts, a dairy farmer. Ghislain Zuccolo, the PMAF director, took an internship in 1993 with CIWF in England, and when he returned to France in 1994, he and Charles Notin, with the aid of CIWF, created the PMAF in France. The PMAF does not overtly promote vegetarianism, but rather focuses on cruelty to farm animals. With its Anglo-Saxon influences and international ties, the PMAF engages in much more lobbying and campaign-style activism than other French organizations. Its major campaigns center on breeding, transportation, and slaughter. In 2012, it won a campaign to enlarge battery cages for egg-laying hens from 550 square centimeters to 750 square centimeters. Now, its goal is to abolish the battery cages altogether (Welfarm 2015).

Muriel Arnal founded One Voice in 1995. Originally called Aequalis Animal (Animal Equality), it claims to be the first group in France "overtly" for the rights of lab and fur animals. They also fight for circus animals, farm animals, and companion animals. With more than 20,000 members and a trimestrial magazine called *Noé* (Noah), this is one of the largest French animal rights organizations. The group specializes in campaigns and lobbying lawmakers. But perhaps this organization's popularity can be attributed to their minimal promotion of vegetarianism and their heavy emphasis on companion animal protection. Anti-fur and anti-testing campaigns often focus on banning the use of companion animals for these purposes, not banning the use of all animals.

The French vegetarian movement was in turmoil during much of this time. After the death of its first president, the Association Végétarienne de France had over six presidents between 1971 and 1980, when it dissolved as an organization. In the meantime, Jean-José Ventura, an AVF member, founded the Union Nationale des Végétariens (UNV) in 1973, which lasted until 1988. Irene Fuhrmann, the last president of UNV, founded *Alliance Végétarienne* as an independent trimestrial journal in 1985. In 1992, Lionel and Marie Reisler took over the journal, and in 1995 they founded an association by the same name. In 2007, Alliance Végétarienne returned to its roots, changing its name back to Association Végétarienne de France.

AVF is centered in Paris and has delegates throughout France. While AVF has literature on nearly all topics concerning vegetarianism, their specialty is arguably the health aspects of vegetarianism, with numerous tracts on individual nutrients like iron and vitamin B-12. One grassroots organization based in Toulouse, AVIS (Association Végétarienne & Végétalienne des InformationS), specializes in broad-based guides for new vegetarians. Philippe, the principal organizer, has held information tables at Toulouse markets nearly every Sunday since its foundation in 1997, and he also produces and distributes a vegetarian starter guide and a book of recipes.

The resurgent interest in vegetarianism in the French movement coalesced in 2001 with the creation of Veggie Pride, a march and rally held annually in Paris. Veggie Pride was explicitly patterned after gay pride parades, with the intention of getting vegetarians to come out of the closet and show their "veggie pride." Organizers specifically state that this march promotes vegetarianism for animal rights reasons, not health or the environment. The first march mobilized about 200 people, and subsequent marches have hovered between 400 and 500 participants. Veggie Pride has continually attracted participants from outside of France, and now Veggie Pride parades are organized in dozens of cities around the world.

These new vegetarian organizations, the farmed animal organizations, and the contemporary animal protection organizations remain largely separate from one another in France. Despite the adoption and creation of the various animal rights philosophies by French activists, the second wave French animal rights movement does not resemble the U.S. movement, nor second wave movements in other countries, in maintaining a focus on farmed animals and vegan outreach.

There is a clear divergence between the French and U.S. movements during this second wave. This split is all the more perplexing when one takes into account the remarkable similarities in animal protection, vegetarianism, and first wave animal rights activism in the two countries. Since second wave animal rights activism focuses on factory farming, one would think that the strong pro-small farmer, anti-globalization, and anti-GMO movements in France, not to mention their strong history of animal protection, would lay the groundwork for a strong second wave animal rights movement. Why has this particular form of contemporary animal rights activism not succeeded in France? Why, especially, since it succeeded in the U.S., a movement with such a similar trajectory? I answer these questions in the following chapters, looking at the cultural resources available to activists, and how activists choose from among those resources. Taken together, I show how the U.S. movement has enjoyed more cultural opportunities, and has taken greater advantage of those opportunities, than has the French movement, thus explaining the differential outcomes of the two movements.

Part II
Cultural Resources

3   Environment and Religion

This first section of the analysis, Chapters 3–6, investigates the dominant culture in each country, to see how it shapes social movement processes. In these chapters, I ask how existing culture shapes a movement's messages, and the reception of those messages. I answer this question by analyzing the cultural and symbolic resources accessible to animal rights activists in France and the United States. I also investigate how those resources exist and function differently in the two countries. I found significant variations in cultural resources between the French and U.S. movements, the majority of which greatly favored U.S. activists.

Sociologically speaking, this type of analysis is important to understand how movements mobilize cultural resources to promote their interests (Williams and Kubal 1999). This idea comes from sociologist Ann Swidler (1986), who characterized culture as a "toolkit." Culture is not simply a tool people use in everyday life. It can also be a tool for activists, as Rhys Williams (1995) notes, a tool they wield more or less self-consciously. From my theoretical perspective, I view culture as structured in such a way that it molds social actors, even as those actors use cultural meanings—cultural resources—in attempts to change cultural values and habits.

What are these cultural resources, and where do they come from? Cultural resources take a number of forms: formal ideologies (Williams 1995, Williams and Kubal 1999), symbolic-expressive actions (Williams 1995), symbols (Williams and Kubal 1999, Jasper 2006a), cultural meanings (Jasper 2006a), and, perhaps most importantly, the knowledge to use all these tools (Jasper 2006a). These cultural resources, or tools, are also historically and culturally defined. This leads to a central dilemma of social movements: activists must package their demands in ways that are culturally challenging but, at the same time, culturally legitimate enough to be accepted by their audiences (d'Anjou and Van Male 1998).

Scholars have demonstrated the variable and historical legitimacy of cultural resources within one specific culture, and they have even shown how the same cultural resource, religion, can be used to different ends by different movements (Williams 2002). But scholars have yet to analyze how a cultural resource might function in different cultures. How transferable are cultural resources between movements? What are the boundaries of legitimacy for these seemingly transposable cultural resources? To answer these questions, I focus on how the cultural context shapes the cultural resources that activists have at their disposal. Thus in these chapters I pay attention to the variability of cultural resources in two distinct yet interrelated ways: (1) which cultural resources were available in France and the United States, and (2) how those cultural resources resonated within the dominant cultures of those two countries.

Environmentalism: A Shared Opportunity

Activists often see vegetarianism and environmentalism as inherently connected. Concentrated Animal Feeding Operations (CAFOs, also known as factory farms) are a major cause of pollution worldwide, and they emit 21 percent of the total carbon dioxide emissions due to human activity (Calverd 2005). These harrowing statistics have existed for decades. A 1998 U.S. Senate Agriculture Committee report called pollution from CAFOs a national problem and cited livestock waste as the largest polluter of waterways in the United States (Driscoll and Edwards 2014). Even if one were to argue that small local farms are more environmentally friendly than industrialized animal agriculture, it still takes vastly more fossil fuel and water resources to produce one pound of meat than it does to produce one pound of plant-based protein for human consumption. Further, research from the World Hunger Program at Brown University showed that a vegetarian diet could feed twice as many people as a meat-based diet. The study showed that an almost purely vegetarian diet could feed 6.3 billion people, whereas a diet where 25 percent of the calories came from animal products could feed little more than half of that, only 3.2 billion people (Hunger Report 1993).

Both France and the United States have strong environmental movement organizations. In the past decade, both countries have also seen environmentalism move to the forefront of mainstream public and political concern, even beyond the Green political parties that exist in both countries. In France, Nicolas Hulot, an environmental activist, gained such popularity that it came as a surprise when he did not run for president in the 2007 elections. Rather, Hulot used his clout to make environmentalism one of the most important topics of the elections, promoting his *Pacte Ecologique* (Hulot 2006). In the United States, former Vice President Al Gore's documentary *An Inconvenient Truth*, along with Gore's environmental activism, led him to win the Nobel Peace Prize in 2007.

Citizens in both countries are increasingly encouraged to make "green" lifestyle choices, in a process that sociologists call "lifestyle movements" (Haenfler *et al.* 2012, Cherry 2015). By "going green" or engaging in "Meatless Mondays," people can engage in a form of activism without necessarily being part of a traditional movement organization. This lifestyle-based activism often occurs through consumerism, such as buying hybrid cars or local and sustainably grown foods.

Given this increase in environmental consciousness in both countries, one might think that animal rights activists would jump at the occasion to promote vegetarian and vegan eating for environmental purposes. Indeed, both French and U.S. activists saw this cultural shift as an opening in cultural opportunities (McAdam 1994) for promoting their issues. Activists in both countries saw this blossoming environmental consciousness as an opportunity to strategically frame vegetarianism as good for the environment, and they also agonized over the dilemma of promoting veganism for environmental reasons rather than purely animal rights reasons. The primary difference in activists' approaches to promoting animal-friendly lifestyles through environmentalism was that activists in France were more cautious, seeing environmentalists as false friends.

Activists in both France and the United States used the cultural shift towards environmentalism as an opportunity to engage in the strategic framing (Zald 1996) of animal rights issues as environmental issues. These activists saw promoting animal rights for environmental reasons as an effective route. Moreover, they saw the issues as inherently tied together: "It's all so interrelated that you're ignoring other parts of animal rights if you don't talk about the environment," stated Jean (SOS). Going further, Talia worried that the animal rights movement spent too little time working on environmental issues:

> All of these national organizations need to be having massive campaigns to get their own members to dial back their energy and not use SUVs and all of the other things that we need to do to reduce emissions. And we also need to be making massive efforts to get environmentalists to understand that going vegan is a very important way to reduce methane. So I worry. More than anything, I worry about environmental issues impeding our long-term aims. Because if climate change continues as it is, then all of the animals are going to be hurt.

Many activists, like Talia, saw environmental degradation as harming animals. But Talia was not just being instrumental in her beliefs, seeing environmental consciousness as solely a route to animal rights. She went on to say that she believed the environment was worthy in itself, and that she saw herself as working towards environmental rescue in her animal activism. Environmental activism brought some of the activists I interviewed to the animal rights movement—Sebastien worked at the Maison de l'Environnement, and Dylan worked with the Sierra Club and a student environmental organization, before they both became vegetarians and animal rights activists.

Because animal rights activists often saw environmental issues and animal rights issues to be so closely intertwined, participating in certain environmental events became a given. At a meeting of the vegetarian group Burdivega in Bordeaux, the president announced the upcoming Salon de l'Environnement, and said the group was going to participate by having a table at the exposition. Frédérique, the president, said, "This is *the* opportunity for us to talk about vegetarianism." The only point of discussion was who was going to staff the table, not whether the group wanted to have a table in the first place.

Some activists in France said they wanted to capitalize upon the newfound interest in environmentalism because they thought that their targets simply did not care about animals. Animal cruelty was an insufficient hook for the movement, and activists should capitalize upon their targets' environmental consciousness for animal rights purposes, as Carol explained:

I've been thinking lately that I've got to try and focus on ecology and the environment. Because it's a big thing at the moment. Everyone's talking about it, schools are talking about it, how to be a good ecologist, and all that [. . .] I think we should stop talking so much about cruelty to animals, because when we say eating meat is cruel, they just shrug their shoulders and go on. And they'll still eat it. But it's becoming so fashionable to become an ecologist in France, people are asking me all the time, do you save water, do you do this, do you do that? It's really becoming trendy. It's becoming very trendy. I think you've got to think of the public and you've got to fight them on their level. That is the strategy I think we have to develop.

French activists saw France as the worst country for animals in all of Europe, because of its philosophical focus on human rights, because of its animal practices such as foie gras production, and because it was a center for animal testing. Therefore, French activists did not believe animal rights reasons to be the most effective strategy to encourage people to become vegetarian. Rather, activists saw France's blossoming environmental awareness as a cultural opportunity to promote vegetarianism.

One of the reasons that so many activists in both countries favored using environmental arguments to get people to become vegetarian was that they hoped that becoming vegetarian would lead people to discover more about animal rights. Fran (SOS) saw this as a viable path, given her own history:

I think that you could use the way that would get people interested, which could be health, or a lot of times the environment. I think if you can start in on that idea, then you learn the benefits of other things, and I think then they could become, like if they become vegetarian for the environment, they might also do it for the animals later on when they learn more and more about it. It's like, I did it for the animals, but then once I found out about health and the environment, it was just like an added bonus.

Fran's case demonstrates the process of commitment as described by sociologist Howard Becker (1960), where commitment to a certain line of action leads to unanticipated positive consequences in other areas. Fran became vegetarian for animal rights reasons, and then she realized vegetarianism also benefited her health and the environment. She, and other activists, thought a similar process might occur if people became vegetarian for environmental reasons. That is, they would see the positive consequences for animals, and would then become further committed to their vegetarianism.

However, many activists remained skeptical of this route. They thought the environment was an insufficient reason to get people to become and stay vegetarian, for numerous reasons. Yann (Collectif Antispéciste de Paris) objected to the strategic framing of vegetarianism as environmentalism because "it does not fundamentally change the philosophy, the relationship towards animals." He continued:

I don't think they're effective because they talk about health, the planet, without any theory behind it. If people are vegetarian in order to improve their own little lives, that's completely selfish. There's no reflection on animals—they have the same status as an omnivore would give them. It's better for people to go vegetarian for the animals, but for them, for health, it's fine if they don't eat animals, but the theory behind it would be the same as an omnivore.

Yann preferred to promote vegetarianism for animal rights reasons, because he saw humanism as a primary obstacle to animal rights. Without changing people's anthropocentric views, the animal rights movement would never advance. Going further, Jenna (Vegan Outreach) noted that many people would not change their lifestyles simply because they believed in environmentalism. She said that "going 'green' is kind of a buzzword these days," so activists are tempted to take an environmental approach. But Jenna saw a problem with taking a multi-pronged approach to promoting vegetarianism:

I think it's a lot of information for people to absorb all at once. And we're pretty selfish. I mean, if we're thinking about our health, there are so many things people are instructed to do and not much of it ever gets done. And the environment, people have known about environmental issues for a long time and we're still driving more than ever. We're still using more energy than ever. We're still consuming more plastics and more nonrenewable resources than ever. And I think just trying to tell them to stop eating meat for the environment is a difficult—it's hard for them to put those two things together.

Jenna noted that people have long known about environmental issues, but that that knowledge has not changed their behavior. Therefore, she wondered about the effectiveness of promoting vegetarianism for the same reasons that have moved people to do nothing in the past. Jenna also noted that taking a multi-pronged approach, meaning promoting vegetarianism for animal rights reasons as well as health and environmental reasons, resulted in simply too much information for people to handle. These problems highlight the fact that people are "cognitive misers" (Bless *et al.* 2004), and they employ various heuristic processes such as forgetting in order to deal with all of this information. That is, people may simply forget the information if they are given too much to process.

Most activists saw using environmental arguments as a strategic choice, and as a dilemma that came with trade-offs, rather than a clear-cut, solely positive decision. As what seems to be an unintended consequence to framing processes, activists encountered what sociologist James Jasper (2006a: 127) called an "extension dilemma," when they widened their interests to gain new adherents. The trade-off for gaining adherents through such breadth is that one loses the depth of one's argument. Activists in both countries saw the environment as a potentially useful argument, but they still believed animal rights to be the strongest argument—they saw animal rights as a more in-depth argument that engendered more commitment to vegetarianism than did environmental reasons. Suzanne (Vegan Outreach) saw the "blossoming of environmental consciousness" as an opportunity to "tweak people's moral center," but she still favored animal rights arguments:

> I think we should always approach it as an ethical question. And I think the environment fits into that very nicely. Basically where I come down is we should never engage somebody's self-interest because self-interest keeps you eating meat. It keeps you doing the quick and easy, convenient thing which is probably not going to be very kind to animals because that's the status quo.

Suzanne summarized one central aspect of the dilemma of using environmental arguments to gain new vegetarians: people will still claim that eating small amounts of meat does not hurt the environment. Using ethical arguments would engender more wide-sweeping changes and would disallow eating any animal products, no matter how infrequent. The implications of these claims are not mere hyperbole. A participant from a previous project I conducted on veganism (Cherry 2003) proves their points: "I think that the main thing again is, for the reasons that I'm doing it, if it's for environmental sustainability and health reasons, then small amounts occasionally isn't really going to have that detrimental an effect." Thus capitalizing on cultural opportunities is a double-edged sword.

French activists, more than U.S. activists, remained skeptical of using environmental arguments to further their cause because of shortcomings they saw in the environmental movement. Activists saw environmentalists as "false friends" and as useless for coalitions because of their lack of support for animal issues. René critiqued the Green Party for having a leader who supported *corrida* (bullfighting): "The representative of the Green Party, Noël Mamère, is a huge fan of corrida, so from there, even the political parties who are concerned about the environment are not really concerned about animals." While René lauded the Green Party for its left-wing politics, he bristled at their lack of concern for animal issues.

One might argue that the Green Party is primarily concerned with environmental issues, making animal issues a tangential subject, but even environmental conservation organizations did not extend their support to animal rights campaigns in France. Antoine Comiti, an activist with the anti-foie gras group Stop Gavage, said that many animal protection organizations supported the ban of foie gras. However, the Ligue pour la Protection des Oiseaux (LPO), the French branch of BirdLife International, did not support the ban, as Antoine explained:

> It's clearly one of the areas where there is a lot of support, even from traditional organizations, like those for dogs and cats. The difficulty, where it isn't working, is with ecological organizations. We thought at the beginning that we would have a lot of success with ecological organizations, but that hasn't been the case at all, even those who care about birds, like the LPO in France.

Echoing Yann's concerns that environmentalism does not subvert the anthropocentric view that humans have towards animals, Antoine explained the LPO's lack of support by saying it was not surprising, because "these are humanist organizations who defend the environment and the earth for humans." An undercurrent of these concerns about environmentalists as false friends is that if a person is an environmentalist, then he or she should support animal rights issues. This underlying value infused the entire French animal rights movement, where activists valued a consistency of thought and action. (I will analyze this value in more detail in Chapter 7.)

Culture can create opportunities or barriers for social movements. The increased interest in environmentalism, for example, opened up new paths for animal rights activists. Understanding the symbols, ideologies, and arguments available to social movements necessitates an attention to cultural resonance, which Williams and Kubal (1999: 234) describe as "a contingent process based on an alignment of legitimate cultural expressions, dominant ideological formations in society, and the cultural resources used by movement actors." The environment was a cultural resource available to both movements, which worked in favor of both movements. In the remainder of this chapter, and in the following chapters in this section (Chapters 4, 5, and 6), I pay attention to the variability of cultural resources in two distinct yet interrelated ways: 1) what cultural resources were available in France and the United States, and 2) how those cultural resources resonated within the dominant cultures of those two countries. I will show how the exact same cultural resources functioned differently in the two countries, with most of the resources working for the U.S. movement and against the French movement.

Religion

Religious views about animals posed a challenge to animal rights activists in both France and the United States. Non-activists in both countries often claimed that "god put animals on earth for us to use." The use of religious rhetoric to justify animal use is not surprising in the United States, where, according to a 2002 Pew Global Project Attitudes poll, 59 percent of people say that religion plays a very important role in their lives (Pew Research Center 2002). It is slightly unexpected in France, where only 11 percent of people say religion is important to them. Most surveys point to the widespread religiosity of people in the United States, and the lack thereof in France. French Catholics have decreased in number, from comprising over 80 percent of the population in the early 1990s to only 51 percent in 2007. The number of atheists has risen in that same time, from 23 percent in 1994 to 31 percent in 2007 (Samuel 2007). Because of this difference in religiosity, U.S. activists successfully used religion as a cultural resource in their own work, whereas activists in France did not. Compounding this was the fact that in France, many people believed that vegetarians were part of a religious cult. Using religious arguments would add fodder to this belief, which French activists tried to avoid.

Religion as a Cultural Tool in the United States

At the 2007 Becoming the Change conference on animal rights, Dr. Lisa Kemmerer, a philosophy and religion professor, presented her research on religion and animals. During her talk, she noted the difficulty of promoting animal rights issues to people of faith, because, she said, they often only care about humans. After her talk, one of the audience members said that whenever she talks to Christians about vegetarianism, they respond by saying that god put animals on earth for us to eat. She asked Dr. Kemmerer how she could best respond to people who believed this. The audience murmured in agreement, waiting to hear her response.

Dr. Kemmerer admitted that many activists preferred to use the message of love and compassion from the New Testament of the Bible, but she preferred to use Genesis. She said the Bible passages people use to defend meat-eating all come from after the fall of Adam and Eve, and that the statements before that all point to a vegan diet. So in response to such challenges, she asks religious people whether they would rather follow the statements of an angry, frustrated god, or the original, ideal plan?

The audience, primarily from the Bible Belt as the conference was held in North Carolina, was very interested in Dr. Kemmerer's response because this was a common belief used by meat-eaters to justify their actions. Animal rights activists, especially in the South, heard this response from their targets all too often. Meat-eaters have used numerous, specific Bible passages to defend their use of animals to activists. (I always wondered whether they were armed with such passages specifically to defend their meat-eating, or whether they possessed an excellent knowledge of the Bible.) Grant, who was from a religious family in the South, believed such ideas were changing:

> These ideas, that animals are the dominion of man, and that man can do what he wants with animals, are based in the Bible, and in religion. I guess in more than just a Christian or Judaic text. So if you no longer hold to these strict interpretations of the Bible, even if you are Christian, these assumptions that the average person makes, that we are above the animals, seem to be a lot less reasonable—if you don't hold to as literal a translation of the Bible.

It is difficult to say whether such religious beliefs about animals are changing. But Grant also spoke to the bigger issue of religion as a cultural constraint, later saying he found it more difficult to convince Christians to become vegetarians than it was to encourage non-religious people to change their diets and lifestyles.

Perhaps the strongest response to these Christian beliefs has been the founding of religious vegetarian associations. Such associations exist in the United States for Christians, Jews, and Muslims, religions in which vegetarianism is promoted less than in religions such as Buddhism and Hinduism. As Christians posed the biggest challenge to the animal rights activists I interviewed, I focus on Christianity and vegetarianism in this chapter.

To counter these anti-animal rights Christian beliefs, and to promote plant-based diets and respectful treatment of animals, a group of professors, theologians, and activists founded the Christian Vegetarian Association (CVA) in 1999. The group's mission is to support Christian vegetarians, to show how vegetarianism can enhance Christians' faith and spirituality, and to advocate a plant-based diet as part of good, responsible Christian stewardship. Not just vegetarianism, but the status of animals as a whole, centers on the concept of dominion, which many non-vegetarians interpret to mean humans can use animals to their own ends. The CVA responds to this belief in the frequently asked questions on their website and flyers, answering the question "Did God put animals here for our use?" (Christian Vegetarian Association 2015). Using numerous Biblical passages to support their vegetarian stance, the CVA promotes the idea of a "sacred stewardship" rather than an ownership-based concept of dominion.

Further promoting this animal-friendly concept of dominion, Matthew Scully, a former speechwriter for George W. Bush, wrote *Dominion: The Power of Man, the Suffering of Animals, and the Call to Mercy* in 2002. The book has found fans in various religious denominations because Scully assuages fears that animal rights activists want to equate humans with animals. As the reviewer from the *San Francisco Catholic* put it:

> The truly remarkable thing about this book is its assertion that many animals in this world deserve better, not because they are our equals and have rights like our own, but precisely because they are our inferiors and subject to our power. (Writers Reps 2015)

More and more religious organizations are opening to the idea of animal welfare, thanks to the work of religious animal rights and welfare activists. An article in the *Los Angeles Times* (Simon 2001) described the work of a former anti-abortion turned animal welfare activist at Liberty University, a fundamentalist Baptist university founded by Jerry Falwell. Karen Swallow Prior, an English professor at the university, has written editorials for the university journal describing animal welfare as an evangelical concern, and she was invited to lecture on animal welfare at her church. Prior said, "A lot of these ideas get dismissed out of a view that they fit into a conservative-versus-liberal [split]. But there are some issues that transcend that." Matthew Scully's status as a speechwriter for George W. Bush likely helped him to promote animal protection ideas to conservative Christians as well. But not all churches were equally accepting of such ideas. Lorena, who spends a significant amount of her activism time engaging in vegetarian outreach with churches, said that church leaders were insensitive to the issue, and that it took the support of the church members for her to be able to enter churches to spread the message:

> Many people in the Christian leadership, and that are involved in animal rights activism, or vegetarianism, have been bombarded with emails and letters from very, very disappointed Christians, saying that their church—the mainstream churches in North America—aren't very sensitive to cruelty to animals. And they are on the verge of either leaving their churches, or leaving Christianity altogether. So we thought that there is something missing there, and that is education on those issues in the mainstream churches. So we thought, one way to get in is through the members themselves, of the different churches, if they are willing to help us get a foot in, it's much easier to educate the congregation. Which has proven very hard.

Lorena emphasized that many church members are open to the idea, but that the primary challenge comes from the church leadership. Lorena was the only activist I interviewed who had done such outreach in churches. More often, activists encountered Christians in their everyday work. This was especially true in the South, where I conducted much of my U.S. fieldwork. Activists capitalized upon this demographic fact, using Christian Vegetarian Association (CVA) flyers in their work. Dylan (SOS) saw these Christian flyers as a way to attract people to the group:

> One thing that is popular around people here, being in the Bible Belt, is on being vegetarian from the Christian point of view, the Christian argument for vegetarianism. That gets a lot of people coming to the table that I don't think otherwise would have paid us any mind at all.

While SOS does not affiliate with the CVA, some of its activists are Christian, and even those who are not have leafleted using CVA flyers at numerous religious events, such as Christian concerts or speeches, including when the Reverend Al Sharpton came to the university. Activists reported that audiences were very receptive to the message, saying that most people took the flyers. SOS also envisioned reaching out to the various campus ministries and giving them CVA flyers, although this plan never came to fruition. Thus even though many SOS activists were not Christian, they saw the utility of Christian arguments for animal rights.

Even in their personal conversations with others, activists sometimes used Christian rhetoric to explain their beliefs in animal rights. Austin did this because he thought the term "animal rights" was sometimes "counterproductive," and it might be too radical for the people with whom he was interacting:

> I usually don't use the term animal rights. I do believe that animals have individual rights. For example, the right to live, the right to eat, the right to be comfortable, the right to have freedom of space, the right to be taken care of. I kind of prefer, though, when I'm talking in discussion, I'll use more of a reverence for life approach, and kind of using the dominion perspective, or the kinship perspective, of humans having a responsibility to care for animals, not only because of their rights, but because of our own.

Austin described using the Christian concept of dominion to explain his beliefs on animal rights because it effectively countered the belief that the term "animal rights" was too radical. But, as I elaborate below, this strategy was only available to activists in the U.S., for using a dominion approach in France may get one branded as a cult member.

Grant grew up in a Christian household, but was no longer a Christian himself. Nonetheless, he said his outlook and practice of his animal rights beliefs was influenced by his parents' Christianity:

> My outlook on vegetarianism is sort of like a tweaking of my parents' Christianity. Well, maybe not the way that they're Christians, but growing

up in a Christian household—I'm not a Christian anymore, but, I guess you read about these things, like "Non-believers will see your actions and will understand why you are a Christian, and that will be your witness." I mean, they're all religious terms, but I kind of, I guess I've sort of implemented that in my take on animal rights.

Even activists who were not Christian used Christian rhetoric to explain their vegetarianism and their beliefs in animal rights to others. Grant went on to say he wanted people to see why he was vegetarian, to be a "positive personification" of an animal rights activist, and he used Christian terms like "witnessing" to describe this strategy of leading by example. Thus even activists who were not, or were no longer, Christian used religion as a cultural resource in their work.

Religion as a Cultural Challenge in France

When I went to France to conduct my fieldwork, the French activists were all curious about the movement in the U.S., and they wanted to know what types of literature and resources U.S. activists used. So, when I went home for a few weeks during the middle of my fieldwork, I returned to France with numerous examples of flyers and literature from U.S. animal rights organizations. I gave these flyers and literature to the activists I thought would be most interested. I gave antivivi-section flyers to ADS, who focused on vivisection, and vegetarian starter guides to activists who founded Veggie Pride. I hung on to the Christian Vegetarian Association flyers, uncertain who might be interested in them.

I thought of giving the CVA flyers to Diana (Association Végétarienne de France), who lamented the French lack of collaboration with groups like the Seventh Day Adventists. But when I met Fabrice (Animale Amnistie), he expressed an interest in the flyers. I brought them to a tabling event one day and showed him the CVA flyer. Fabrice laughed, and said, "You really use that?" I said yes, that SOS was not a Christian group, but it was a useful flyer because so many people in the South were religious. Fabrice took the flyer and said, "Here in France, we could never do this," placing the SOS flyer and the CVA flyer side by side on the table. "France is a secular country," he continued, "which they take not just to mean that the church and state are separate, but that we should be against religious groups."

Fabrice asked when and where we use the flyers, and whether we always have them on our tables. I said that most of the flyers we used were basic vegetarian and animal rights flyers, but that SOS does usually have the CVA flyers on hand because one of the most common responses SOS receives from passersby was that "god put animals on earth for humans to use." I went on to explain that SOS sometimes purposefully leaflets with the CVA tract, like at Christian concerts. Fabrice turned to me and asked, "What? Christian concerts?" I explained that Christian bands often put on large concerts, and that SOS leafleted at one called "Harvest Fest," called such because the organizers say they are "harvesting souls for the lord." Fabrice laughed, and said, "I must visit this country of yours and see your unusual ways."

Fabrice's reaction to the CVA flyer provides a good introduction to French activists' views towards the use of Christian rhetoric. Fabrice was astonished that we would use such flyers, and he was equally astounded by the very public nature of Christianity in the U.S. Even though so few French people claimed religion to be an important part of their lives, Christian beliefs towards animals proved a significant challenge to animal rights activists in France. But unlike U.S. activists, who then used religion as a resource to promote animal rights and vegetarianism, French activists did not use religious rhetoric. This was partly because many French activists saw animal rights as a secular ethical issue. More so, it was due to the fact that French people saw animal rights activists and vegetarians as being in a cult. French activists tried to avoid this charge by avoiding any religious references in their work.

As in the United States, French activists found Christian beliefs about animals to be a challenge to their work. Some activists spoke of this challenge in a historical fashion, blaming the anthropocentric aspects of humanism on their Christian roots, as Sebastien said: "With all the roots there are in religion, in Christianity, in Judaism, the exclusive side of humanism is very, very strong there. The sacredness of human life is very, very strong." David went further, claiming that Christianity and humanism dominate the entire world:

> The main challenge is a tradition that transformed itself into the official ideology of humanism: only humans count. I think if we don't address this problem, we won't get very far. Now there are other questions tied to that, in relation to the fact that this ideology is based on Christianity, in relation to the fact that Christianity is the central culture of the Western world, and that it's the Western world that dominates the world.

David and Sebastien both challenged the precepts of humanism, but they both saw Christianity as being the core of humanist beliefs. French historian Maurice Agulhon (1981) saw this as well, describing a tension between secular humanism and animal protection. Hervé saw these same issues but also faced the challenge of simply talking to Christians who believed that god put animals on earth for humans to use:

> For me, also, especially when talking to my parents, is when they start talking about god. I don't think they're believers, but it's happened. "It's god, it's like that." I don't believe in god. And that's difficult to discuss. So for people who are religious, I think it's not easy to think that humans are mammals, like other animals, who evolved differently.

Hervé described his parents' religion as a challenge, and other activists described Christian beliefs about animals to be a challenge to their work. However, I did not witness any French passersby using religious reasons to defend their meat-eating. Rather, it was the passersby who accused animal rights activists of religious activities.

Activists as Cultists in France

Given the lack of religiosity in France, and the secular nature of French culture, French activists did not use religious rhetoric because such frames would not resonate culturally. But this avoidance was due to more than French secular culture or French activists' atheism. I found that French animal rights activists avoided religious rhetoric as a frame because they wanted to avoid being accused of being in a cult.

French people believed that animal rights activists, particularly those who were vegetarian or vegan, were in a cult. For example, while tabling with the Collectif Antispéciste de Paris one day, I spent the day talking to all of the people who passed the activists' table. One young man who looked at the table as he walked past told me, "I shit on them." Thinking perhaps I misheard, I said, "Excuse me?" The young man repeated, "I shit on them," holding his rear end and squatting for emphasis. I asked if he said that for any particular reason, and he said, "They're a cult. A cult!" I learned this was a common claim, and most of the French activists I interviewed claimed that people believed they were in a cult:

> Either you have the image of Brigitte Bardot, cats, dogs, the grandmother types from the B.B. period who have been active quite some time for dogs and cats, or else you have the image of cults. Vegetarianism is extreme for them, they think it's crazy. It's a rather negative image of activists, of vegetarian activists. (Yann)

> I think a lot of people have bad ideas, have bad information, who mix up too many things, who think that people who are activists are part of a cult. There are people who still think that. (Emmanuel)

> In France, vegetarianism has a hygienic image, or hippies, or even cults. Not a good image. (Sebastien)

Some activists said their own families thought they were in a cult because of their animal rights activism. Others said the issue was not simply that French people thought vegetarians were in a cult, it was that vegetarians *must* be in a cult—why else would they want to be vegetarian? Christine (AVF) explained this reasoning:

> For many French people, to be vegetarian is not normal, and you must be part of a cult to be like that. That's because of the importance of food in France, the importance of meat in France. There is so much education about meat in France that people do not understand if you do not eat meat. It's weird because very few cults claim to be vegetarian, but it seems so weird to people because to them, it's natural to eat meat, so they call us a cult.

If so few cults in France actually were vegetarian, then where did this notion of a cult come from? David explained that the Cathars, a religious sect that flourished in France during the twelfth and thirteenth centuries, practiced vegetarianism and that this influenced modern day beliefs about vegetarians, sects, and cults. More recently, André (AVF) explained this belief by basing it on people practicing vegetarianism in dangerous ways. He said his group could not present vegetarianism to children and never developed any material for children, because of these beliefs:

> Because vegetarianism, for children, is often associated with the notion of cults. There have been many examples in France of cult groups who practiced vegetarianism in an unknowledgeable way. Consequently, for an adult, sure, he's already grown, he's more resistant, but for a child, that can have grave consequences from a health point of view. That's why that is a dangerous subject. We cannot talk in school, and school, for example, is an area of collective dining. We have a few things for schools, letters, but nothing for the time being.

Perhaps André was speaking of the same "cult" that a different passerby at a CAP tabling event mentioned. He said he had seen a television show about a cult who had raised their children vegan, and he said they became malnourished and almost died. Diana said the assumption that vegans are in a cult or sect constrained AVF's ability to work with vegetarian religious groups, and she explained that part of this fear of sects and cults came from the French government:

> The French consider the Mormons and the Jehovah's Witnesses as terrible—well not terrible, but really worrying sects. Whereas we are so accustomed to having the Mormons and the Seventh Day Adventists, they're just lovely little minorities that just get a bit irritating when they come to the door on a Saturday morning. So they're here, there's a big *chasse aux sects*, a big witch hunt that's been going on for years against sects. So anything that's slightly eccentric, new-agey, or religious, or bizarre, like vegetarianism or animal rights, it's considered sort of dangerous, like that sect stuff. So we have to be very careful.

In 1995, the French National Assembly approved a report on cults in France which recommended strong anti-cult laws. Many of these laws were subsequently passed in the early 2000s. The report included numbers of adherents to hundreds of cults and sects in France, including Mormons, Jehovah's Witnesses, Seventh Day Adventists, Christian Scientists, Scientology, Nichiren Shoshu, and Raelians. The report never specifically named vegetarianism or veganism, but it did warn of "the promotion of new food practices" (Assemblée Nationale 1995). However, as many of the minor groups mentioned in the report were Buddhist or Hindu sects, vegetarianism or veganism were likely part of their practices. I also found several anti-cult websites that promoted the idea that vegetarians and vegans were all part of a cult, as well as many internet forums focused on vegetarianism and veganism, where vegans lamented that their families believed they had joined a cult when they became vegan.

How did the belief that vegetarians and vegans were in a cult affect animal rights activists? As André mentioned, his group could not enter schools to promote vegetarianism, because speaking to children on the subject made them look like a cult. Animal rights activists also received bad press in the media, which referred to them as cult members. Diana noted this accusation of cult status from the media in a report on an event that the AVF did for World Vegetarian Day:

> So you just, for example, on World Vegetarian Day three years ago, we had a homosexual member who wanted to arrange a vegetarian buffet lunch to celebrate World Vegetarian Day in his local church in Paris, which was a Christian church largely oriented toward homosexuals. Well, we ended up, the media announced that we were a homosexual vegetarian sect, or something ridiculous. I mean, just because one person out of 50 happened to be homosexual, and happened to put a buffet on in his church, for Pete's sake.

These public accusations made activists avoid collaborating with any groups that might be considered cults or sects. In the vegetarian society with which Diana worked in New Zealand, she said they had cooking demonstrations by and speakers from the Seventh Day Adventists, but they could never do such a thing in France.

More than blocking collaborations and coalitions, the fear of being called a cult also affected the inner workings of animal rights organizations. For example, nearly every animal rights organization in France publicizes that they are *non-confessionelle*, meaning non-denominational. Further, when Animale Amnistie formed and created their bylaws, one of the members specified that they needed to be certain that "we can kick someone out if they call us a cult." French animal rights organizations went to great pains to avoid looking like they had anything to do with cults. When I attended the 2007 General Assembly of the Association Végétarienne de France, I witnessed them change their name from "Alliance Végétarienne," because they felt the word *alliance* sounded like a cult:

André Méry:	The first proposed change is changing the name from Alliance Végétarienne to Association Végétarienne de France. Some people didn't like the name, especially the *alliance* part. The new name is more professional.
Audience Member:	For some, *alliance* might sound like it's a federation of associations.
Audience Member:	If we contact journalists, now this is an emblematic name. We wouldn't have to explain who we are. It's all in the name. We're an association, we promote vegetarianism, we're based in France.
André Méry:	Does anyone have any comments?
Audience Member:	*Alliance* sounds like a cult.

After someone said that *alliance* sounded like a cult, everyone in the room murmured agreement. When they took the vote, all but a couple of the 50 or so members in attendance voted for the name change. The fear of association with cults and sects ran through the General Assembly meeting. The group also voted to change the bylaws to reflect the non-cult status, adding a line that read: "This association is secular and apolitical." These changes were the only two that went through without any debate or argument. In fact, they were the only two changes made to the bylaws at the General Assembly, because the group members did not agree on any of the other proposed changes. The other changes were largely bureaucratic, though important to the functioning of the group. But the seeming ease with which the group made changes in their name and bylaws to demonstrate their non-cult status speaks to the fear of cult accusations.

Thus while the environment served as a cultural tool for both movements, religion as a cultural tool benefited the U.S. movement and worked against the French movement. U.S. activists were able to use Christian rhetoric to promote animal rights issues, and organizations such as the Christian Vegetarian Association engaged in vegetarian outreach to Christians. In contrast, in France, animal rights organizations suffered from being portrayed as cult members, and they tried to avoid any association with religious movements or organizations because of these cultural beliefs about vegetarians and vegans.

4 Health

Beliefs about what constitutes healthy eating are socially constructed (Keane 1997). While dietitians and doctors can tell us what nutrients we need in order to survive, the way in which we obtain those nutrients varies greatly. Beliefs about the healthfulness of vegetarian and vegan diets are also culturally bounded. Activists in the United States benefited from, and capitalized upon, beliefs that vegetarian and vegan diets were healthier than a meat-based diet. Activists in France, however, did not benefit from this cultural resource. Instead, beliefs about the dangers of vegetarian and vegan diets plagued their work and posed a significant challenge to them.

Veganism as Healthy in the United States

In the United States, meat has gone from being seen as supremely healthy, the ideal food, to being seen as questionable and sometimes dangerous (Fiddes 1991). In the late twentieth and early twenty-first centuries, major meat-borne illnesses such as BSE (bovine spongiform encephalopathy) or "mad cow disease," hoof and mouth disease, and E. coli outbreaks have contributed to this vision of meat as dangerous. In the past few years, numerous recalls of meat have also added to this view. In February 2008, the USDA issued the largest meat recall in history—143 million pounds of beef—because a California meatpacker allowed "downer cows," or sick and non-ambulatory cows, to enter the food supply.

Medical research has shown that diets high in animal protein from dairy and eggs are associated with cancer, whereas plant-based diets are associated with lower mortality (Levine *et al.* 2014). In popular culture, the popularity of Eric Schlosser's 2001 book *Fast Food Nation* hammered home the idea that animal products, especially factory-farmed, mass-produced, and mass-distributed animal products, are bad for human health, the environment, and animals.

Paralleling this idea of meat as dangerous is the view of vegetarianism and veganism as healthy. The American Dietetic Association published a position paper with the Dietitians of Canada in support of vegetarian diets: "It is the position of the American Dietetic Association and Dietitians of Canada that appropriately planned vegetarian diets are healthful, nutritionally adequate, and provide health benefits in the prevention and treatment of certain diseases" (American Dietetic Association

2003: 748). This position paper goes on to laud the benefits of a vegetarian diet for preventing heart disease, obesity, hypertension, diabetes, osteoporosis, and many other diseases and illnesses. Many health insurance companies even offer discounts to people following the Dean Ornish "Lifestyle Management Program," a program designed to combat heart disease and other illnesses, and which is based on a vegetarian diet (Preventative Medicine Research Institute 2015).

These medical claims that vegetarianism is healthy, even healthier than meat-based diets, do not apply to adults alone. The American Dietetic Association also promotes vegetarian and vegan diets for humans at all stages of the life cycle:

> Well-planned vegan, lacto-vegetarian, and lacto-ovo-vegetarian diets are appropriate for all stages of the life cycle, including pregnancy and lactation. Appropriately planned vegan, lacto-vegetarian, and lacto-ovo-vegetarian diets satisfy nutrition needs of infants, children, and adolescents and promote normal growth. Vegetarian diets in childhood and adolescence can aid in the establishment of lifelong healthy eating patterns and can offer some important nutritional advantages. (American Dietetic Association 2003: 754–755)

Dr. Benjamin Spock, a leading expert on children's health, promoted vegetarianism and veganism for children in the seventh edition of his best-selling 1998 book *Baby and Child Care*. The reaction of other doctors and nutritionists was not that of whole-hearted support. Many still called it risky, difficult, and dangerous (Brody 1998). Children's vegetarianism is a touchier subject than vegetarianism for adults. Nevertheless, these currents all point to a vision of vegetarianism and veganism as healthy, and healthier than eating meat.

Even though doctors and dietitians promote vegetarianism and veganism as healthy, this does not mean that people will change their diets or even believe their claims in the first place. More people are taking their health into their own hands, self-diagnosing with the help of internet resources like WebMD. Add to this a healthy postmodern distrust of the universal truths promoted by the medical establishment, and we can see that not everyone will be swayed by the medical establishment's promotion of vegetarianism and veganism. Jenna (Vegan Outreach) also noted that it was easier for people to add items to their diet than to remove them:

> It's much harder for people to eliminate things from their diet than it is too add something in. For example, you see the success of supplements and people feeling good when they include green tea or wine or chocolate in their diet for the antioxidants. But it's much harder for them to say, "Okay. I'm not going to eat dairy anymore because of the negative effects it has."

It is highly likely to be easier to add decadent foods like chocolate and red wine to one's diet than to take out comfort foods like meat and cheese. Stewart (Vegan Outreach) also noted that, despite the growth of vegetarianism, meat consumption has actually increased:

You're up against a society that has gone the complete opposite direction over the last several decades where meat was once a, percentage wise, a relatively small part of our diet. And now, for some people, it's 90 percent of their diet. They're having meat for breakfast, lunch, and dinner and they're *so* reliant on it.

One might think that since the advent of the contemporary animal rights movement, which centers on promoting veganism, meat consumption would have declined. On the contrary, the average annual per capita consumption of meat and poultry in the United States has steadily risen from 196.4 pounds in 1980 to 221.2 pounds in 2006 (National Beef Cattlemen's Association 2015). This is a whopping increase from the mid-twentieth century, when in the 1950s Americans consumed 138.2 pounds of meat (including poultry) per capita (United States Department of Agriculture 2002).

Despite these numbers, activists were not dismayed. Rather, they saw the increase in meat consumption as leading to an increase in health problems, which would, in turn, lead to an interest in vegetarianism, as Justice (SOS) explained:

Now, more than ever in the past, physicians and people, consumers, people in the medical industry, scientists, are linking diet to health. And I think *that* is going to affect how people choose to eat. The products that they buy, I think people are going to be more willing to purchase and support what they see as health foods or alternative foods, which I think can only create a ripple effect that leads to a greater understanding of vegetarianism and veganism and animal-rights. I mean, I got into it for health reasons, and it just progressed very naturally, and then it became more about morality and animal-rights more so than about health.

Justice optimistically believed that the health problems caused by such rampant meat consumption would lead to an increased awareness of and interest in vegetarian and vegan foods. Her personal foray into veganism also echoed sociologist Howard Becker's (1960) theory of commitment, in that she committed to one action and subsequently experienced other, unforeseen benefits. Originally interested in healthy eating, Justice learned of the benefits of her diet for animals, and subsequently became so interested in the animal rights argument that she became president of her university's animal rights group.

Animal rights activists in the United States often took such a long-term view on the state of their movement. Eric, one of the faculty advisors for Speak Out for Species (SOS), spoke of how vegetarians and vegans have benefited from an increased awareness of the health aspects of vegetarian and vegan diets:

I think a lot of that comes back to my slow evolution to where I am now, it would have been much easier had I had that [information and support]. I had to pretty much seek out information on my own, and I had to do it in a college environment where all the things I was starting to think about put me out of the mainstream, and just thinking about a speaker we had at SOS a few weeks ago, we had a registered dietitian come to speak, and how great that would have been when I was in college, trying to survive on grilled cheese and French fries.

Eric spoke of when SOS invited registered dietitian George Eisman to speak at the University of Georgia. Eisman was a faculty member in Dietetics and Nutrition at several universities, and he created the first accredited program in Vegetarian Studies. The following year, SOS invited "mad cowboy" Howard Lyman to speak, again on the health benefits of a vegan diet. Both events were among the highest attended of all SOS-sponsored events up to that point, with 85 people attending Eisman's talk, and a whopping 220 at Lyman's talk.[1]

Thus many U.S. doctors and dietitians believe vegetarianism and veganism are healthy, and audiences will turn out in droves to learn about the benefits of these diets. But it is also important to understand the real changes that come about as a result of these beliefs. Animal rights activists have garnered support from legislators to provide vegan options on public school menus, a huge accomplishment. Amber worked on one such campaign, which she described as a success:

> [The campaign] seeks to get plant-based options in children's schools, in the public school system. We worked with some legislators in California, with a group that was already active there, and they were actually able to pass legislation mandating that vegan options be available to children in their entire school system, their entire school district. That is a particular success because it is mandated, and it is an entire school district.

She found the difficult part to be not passing the legislation, but rather implementing the program, because of the requirements for cost and nutritional ratios, a process on which her group continues to work. Thus activists in the United States enjoyed the support of doctors, dietitians, and even government legislators, who helped promote the idea that vegetarian and vegan diets were healthy. The permeation of such beliefs in U.S. popular culture, from *Fast Food Nation* to Lisa Simpson being a vegetarian, provided animal rights activists with a powerful cultural resource with which they could promote vegetarianism, veganism, and animal rights.

Using Health Arguments and "Health Crazes" in the United States

How did U.S. animal rights activists use these cultural resources to their advantage? Or, given the dilemma that activists faced over using environmental arguments to promote vegetarianism, did they use health arguments at all? There was much less debate

1 Thank you to SOS faculty advisers Wendy Moore and Eric Griffith for providing attendance numbers.

over using health arguments, though activists did see quandaries similar to those surrounding environmental arguments. Amber described a central problem when she explained how her group evaluated the success of their strategies and tactics:

> It's hard to tell which tactic to use, so we mix it up. And that more people will try vegetarianism or veganism for their own personal health reasons. So a lot of people focus on that. However, the fail rate is higher than if they do it for the animal-rights reasons. So if they are motivated by a strong desire to help the animals, they are more likely to stay vegetarian or vegan than if they do it for their own personal health. So again, what do you choose? Do you choose the path that gives you the stronger converts, or the path that maybe gives you more quantity-wise?

Amber did not cite specific studies, but said she had read reports from Faunalytics that found that people who become vegetarian or vegan for animal rights reasons remain more committed than people who do so for health reasons. This did not stop her group from using health reasons, however. Jack Norris, the co-founder of Vegan Outreach and a registered dietitian himself, gave a number of explanations as to why his group did not focus on health:

> There's a number of reasons why. One is that we are trying to create a grass-roots movement that convinces people to see animals differently to a large extent. Our target audience, which is people we think are most likely to change and make a permanent change in their lives, are at an age in their life where they are not as concerned about chronic health problems as older people are, say, once you hit your forties or something. So they're really not motivated much by health reasons. So it would be kind of wasted on our best audience to do something like that.

Jack went on to explain that if people only cut animal products from their diet and ate "what's left over out of the 'Standard American Diet,'" they would be hungry and unhealthy and would tell everyone how horrible a vegan diet was. As part of Vegan Outreach, Jack created and manages a website on vegan health. While he obviously believes a vegan diet is healthy, he was more interested, as he said, in encouraging people "to see animals differently." Thus Jack and Vegan Outreach did not use health arguments to further their animal rights cause, but they did provide resources on healthy eating for people who want to become vegetarians or vegans.

Most activists and animal rights organizations, despite their misgivings about the commitment of people who become vegetarian or vegan for their own health, availed themselves of this particular cultural tool. They saw health as a resource they could use to target the aging population of baby boomers, people worried about the "obesity epidemic" in the U.S. (Saguy 2013), and as a curative diet for those with certain illnesses. Activists also saw the U.S. obsession with various "health crazes" as an opportunity to promote vegetarianism. In a country where millions of people adhered to the Atkins Diet, Carrie (SOS) saw the health aspects of vegetarianism as having an equal potential for such popularity:

All the health crazes. I think that could be really helpful. If we could make people understand that a vegetarian diet is really healthy, and good for your weight, which is something that everybody—I mean, I guess it's not always good for your weight, but if you do it right, it could be. Better than the Atkins Diet. If he got that much of a following, it seems animal rights activists could.

The Atkins Diet, developed by Dr. Robert Atkins in the late 1960s, surged in popularity in the early 2000s. Advocating a low-carbohydrate and high-protein diet, which usually translated into high meat intake, the diet became the target of much criticism from nutritionists and animal rights advocates. Activists level the same critiques towards the heavily meat-based "paleo" diet that is so fashionable in the 2010s.

Activists certainly capitalized upon America's diet obsessions. Rory Freedman and Kim Barnouin wrote *Skinny Bitch* in 2005, described on the book cover as "A no-nonsense, tough-love guide for savvy girls who want to stop eating crap and start looking fabulous!" But this is no ordinary weight-loss book. It promotes a strictly vegan diet, contains a wealth of information on animal rights, and debunks perceptions about meat and health in a chapter entitled "Have No Faith: Government Agencies Don't Give a Shit About Your Health." When Victoria Beckham was seen holding a copy of it in a Los Angeles store in May 2007, the book became a best-seller in England and the United States (Rich 2007). It was number one on *The New York Times* best-seller list for paperback advice for 19 weeks, and remained on the best-seller list for over a year after that. The authors have since written several others books aimed at men, pregnant women, and couples.

While *Skinny Bitch* focuses on weight loss, other organizations promoted vegetarianism and veganism as ways to combat heart disease and other health issues, and they tried to target the aging baby-boom population on this issue. Many activists worried that promoting vegetarianism for health reasons hit upon people's self-interest rather than interest in helping animals. However, it did not stop their organizations from using a health argument in their activism. The same debate existed in France, although with vastly different resources available for promoting veganism for health reasons.

Veganism as Deadly in France

The discourse surrounding health, vegetarianism, and veganism in France took nearly the opposite form to in the United States. In contrast to the American Dietetic Association, which supports vegetarianism and veganism at all stages of life, the main French dietetic association, Association des Dieteticiens de Langue Française, has no such position paper and no information on vegetarianism or veganism. French animal rights activists thus viewed the medical establishment as a primary challenge to their work.

A lack of critical discourse at the medical level alone does not necessarily characterize the universal condemnation in France of the healthfulness of vegetarianism and veganism. People widely believe that vegetarianism leads to severe and dangerous vitamin deficiencies. This belief is best summarized in an exchange between Stephanie Rebato, a vegetarian actress and PETA France supporter, and Jean-Pierre Coffe, a former actor turned regional cuisine expert, on the talk show *T'Empêches Tout le Monde de Dormir* in October 2006. Though the pair were originally invited on the show to discuss the fur trade, the conversation turned to vegetarianism, which Stephanie Rebato attempted to promote for health reasons:

Stephanie Rebato:	I'd like to specify that people do not have to eat meat in order to be in good health.
Jean-Pierre Coffe:	Now that, oh, that, you have no proof to say that.
Rebato:	Many people are vegetarian for their health.
Coffe:	Bring a scientist who says this.
Rebato:	On the other hand, fur is a debate that we can't just pass off.
Coffe:	[louder] Bring a scientist who says this!
Marc-Olivier Fogiel [talk show host]:	Don't piss Stephanie off, be careful!
Coffe:	You accused the furrier of counter-truths. Now I accuse you of counter-truths. Bring with you, next time, bring with you . . .
Rebato:	[interrupts] Why are you defending this man?
Coffe:	[continues] Bring the man with you who says meat is bad for your health. I defend the same combat as you. But I find you excessive, and useless, in this combat, because excessiveness is unpleasant! [Measured, but getting louder with each word.]
Rebato:	But . . .
	Both Jean-Pierre Coffe and Stephanie Rebato are cut off when the audience starts applauding and cheering for Coffe's comments.

The two main characters in this exchange are metonyms: Stephanie Rebato standing in for animal rights activists in France, and Jean-Pierre Coffe standing in for the typical French person who lauds tradition, gastronomy, and *produits du terroir* (regional specialties). Coffe, a popular expert on cuisine, who has written over a dozen culinary guides and cookbooks, challenged Rebato to prove that vegetarianism was healthy. Many popular chefs in the U.S., such as Anthony Bourdain, are noted for their disdain of vegetarians and vegans, arguing that plant-based food is not cuisine, and vegetarians and vegans are ignorant of "good food." While Coffe certainly agrees with those chefs, here his primary critique was of the healthfulness of vegetarianism. Coffe demanded to see a scientist, or any man (*le monsieur*, he said) who claimed vegetarianism was good for one's health.

This exchange between Rebato and Coffe is intended to give readers a taste of the vitriol launched at vegetarians in France. French objections to the healthfulness of vegetarianism usually took more nuanced forms. People saw vegetarianism as a medical problem, as provoking vitamin deficiencies, and it received no support from the medical establishment or from legislators. Many French activists spoke of wanting to become vegetarian when they were in their teens, but they said their parents opposed this move. This phenomenon also occurred in the United States, but the difference was that in France, these activists' parents would often consult doctors or nutritionists, who further denounced vegetarianism. In the U.S., such doctors might simply counsel parents to inform themselves on how to prepare well-balanced vegetarian meals.

This medical critique proved so strong that even people who believed in animal rights and who personally knew many healthy vegetarians and vegans questioned their convictions in light of doctors' critiques. For example, I met Pierre, from Paris, at Les Estivales de la Question Animale, after which he decided to become vegetarian. I saw him again at an Association Végétarienne de France dine-out in Paris, where he said he was doubting his decision. He had consulted a nutritionist, who told him he was too young—at age 19—to become vegetarian, and that if he did, his muscles would weaken and he would no longer be able to play sports. Two other attendees sitting near us said that nutritionists and doctors hate vegetarianism because they do not study it in school, thus they believe people need meat and animal products to survive. They said vegetarian nutritionists would tell him otherwise.

This threat of vitamin deficiencies surrounded the idea of veganism in non-vegans' discourse. Carol, a woman from Scotland who had lived in France for almost 20 years, saw this as a specifically French problem, and she contrasted France with Britain, where she said it was "how things should be" as regards animal rights. When I asked her to explain further, she said:

> Awareness, public awareness. So that people are aware of the issues, and are basically sympathetic, even if they do nothing about it. Even if, a British person, even if a British person eats meat, they know why people don't eat meat. They know that. And sometimes they feel guilty about eating meat, but they still do. I mean, British people know that things are tested on animals, they know these things. Even if they don't fight to eradicate these things, they know. They still know about it. They know what vegetarianism is, and they know why. Whereas in France, that's not the case. Not yet. And I'll say that most British people now realize that a vegetarian, vegan diet is better for you. That's not what you get in France. That's just a, there's a big fat problem with awareness, really. And they're not considered whackos and cranks any longer. But in France we are.

Carol's outsider perspective shed light on the French idea that vegetarians would all die of vitamin deficiencies, and she blamed this misconception on a general lack of public awareness. Where does such awareness come from? In the United States, the support of doctors and dietitians helped spread the belief that vegetarianism was healthy. But such professionals in France did not share this belief with their U.S. and U.K. counterparts, as Diana (AVF) explained:

It's an immediate, extremely narrow-minded assumption that it's going to be bad for your health, that you're going to be dying of deficiencies. There's a lack of willingness in France to look to outside research, other countries, other cultural references. They are incredibly chauvinistic like that. It doesn't occur to them. I mean, you get, the doctor Jean-Marie LeCerf, the Institut Pasteur de Lille, which is the reference, like the British Medical Institution, for Pete's sake, he's in the nutrition section, and he's the great pioneer of vegetarianism, or what he calls "alternative menus," because of the importance of reducing meat consumption for health. He will turn around and say on television, just five or six years ago, "One can be vegetarian for several years without any risk, provided one is very careful of one's diet, of finding a balance." Now that shows a tremendous contempt for international literature, scientific literature, and for simply opening his eyeballs and seeing what's been happening in India for millennia.

Diana, an activist who moved to France from New Zealand 18 years ago, saw the French doctors' and dietitians' lack of looking to sources outside of France as the primary problem in maintaining the idea that vegetarianism was unhealthy. Not only did French doctors ignore non-French sources, but the French medical establishment enjoyed a hegemony in France, making it a primary challenge to animal rights activists. André, the president of the Association Végétarienne de France, cited the medical establishment as an even bigger constraint than animal cruelty: "Animal mistreatment, that it is cruel to kill them, people can come to recognize that, but in my opinion, the medical establishment is the biggest obstacle." He believed people would come to see killing animals as cruel sooner than they would come to see vegetarianism as healthy. Thus French people, medical doctors or not, steadfastly believed that a vegetarian or vegan diet was extremely unhealthy, and would lead to severe vitamin deficiencies.

Capitalizing on Misconceptions about Vegetarianism in France

These cultural beliefs would seemingly point to French activists *not* using health as an argument for veganism and vegetarianism. On the contrary, this did not stop activists from trying to use health arguments, despite their lack of cultural resonance. To combat such anti-vegetarian rhetoric in the French culture, animal rights activists capitalized upon misconceptions of vegetarianism, even potentially detrimental ones such as *néo-végétarisme* or "new vegetarianism," discussed in more detail below, which is essentially meat reduction (Briet 2010). Activists also attempted to make the most of heath crises and governmental healthy eating programs, though many critiqued using a health argument to promote vegetarianism for the same reasons they opposed environmental arguments.

At tabling events, passersby often contradicted the health claims of animal rights activists who promoted vegetarianism. To those who said that vegetarians and vegans would surely die of vitamin deficiencies, a common response was, "How can you explain that we are all standing here?" Bernadette, a vegetarian since birth, now vegan for the past few years, often used her own healthiness as a counter-example for people who claimed vegetarians could never be healthy. She recounted one such encounter at a tabling event in our interview:

> In fact, this bloke once told me that you couldn't be a vegetarian or a vegan and be healthy. It just wasn't possible. And so once again, I said, "I've never eaten meat, and I've never had any health problems at all." And he just stood there and said, "No, that's not true." I said, "Come on, I know that I'm a vegetarian, I know I've never had meat, and I know I'm healthy." He said, "No, you're lying, it's not possible." He said, "Even if you are a vegetarian or a vegan, you've got no strength. You couldn't run, for example. It's physically impossible for you to run." I said, "I could run up and down the street and prove it to you, if you want." But he just wouldn't listen.

Bernadette's physical existence as a vegetarian since birth did not convince this person that vegetarians could be healthy. While Bernadette reacted in a straight-forward manner, other activists tried to take a lighthearted approach and made fun of such misconceptions. For example, at an Association Végétarienne de France dine-out, one attendee brought a magazine on organic food, the "special edition on protein." One of the articles claimed that vegetarians were all weak, anorexic, no fun, and had vitamin deficiencies. The woman who brought the magazine passed it around the tables, along with a card that we all signed. On the card she wrote, "Tonight we had a gathering of a bunch of weak, skinny, deficient, boring people. We all weigh 55 pounds, except for Jacques, who is the fat one at 65 pounds." She went on to explain how the author was completely wrong about vegetarian food, and how he needed to recognize the diversity of vegetarians and vegetarian food. Of course, reacting with humor to the claim that vegetarians are no fun was a stra-tegic move in itself. But this reaction speaks to the larger strategy of attempting to capitalize upon the misconceptions of vegetarians.

One such misconception of vegetarianism in France was *néo-végétarisme*, or "new vegetarianism," which does not mean cutting out animal products or meat from one's diet entirely, but rather simply cutting down on meat (Briet 2010). Despite its potential to harm the animal rights movement by reducing vegetarian-ism to not eating steak three times a day, some activists saw it as a potential tool in their already meager toolkit, as Diana (Association Végétarienne de France) explained

> They've even appropriated vegetarianism in France and adapted it to their own cultural context by inventing what is called "*néo-végétarisme*." You know, neo-vegetarian. It's sort of a food trend amongst young people, where they are reducing their meat consumption, and they're switched onto fruits and vegetables, because it's fashionable. So it's interesting, to me, to see the aspect of vegetarianism that's got the most publicity in recent years has been this *néo-végétarisme*, which isn't true vegetarianism at all, because they still have a big red steak every so often if they feel like it, or they have fish when

they feel like it, so it's sort of, I think that phenomenon is a direct reflection of French society, which is faithful to its traditions, but which prides itself on creative cooking, and which prides itself on their cultural innovations. I think it's a superficial phenomenon; however, I am happy to ride the wave, to ride the back of that, to try to encourage people to come to a deeper kind of ethical commitment of vegetarianism.

Diana claimed she was happy to "ride the wave" of *néo-végétarisme* to use it as a path to "true" vegetarianism. Later in the interview, Diana also mentioned health crises, such as mad cow disease, cholesterol, and obesity. As these health issues became more and more prominent, animal rights activists prepared to use them as reasons to become vegetarian and vegan.

Cultural Opportunities and Obstacles in France

Activists also used more quickly emerging crises, such as tainted meat, in their work. Jérôme described one such demonstration that PETA France attempted:

About a year ago, there was a dozen people who were hospitalized, of which a few died, from food poisoning from eating meat. PETA England asked us if we could do an action to exploit this current event, to promote vegetarianism. It was an excellent action, which consisted of lying in coffins and saying "Meat kills, go vegetarian" in front of Fouquet's in Paris, on the Champs Élysées.

PETA is known for its opportunism, as with their "payback time" demonstrations when bird flu began spreading throughout the world in 2005 and 2006. This particular demonstration was canceled not because people found it to be in bad taste, but because it happened at the same time as the riots in the Paris suburbs in fall 2005. PETA France organizers realized they would not be able to compete with the riots for the press's attention and canceled the demonstration

French animal rights activists tried to lobby politicians to get them to support vegetarian eating. Association Végétarienne de France runs a campaign to get vegetarian menus in collective dining facilities, and they attempted to garner support from politicians. At the General Assembly of the association in January 2007, André Méry reported back on the campaign. He said the Association Végétarienne de France sent letters to députés (Parliament members), but said it was "not a very effective route." Three of the five députés contacted responded, and André said, "You can see that they don't care." He showed the three negative responses on his Powerpoint, which read:

A vegetarian diet cannot always satisfy the body's need for iron, notably in women and children, since meat and fish products hold high quality iron, which is difficult to replace with plant-based foods, for which the iron is less readily absorbed.

The establishment of specific measures may be considered solely if the child is the victim of health problems that have evolved over a long period.

Since 2001, France has equipped itself with a politics of nutrition through the national nutrition health program [programme national nutrition santé, PNNS]. It is, of course, in the interest of the chiefs of collective dining services, as it is of its users, to refer to the recommendations contained in this program

On this slide, André said, "See, the first one says that you need to eat meat for iron," and the audience groaned. But the third quote represents another path where animal rights activists tried to promote vegetarianism for health reasons. This national nutrition program seemed like it could provide an opportunity for AVF to promote its campaign for vegetarian menus in collective dining services, but in practice, it did not, as André explained in our interview:

Politicians consider this campaign to be sufficient, and prefer to have colloquia or studies based on this official campaign, which does not question meat at all, which asks people to just change their food habits a little bit, and the rest, they consider secondary. Vegetarianism is considered excessive and useless for health, you just have to change your diet a bit, eat less sugar, exercise more, eat less processed foods, eat more fruits and vegetables. That's the official orientation. There is no positive reaction to this campaign at the political level.

Here we can see a direct contrast to the successful campaign run by a U.S. organization to implement vegan menus in school systems in California. The U.S. group needed to make their vegan menus conform to the nutritional requirements already in place, but the Association Végétarienne de France did not have that opportunity because politicians saw the national nutrition program as sufficient.

Debates over Health Arguments in France

Finally, in addition to all of these constraints to using health arguments in France, French animal rights activists also engaged in debates over whether to use health arguments at all. Just as activists questioned the appropriateness of using environmental arguments, they believed health arguments were insufficient because they did not question the anthropocentric philosophies surrounding human–animal relationships, and they did not necessitate serious lifestyle changes.

For example, when tabling with Philippe (AVIS; Association Végétarienne & Végétalienne d'InformationS) in Toulouse one day, we discussed the recently passed smoking ban in France. Philippe said that the only time that people change their behavior is when they are forced to do so, like with the smoking ban. He said when the warning labels on cigarettes appeared, they did not change people's smoking habits. What was ironic, he continued, was that in France it was "cool" to oppose genetically modified foods, and that many people claimed the reasons for their opposition were health-related. However, he said, people only used health as a reason to be anti-GMO, and did not relate that argument to smoking. Philippe said smoking was never good for your health, but people continued to smoke anyway. This is why, he clarified, the health argument does not work in France for eating meat, because people can say that they could eat just a little meat and it would not be bad for them.

Going further, and echoing French activists' critiques of environmental arguments, activists avoided health-based arguments on the grounds that they do not question the status of animals. Encouraging people to become vegan was not the only goal—veganism was one part of animal rights, and activists did not want to promote one part at the expense of others, as Nathalie (Collectif Antispéciste de Paris) explained:

> There are people who use a little bit of all sorts of tactics so people will become vegetarian. For many people, the essential is that they become vegetarian, and not necessarily why they become vegetarian. If you want my opinion, for me I think it's very important that people become vegetarian for the animals, not because it's good for their health, because that means they are still speciesists and they can still wear fur or leather, use products tested on animals, etc. For me, that does not denounce the problem in itself. I am vegetarian and also antispeciesist, and my vegetarianism is for the animals. There may very well be fewer famines if there were more vegetarians, and it's probably good for the environment, but for me, those are still speciesist arguments because they don't take into account the animals at all—and I haven't even talked to you about health.

Nathalie claimed the health argument was the "worst" of all because it only takes the individual into account. As explained earlier, most animal rights groups focus on vegetarianism and veganism in their campaigns, because that affects the largest number of animals. However, that does not mean activists wanted people to stop at vegetarianism and continue to wear fur, as Nathalie said. Another reason activists found fault with using a health argument was that it did not create more activists, which was what the animal rights movement needed, according to David:

> Someone who becomes vegetarian for her health does that for a selfish reason and thus will not become an activist. That will not augment the number of vegetarians exponentially; it will just create one more vegetarian. If we really want the movement to concern society as a whole, then every vegetarian that we create, we must make them an activist [. . .] It is like that that it will propagate, that it will become a popular movement, a mass movement.

In this sense, we can see how health arguments were even more objectionable to some animal rights activists than environmental arguments. With environmental arguments, there were at least chances to create coalitions with environmental activists. Using health arguments does not create a social movement. It would instead, David said, create a mass of people "solely capable of taking into account its own selfish interests."

The French organizations and activists who used health arguments to further their cause primarily included groups that were branches of, or that were influenced by, Anglo-Saxon animal rights groups. The French branch of the U.S.-based PETA had no qualms about using health arguments, as Jérôme noted when explaining the French movement's reaction to PETA's media-attracting tactics:

> That's a theory regularly raised by French activists, that the culture in France is too different by this history of culture, of nudity. I'm not hiding myself, there are people, antispeciesists who don't like PETA precisely because, especially what angers them is that we don't speak only of animals. We have no scruples about using health arguments, for example, for the good reason that we think that we can more easily convince someone with multiple arguments.

As I will demonstrate in Chapter 7, such a pragmatic approach of using multiple arguments is a primarily U.S. (and Anglo-Saxon) strategy. Working for one such organization, Jérôme believed that using multiple frames, or casting a wider net, would result in winning more people over to the animal rights cause.

The Association Végétarienne de France, another group highly influenced by Anglo-Saxon organizations, also employed multiple arguments to promote vegetarianism. AVF takes a four-pronged approach, promoting vegetarianism for the animals, for people's health, for the environment, and for reducing hunger in developing countries. While all of the AVF activists I interviewed were vegetarian or vegan for animal rights reasons, they employed multiple arguments in their activism. Frédéric explained that AVF accepts all points of view and they have activists who became vegetarian and vegan for the animals as well as for health reasons or the environment. He was vegetarian for animal reasons, which he believed made a stronger case for vegetarianism:

> When I became vegetarian, I was vegetarian for the animals. But I discovered that it was good for your health, even better, that's good, and for the environment, great, that's perfect! My personal conviction is that there are arguments like that, one, two, three, like wagons on a train. There's a locomotive, and the locomotive is the motor. For me, the locomotive is vegetarianism for the animals. That doesn't mean that the others aren't important, they are important, but that means if I were vegetarian for health reasons, if I get sick, for example, if the day that I get better I eat meat, for example, you see, that's what they might tell themselves. The environment, what does that mean, does that mean that if one day we had no more pollution, if we had less pollution that we could still eat meat?

Frédéric went on to say that he used health and environmental arguments if he thought that was what primarily interested the person, and that he hoped that becoming vegetarian for those reasons would open up their eyes to animal rights. However, he still maintained that health and environmental reasons conjure less commitment to vegetarianism than animal rights reasons.

Most French activists believed animal rights reasons were strongest for winning new vegetarians and vegans. André agreed with this but saw a real need to focus on health reasons, given the dearth of information about the healthfulness of plant-based diets in France:

> You can notice, by the questions you receive from people in *salons* [discussion groups], or people who contact you from all over France, that the primary questions from people, their main worries are about health. Thus maybe it's good to project shocking films, or to do shocking actions, maybe, but I think that the most important is to do an in-depth work on the question of health, to do a scientific study, to call on all the medical studies there are on the subject, in order to show people that they have not only nothing to worry about, but they have everything to gain, in fact. And that seems more important to me, that's mainly what motivates me. Well, it motivates me by force, because I have noticed that these are the questions that people ask, so we have to address these issues.

French activists found themselves in a quandary. On the one hand, they did not want to use health reasons to promote vegetarianism and veganism, since that did not question the anthropocentric philosophies that put humans superior to animals. On the other hand, given the lack of information on health, many people had questions about the topic, and thus activists felt compelled to answer those questions.

In this chapter we have seen how health arguments added yet another tool to U.S. activists' tactical toolkit. U.S. activists were successfully able to use health arguments to promote vegetarianism and veganism, especially with the backing of organizations such as the American Dietetic Association. In contrast, French activists were not able to fully rely on using health arguments, whether for ideological or practical reasons. Either French activists avoided such arguments because they believed they contributed to speciesism, or they attempted to use them but failed because of the strong anti-vegetarian sentiments from the general public and from the medical establishment.

5   Food

Vegan food is both a goal and a means for promoting animal rights. Although the overwhelming majority of people in France and the United States eat meat, activists used vegan food as a cultural resource when promoting veganism for animal rights reasons. Animal rights activists in both France and the United States hold several nation-wide events promoting vegan food. In the United States, activists hold the Great American Meatout event, where several vegan companies donate free food samples and coupons to activists for their events. In France, activists celebrate Vegan Day by perfecting vegan recipes for traditional French foods such as *pain au chocolat* or *crêpes* that they cook and serve at their events. The U.S. Meatout events typically celebrate the ease with which one can eat pre-made vegan food products found in mainstream supermarkets. The French vegan events typically showcase ways to celebrate French culinary traditions without using animal products. In this chapter I explore the cultural and structural reasons behind using food as both a goal and a tactic, as well as how and why those two aspects differ between countries. I discuss French gastronomy, *patrimoine culturel*, vegan food in France, and vegan food in the United States. In doing so, I will show how the same cultural resource—food—functions differently in different countries.

Gastronomy

Gastronomy differs from mere cuisine. Gastronomy began in France, and is typically French. It is born of modernity, and influenced by the scientific process. Cultural sociologist Priscilla Parkhurt Ferguson (1998: 602) calls gastronomy "the systematic, socially valorized pursuit of culinary creativity." Jean Anthelme Brillat-Savarin, one of the founders of the French gastronomic field, first defined gastronomy as:

> the reasoned comprehension of everything connected with the nourishment of man. Its aim is to obtain the preservation of man by means of the best possible nourishment. It attains this object by giving guidance, according to certain principles, to all who seek, provide, or prepare substances that may be turned into food. Gastronomy, in fact, is the motive force behind farmers,

vinegrowers, fishermen, and huntsmen, not to mention the great family of cooks, under whatever title they may disguise their employment as preparers of food. (Brillat-Savarin 1994 [1825]: 52)

The origins of the French gastronomic field are found in culinary institutions associated with the aristocracy but, over the course of the second half of the nineteenth century, gastronomy transformed into "a fundamental attribute of 'Frenchness,'" according to Ferguson (1998: 635). Structural factors in France, such as links to the literary field, specific sites dedicated to gastronomic production and consumption, as well as the institution of gastronomic authorities and standards, all served to establish French gastronomy as a national cultural field. Going further, Ferguson (1998) claims the concept of a gastronomic field does not make sense for U.S. culture or cuisine for numerous reasons, most notably because of the sheer size of the United States and its cultural pluralism. There is no "American cuisine" exemplifying or existing in the entirety of the country, save fast food. Thus the gastronomic field is a culinary institution and practice particular to France.

Pierre Bourdieu (1993) notes that fields are dynamic relationships, and are never fully formed, with constant struggles between fields, sub-fields, and actors within fields. In this sense, animal rights activists are not exactly actors *within* the gastronomic field, though they do target it, and their influence is felt and resented there. Within the gastronomic field, one huge shakeup in France came in 2001, when Alain Passard changed his three-star Michelin restaurant, l'Arpège, to a vegetarian menu. In fact it was not quite vegetarian, as Passard continued to serve seafood and some poultry dishes, but Passard and his critics proclaimed it as such. The lack of pork and beef products—even foie gras—combined with Passard's self-proclaimed vegetarianism, caused an uproar in the culinary community and was called "blasphemy," as reported by *The New York Times*:

> In a country where vegetarians are few and considered rather abnormal, his leap across the food barrier has become the gastronomic talk of the moment. The media have examined it with attention usually reserved for political scandal [. . .] But there is still respect for tradition. And this means that every civilized meal should include fish, fowl or beast. The arrival of "le fast food" from overseas was already a blow. But now that such pillars as "le steak" are under attack from one of France's own cardinals of food, even blasé Parisians are demanding explanations. Some have berated Mr. Passard as if he were a warmonger. "Surely you are offending your colleagues who are still cooking meat," said a caller, interrupting an interview in the chef's crowded office. (Simons 2001)

French gastronomy seemingly equates with meat-eating, as Passard went on in his interview to say that while other countries appreciate vegetables and vegetarian cooking, "in France we still have to invent it." Animal rights activists noted that an appreciation for food and cuisine *could* translate into a positive force for veganism and animal rights, but they saw the French gastronomic tradition as too heavily steeped in meat to change quickly or easily, as Frédéric (Association Végétarienne de France) explained:

> I see more handicaps in this country, vis-à-vis food, because we function a lot with tradition, and you get the impression that people are very attached to their traditions, and eating, for example, in Lyon, here you are in a city with a huge tradition of eating pigs, for example, sausage, things like that, specialties. There are andouilettes, those are made with the entrails, and people are very attached to that. You get the impression that if you take that away, you are harming them. And frankly, that comes up whenever you have a discussion with non-vegetarians, when you say, "It's possible to eat good vegetables, too," and they say, "Yeah, but come on, a good sausage!" You see, they can't set it aside. It's in the culture, it's attached to their culture.

Changing the French gastronomic tradition did not come easily, even when respected insiders make those changes. Culture is not infinitely malleable (Hays 1994), and in this case, the French gastronomic tradition seems more rigid than malleable at all. Tali, for example, noted this rigidity when describing traditional French dishes, none of which were vegetarian, much less vegan:

> What is typically French is attachment to tradition, under the pretext that it is a tradition so it must be kept. It's that, the refusal to change. That foie gras is a tradition, French food—you don't even have one typical French dish that is vegetarian. You open up a French cookbook, and there's nothing without meat. The French tradition is meat everywhere.

Although fields do change and evolve, the French gastronomic field has yet to open up to vegetarian and vegan cooking. French gastronomy is synonymous with eating meat. Moreover, French people do not see vegetarianism or veganism as a potential avenue for gastronomy—they see it as an insult. Just as French chefs critiqued Passard for avoiding meat, waiters admonished vegetarians who dared to dine in gastronomic restaurants. Bernadette described a vegetarian friend's encounter with a waiter at a French gastronomic restaurant, where she realized there was not one dish without meat on the menu:

> So, being a vegetarian, she asked them very politely if she could have a dish without meat. She said, "Can I have this dish, but without the," I forgot whatever kind of meat there was in it. And the bloke just literally insulted her, yelled at her, and said, "You can't change French culture. Eating meat is part of who we are. It's a personal insult that you try and modify that with your vegetarianism." That kind of thing. He was really, really aggressive towards her. So obviously they just left, they weren't going to eat there after that. But typical example. It's as if you were attacking them personally. Trying to change their culture.

Thus gastronomy is synonymous with meat. Passard's Arpège has kept its three-star Michelin rating, but it has not exactly caused a vegetarian revolution in French cuisine. Many French animal rights activists lamented this inertia, especially when comparing France and Britain. They said they believed animal rights and vegetarianism took off so quickly in Britain because of their lack of haute cuisine, but more often, they explained that gastronomy meant more than just food to the French, as did André (AVF):

> Even if I make a comparison with British culture, for example, I think that the British were also huge meat eaters, huge hunters, and they had a very, very strong speciesist culture. And yet they succeeded in breaking this and created a very well-developed Vegetarian Society. So you can talk about these sorts of things in France, too, there's the culture of meat, good cuisine, but is that sufficient? I think it's very mixed up in France. There's a tradition of cuisine, but also, there's a philosophical tradition to consider animals as inferiors.

André and other activists pointed to tradition—not just culinary, but also philosophical—when explaining the challenges to the animal rights movement in France. In addition to the tangible, material culture of the meat-based gastronomic tradition, France carried a strong anthropocentric philosophical tradition of humanism. These traditions, these aspects of French culture are structural because they are supra-individual and constrain action. Considering these material and immaterial traditions, we can see how culture cannot simply be "thought away" (Polletta 1999). In France, the desire to protect these traditions was so strong that legislators passed laws to protect them as carriers of *patrimoine culturel*, or cultural heritage.

Tradition and *Patrimoine Culturel*

France prides itself on its culinary traditions. Many other traditions involving animals hold a special place in French culture, notably hunting, the production of foie gras and the practice of *corrida* (bullfighting). Each region specializes in a different animal tradition, as Emmanuel (AVF) explained:

> The particularity in France is that France is a country of tradition. Certain regions of France are linked to hunting, to the exploitation of animals, in general, and, and I'd say that the most shocking for me is hunting, but there are other domains, like corrida. In the North, it's probably more the breeding of pigs in Brittany. There are a lot of regions in France that are very traditional, so what we do in Paris is not what one does in Nîmes for corrida, or what you can do elsewhere, for hunting, for example.

Emmanuel saw hunting as a huge obstacle, which is understandable in context, since France has the highest number of hunters in Western Europe (de la Chesnais and Hofstein 2013). However, there are far fewer hunters in France than in the United States. Approximately 1.8 percent of the French population

(Fédération Nationale des Chasseurs 2015), compared to 6 percent of the U.S. population (U.S. Fish and Wildlife Service 2011), are registered hunters. But in France, this tradition of hunting was so strong that it became a political party, Chasse-Pêche-Nature-Traditions ("Hunting-Fishing-Nature-Tradition," or CPNT), founded in 1989. CPNT counts numerous mayors among their ranks, but has yet to find success in electing national legislators. Frédéric Nihous, the CPNT candidate for the 2007 presidential election in France, took 1.15 percent of the vote, coming in 11th of 12 candidates. In the 2012 presidential elections, Nihous supported Nicolas Sarkozy, because Nihous did not get the 500 signatures necessary to appear on the first-round election ballot.

Emmanuel also mentioned the importance of *corrida* in the south of France—another tradition promoted by CPNT, but, more importantly, one protected by French law. In France, the traditions of foie gras and *corrida* were so respected that when threatened by European Union laws, the French government created legal exceptions for them as carriers of *patrimoine culturel*, or French cultural heritage. Article 654-27-1 of the French Code Rural et de la Pêche Maritime (the set of French legal codes on rural and agricultural issues) states that "Foie gras is part of the cultural and gastronomic tradition that is protected in France. Foie gras refers to the liver of a duck or a goose specially fattened by forced-feeding."[1] On *corrida*, Article 521-1 of the Penal Code states the following:

> The unnecessary infliction, in public or otherwise, of serious maltreatment towards or the commission of an act of cruelty on any domestic or tame animal, or any animal held in captivity, is punished by six months' imprisonment and a fine of €30,000. As an additional penalty, the court may impose a prohibition, permanent or otherwise, against keeping an animal. The provisions of the present article are not applicable to bullfights where an uninterrupted local tradition can be shown. Nor do they apply to cockfights in localities where an uninterrupted tradition can be established. The penalties set out in the first paragraph apply to the creation of any new center for holding cockfights.[2]

Cockfighting was popular in the north of France in the nineteenth century, but now it is more of an issue in the overseas departments and thus not a primary focus of mainland French animal rights organizations. But foie gras and *corrida* are central concerns of many French activists. Organizations such as FLAC (Fédération des Luttes pour l'Abolition des Corridas, or the Federation of Corrida Abolitionists) and CRAC (Comité Radicalement Anti-Corrida, or the Radical Anti-Corrida Committee) are single-issue organizations mobilized against *corrida*, and Stop Gavage is a single-issue organization focused on foie gras (*gavage* refers to the method of force-feeding).

---

1 My translation of the following, since this set of French legal codes does not have an official translation: "Le foie gras fait partie du patrimoine culturel et gastronomique protégé en France. On entend par foie gras, le foie d'un canard ou d'une oie spécialement engraissé par gavage."
2 Official translation found at: www.legifrance.gouv.fr/Traductions/en-English/Legifrance-translations (retrieved January 20, 2016).

Despite the small numbers of CPNT elected officials, most French politicians support protecting foie gras and *corrida* as *patrimoine culturel*, as Yann (CAP) wryly noted:

> Everything that is tradition, hunting, foie gras, the gastronomic culture, there's really an argument that it's tradition, that we must conserve the French patrimoine. For example, in the National Assembly, the only time that the Left and Right agree is on the European law against foie gras. That's when the Left and Right agree to vote for a specific French law to conserve the tradition of foie gras. That shows that everyone agrees, there is no opposition. For them it was obvious that they had to conserve this French tradition above all.

European Union legislation did not threaten hunting, but it did threaten foie gras and *corrida*, and thus French politicians responded by passing laws to protect both practices as carriers of cultural heritage. It can be difficult to pass laws without relatively widespread support for the measures. Litigation is ineffective until there is an "interest convergence" (Bell Jr. 1980)—until public opinion is on the movement's side. Scholars have also shown how litigation and legislation often lag behind public opinion (Rose 1968, Bernstein 2003). Moreover, laws do not dictate cultural beliefs—it is more often the opposite. Thus many activists chose to look at these issues through multiple lenses. Groups such as Stop Gavage, Welfarm, and L214 centered on legislative issues; "L214" refers to the set of legislative codes the group wishes to change. Many other groups primarily focused on cultural aspects, viewing foie gras and *corrida* as cultural practices to be combated symbolically. Virginie (CAP) said, "Symbolically, it's very important—hunting, corrida, foie gras. These are symbols, in fact, really very strong, and thus it's important that we mobilize against them symbolically."

But foie gras represents more than a cultural practice of the rich French gastronomic tradition. While foie gras is available year-round, it is most associated with Christmas, when the vast majority of foie gras is sold and consumed. Concurrently, this is when most animal rights activists ramp up their anti-foie gras actions. At a meeting with the Collectif Antispéciste de Paris in October 2006, when they were planning their upcoming events, Ivora said it would be good to do something against foie gras, because it is "*the* thing you put on the table" at Christmas. Yann said that when you do something against foie gras at Christmas, it's like you want to "kill Christmas." Nathalie laughed and said she wanted to kill Christmas anyway, so that was no problem for her. Everyone laughed, and then Yann said, "But how do you get past tradition?" Everyone went quiet for a moment, and then started debating whether or not to use health arguments, and the best vegan faux foie gras to use for a tasting. But Yann's comment about trying to "get past tradition" pointed to the larger problem facing animal rights activists.

Foie gras production did not denote mere breeding practices; it exemplified long-standing traditions so strongly valued that French legislators put them into law. Moreover, legislators posited these practices as part of the French national identity, to be upheld against the meddling influences of the European Union, as Antoine Comiti of Stop Gavage described:

To see it as something against France, that's, for example, at Brussels, the European Commission, or the countries in the north of Europe, or the Americans, against the traditional French product. Something like the foreigners against the French, and often on foie gras, it's positioned like that. That's a difficulty that stems from the fact that the French movement is not yet visible enough.

These traditions protected by legal standing exemplify the importance of gastronationalism, which sociologist Michaela De Soucey (2010) describes as a way for countries to resist the homogenizing forces of globalization in food. Through gastronationalism, foie gras became a symbol of national identity for France.

France is a country proud of its traditions and slow to change, especially for outside influences such as fast food. Sociologist Rick Fantasia (1995) outlined three points of view on the infiltration of fast food into French society. One, championed by Claude Fischler (2001), sees the emergence of fast-food restaurants in France as simply part of the global circulation of culinary practices. Another sees France as "immune" to outside influences, because, as French sociologist Michel Crozier states, "for many French people there is an association that good food is French and fast food is American and foreign and bad" (Greenhouse 1988). The third perspective characterizes the French response to European initiatives that endanger the production of foie gras. In this view, French cuisine is not immune, but is seriously endangered by outside influences such as fast food. Sebastien (Stop Gavage) characterized the French image of foie gras as fighting against these noxious influences:

> Take foie gras, for example. There are huge amounts of money at stake, as much by the producers as by the supermarkets at Christmas time. Everything is attached to images of conviviality, of parties, of tradition, of something authentic and real against a fast-paced society, against the fast-food society. Those are really the huge challenges.

As with the growing movements towards local food and "slow food," Sebastien said French people saw foie gras as working against these fast-food and fast-paced societal influences. Moreover, as an emblem of French gastronationalism (De Soucey 2010), foie gras embodies something "authentic and real," truly representative of French national identity. Thus, as Yann asked, how can one get past tradition? How can one fight against a commodity that so deeply represents not just the French culinary tradition, but the French national identity, as Antoine described?

French activists used a number of strategies to combat these forces surrounding foie gras. As mentioned above, some took a legislative approach, but most took a symbolic approach, fighting one cultural image with another. Just as anti-*corrida* protesters frequently held signs saying "corrida: la honte" (bullfighting: for shame), many animal rights activists questioned whether the forced-feeding of ducks and geese in *gavage* was really an identity that France would want to export, as David (Lyon Antispécistes) explained:

In the political parties who are against Europe, and who want to limit the influence of Brussels, the example that always comes up is that Europe wants to outlaw foie gras. There, still, it's the French identity that is constructed on the exploitation of animals. Today, in a hidden manner, the question of animals is at the heart of the debate. And today, in a hidden manner, national identity is constructed in a large part against animals. Our task is to tell French people that the French identity, at one period, was reactionary, Petainist, and almost fascist, and that today it has become an identity of a plural France, a France with integrated immigrants, which is antiracist, etc. In the same way, the identity of France was always profoundly hostile towards animals, so we can say that the identity of France is something other than that, it's an open identity, which can reflect on new problems and which can even be at the forefront of these new ideas.

David described the strategy of showing how the new plural, antiracist French identity should be open to animal rights, or at least open to questioning the animal practices that characterized the old "reactionary, Petainist, and almost fascist" French identity. From a life-course perspective, David's strategy might be lost on an older generation that remembers Petain. Capitalizing on the time period when youths undergo a period of self-exploration, identity formation, and a break from their family (Clausen 1986, Coleman and Hendry 1990), Ghislain, director of the PMAF, saw the PMAF's anti-foie gras campaign as a long-term campaign aimed at younger generations more susceptible to such an opening of spirit:

People who are sensitive to the animal movement, and who support us, often will not support us in the foie gras cause. They tell us, "But we only eat it once or twice a year, and it's so good!" So it's more of a long-term campaign. I think that foie gras, the current generation, like my parents, taking away their foie gras will not happen. It's too permeated in French culture. However, we need to destroy the good image that foie gras has in France, especially with younger generations. We need to develop this idea in adolescents, that foie gras is out of fashion, bad, and cruel, that it's bad to eat foie gras. I think that's how we should do our marketing. Because right now, foie gras has a festive side. When people talk about foie gras they think about Christmas parties, of good times with their family. That's certainly a positive image, and we need to break that. Thus our foie gras campaign, we see it as a long-term campaign.

Just as many U.S. animal rights organizations centered their efforts on reaching young adults, whom they found more likely to change their behavior, and who had more years of potential vegetarianism ahead of them, the PMAF focused their long-term campaign on changing the image of foie gras among young French people. They viewed such cultural change as possible with generational change, rather than trying to change a generation of people who never questioned the goodness of foie gras.

Promoting Veganism in France

Understanding these particularly French constraints to using food as a cultural resource, I now turn to the specific strategy of promoting veganism. Vegan outreach worked much better in the U.S. than in France for numerous reasons. For one, misconceptions about veganism and vegetarianism plagued animal rights activists in France. In addition to encountering beliefs that veganism was dangerous and unhealthy, and that vegans were part of a religious cult, French animal rights activists also faced the challenge of ignorance: many French people simply had no idea what vegetarianism or veganism meant. Only about ten years ago, many French people believed that vegetarianism meant simply that one did not eat red meat. This was the case for Christine (AVF), who is now a vegan:

> I didn't go vegetarian until I was 21, because in France, we have a huge amount of trouble with the definition of vegetarianism, so I had the impression that vegetarianism meant you just don't eat red meat. I stopped eating fish when I was 18, and I went totally vegetarian when I was 21, when I met some vegetarians.

The current popular understanding of vegetarianism in France now excludes poultry, but includes eating fish. I thought perhaps these misconceptions about vegetarianism were relegated to people who had little expertise in the realm of food and nutrition, but this idea was proven wrong on a number of occasions. As just one example, when I attended the 2006 annual meeting of the French Sociological Association, I browsed the books available for sale, and I found one book that focused on food. The one chapter on vegetarianism claimed that vegetarians ate fish, and that vegans mostly practiced new-age religions, which explained their veganism. This misconception promulgated by a purported scholar of the subject shows the extent to which such ideas have spread.

In addition to these misconceptions, negative stereotypes of vegetarians and vegans abounded in France. Sebastien (Stop Gavage) called this a "veggiephobia." British sociologists Matthew Cole and Karen Morgan (2011) have studied "vegaphobia" in journalistic treatments of vegetarianism, echoing some of these stereotypes, which Diana (AVF) described as follows:

> The image of the vegetarian in France is changing slightly, but to a large extent, it's still the image of an old-fashioned, nutcase, eccentrically-dressed, marginal—did I say old-fashioned?—person, who's slightly ideologically focused, a little bit virulent about animal rights and what you should be doing. You should be eating dried peas at three o'clock in the morning for your health, or throwing your bosom out the window at four in the morning and drinking fresh air. It's a bad image that we've had in the past. And we've got to modernize our image. We've got to modernize it without falling into the trap of becoming seen as trendy neo-vegetarians who eat their red steak when they feel like it, occasionally.

But more than old-fashioned, health-obsessed, or simply weird, French people saw vegetarians, and especially vegans, as extremists. French people considered these diets and lifestyles fanatical, just as many of them thought that caring about animals beyond companion dogs and cats was irrational. The problem for the French animal rights movement was that this conception of veganism as unreasonable and excessive also shaped activists' perceptions of what types of actions or discourse they would use in their work. Although none of the activists I interviewed personally thought that veganism was extreme, they sometimes shied away from overtly promoting it for fear that it was too much for their audience to handle.

One way in which these beliefs influenced French activists' strategies was that even when veganism and animal rights support was their goal, activists often asked for smaller changes to avoid completely alienating their audience. In some of my early interviews in France, I tested the limits of such activism by asking activists if they ever rejected ideas for strategies and tactics because they thought they would simply never work in France. Tali and Rob, whom I interviewed together, debated the subject:

Tali: Me, I don't think so, but you see, on this subject, we disagree. We have two points of view. He thinks you have to ask for a lot to obtain a little. Me, I think you have to ask for a little to obtain a little. He really prefers to talk about veganism to people.

Rob: That's different than an action for animal rights.

Tali: Not animal rights, that's just vivisection, fur, vegetarianism. I think you can't talk to an omnivore about veganism. That's too much for them, they wouldn't support it. But that's just what I think.

Rob: But veganism is more than just diet.

Tali: Exactly, that's too much to ask of people. It's like I was saying a moment ago, vegetarianism is already very good. I tell myself that if we just ask for that, we can talk to them about more things afterwards. But we don't feel the same on this subject. He thinks you have to ask for a lot, and I think that when you ask for too much, you shut them down, because that scares them and they run away. Already, when you ask people to stop eating meat and fish, they look at you like you're crazy. Then if you tell them it's meat, fish, eggs, milk, leather, wool . . . [trails off]

These French activists did not favor working for farm welfare reforms, as did welfarist groups such as Welfarm. They actively promoted veganism in their work. However, they questioned the effectiveness of such overtly vegan campaigns.

This timidity towards using the terms "vegetarian" or "vegan" sometimes affected activists' campaigns and even the entire existence of certain organizations. For example, I spoke with a group of animal rights activists, some of whom were helping to start a new periodical called *Végétariens Magazine*. One activist spoke of an encounter with the magazine editor, who said he only wanted to include vegetarian, and not vegan, recipes in the magazine. This activist told everyone that the editor said he did not want to push veganism, but instead wanted to do something a little more mainstream, and that having vegetarian recipes would be shocking enough. Other activists said they feared that just having the word "vegetarian" in the magazine's name would never work in France.

One strategy activists used in order to combat these negative and extreme images of veganism was to try to make vegetarianism look normal. At the General Assembly of the Association Végétarienne de France, the group discussed bringing back the "Mention V" label, which AVF gave to non-vegetarian, but vegetarian-friendly, restaurants to display. Activists supported this idea, saying that it gives "free publicity" to vegetarianism and veganism, and makes vegetarianism and veganism seem banal and normal. Such was Philippe's strategy as well, who has staffed a table on vegetarianism and animals rights at a Toulouse farmer's market nearly every single Sunday since 1997. On such consistency, Philippe (AVIS) said:

> I prefer to privilege actions that are constant, that are visible as often as possible. As I said a moment ago, that's the same principle as advertising, simply put. It must be constantly visible, all the time, and become part of the landscape, so that being vegetarian, or being confronted with something vegetarian, is no longer exceptional, but banal. That's really the basis, that it comes to be considered something normal.

Rather than meat-eating being seen as normal, animal rights activists tried to make vegetarianism and veganism seem normal, or even banal. Many activists who had spent time in Britain noted that vegetarianism and veganism were seen as normal there, and thought that achieving this perspective would indicate success for the French movement. They sought to achieve the "tipping point" at which vegetarianism and veganism would become mainstream and accepted in France.

One final obstacle to the French animal rights movement was the lack of vegetarian and vegan food options. Even if one wanted to become vegetarian, or especially vegan, it would be difficult because of a lack of suitable products on the market. Using the Product Launch Analytics database, which shows the total number of new food products labeled "vegetarian," "vegan," and "no animal products," Figure 5.1 shows the raw number of vegetarian and vegan products available in each country from 1990 to 2014, since the beginning of the "second wave" of animal rights activism that focuses on promoting veganism. The products available in the United States vastly outnumber those available in France. But this is not only due to the different sizes of the countries. Taking into account the difference in total population between France and the United States, the U.S. still has 4 to 15 times as many vegetarian and vegan products in comparison to France, per capita (see Figure 5.2).

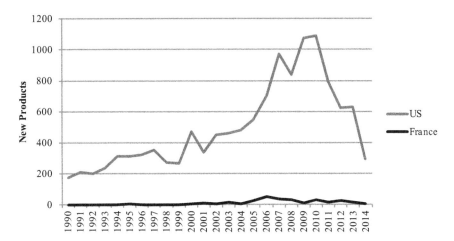

Figure 5.1 New food products labeled "vegetarian," "vegan," and "no animal products" in France and the United States, 1990–2014

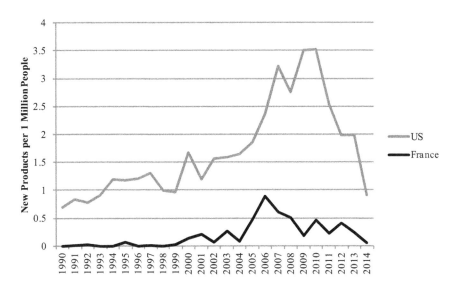

Figure 5.2 New food products labeled "vegetarian," "vegan," and "no animal products" per 1 million people in France and the United States, 1990–2014

The everyday experience of vegans in France included constantly sharing tips on where to find vegan cheese or mayonnaise, or which mainstream products happened to be vegan. These numbers clearly show the difference in the availability of vegan and vegetarian food products between the two countries, and they attest to the relative ease of living as a vegan in the U.S. when compared to France.

When supermarkets and natural food stores did not carry the products French vegans and vegetarians wanted, they used the French website "Veggie Wave" to order such products from abroad. Veggie Wave, the first completely vegan online retailer in France, opened for business in March 2005, only to close in September 2006. The Veggie Wave team sent an email to its supporters to announce the closing, stating that, despite a large number of supporters, they did not have enough orders to continue their business. In 2012, Un Monde Vegan opened in Paris, with both a physical store in the Marais, and an e-commerce site, much to French vegans' rejoicing.

This relative lack of vegan and vegetarian food products did not stop French animal rights activists from using food samples in their activities. They simply used more homemade food, and less store-bought food, when they made food available at events. For the celebration of Vegan Day in Paris, I brought some (German-made) vegan cheese that I found at a natural foods store. While at least 20 other people brought food to the event, I was surprised to see that I was the only one who brought store-bought food and not homemade food. My strategy in doing so was to show potential vegans how easy it is to find such products in stores. I was also doing what was considered normal for U.S. vegan events. This is how I had been trained as an activist, and I was bringing my toolkit to the French arena. This tactic did not exist in their tactical toolkit, and thus none of the French activists brought store-bought foods. They all showcased home-made vegan foods. Despite the lack of readily available vegan and vegetarian foods, French activists still saw food as a way to win people over to the cause, as Virginie (CAP) noted:

> I think that food, in fact, since people really like food, we also make tons of great recipes. And with these dishes, too, by showing that vegetarian food is good, we can, my brother in law, for example, went vegan in one day. The first time we went to a vegetarian restaurant, he said, "This is so good! And when you leave, you're not still hungry!" So we might be able to win people over through their stomachs.

Veganism and Animal Rights Philosophy

Thus far this chapter has outlined the constraints on French animal rights activism when using food as a cultural resource. But I do not wish to mislead readers by focusing so heavily on veganism outside of an animal rights context. While most of the activists I interviewed were vegan, many of them critiqued a focus on veganism that ignored the philosophical aspect of animal rights. André (AVF) saw vegetarianism and veganism as developing a bit in France, but he took greater issue with the lack of development of the philosophical side of the issues:

> The fact is that vegetarianism is not developing in France. Okay, now it's normal, it's accepted, okay, people talk about it more and more, that's true, there are people who eat vegetarian. You're in a restaurant, you order a vegetarian

dish, okay, fine. But it's not developing, I don't feel it's developing in the sense that people understand what vegetarianism is—its spirit, of animals, of their rights. A work of reflection.

The simple fact that it was now easier to find vegetarian and vegan food in France than ever before did not spell success for André. He wanted vegetarianism to develop in conjunction with a deeper understanding of animal rights. Yves Bonnardel, one of the founders of the animal rights journal *Cahiers Antispécistes*, also worked to develop this philosophical side. In our interview, Yves critiqued the focus on veganism and vegetarianism as an identity, rather than as a tactic:

> On the strategic level, I've fought a lot for the fact that people consider themselves as vegetarian or vegan, those are definitions for a lifestyle, or a way of eating, and in our democratic society, we have the tendency to define ourselves in relation to an action, like fair trade coffee. People have the tendency to define themselves by a lifestyle, or a method of consumption, and not a political engagement. For me, to define myself as antispeciesist and against human domination of animals, that's preferable than defining myself as vegetarian or vegan [. . .] We made a brochure, "We refuse to eat meat in order to not kill animals." We didn't use the word "vegetarian;" we defined ourselves by an action, by a motive, an intention, and not by an identity. My critique of Veggie Pride is that it is too "vegetarian identity," whereas I don't care about vegetarianism. It's nothing but a means for me. It's a part of the end, but it's nothing but a part.

Yves mentioned Veggie Pride, an annual march he helped found and organize, which aims to show vegetarian and vegan pride. In doing so, Yves articulated a critique of the new social movement focus on collective identity, a critique I have described elsewhere when analyzing the cultural strategies of the animal rights movement (Cherry 2010). Developing and displaying collective identities is both a strategy and a goal of new social movements (Melucci 1995). Animal rights is a new social movement (Jasper 1997), but while one may hold dear the identity of vegan, vegetarian, or animal rights activist, the animal rights movement is not an identity movement. Animal rights activists do not try to get more people to simply *identify* as vegans, they attempt to encourage more people to reconsider human relations to other animals, and to modify their behavior accordingly. Moreover, previous research has found that claiming a vegan identity is insufficient to maintain commitment to the basic tenets of veganism (Cherry 2006). The fact that so many meat-eaters self-identified as vegetarian was a problem for the French movement. The misconceptions about vegetarianism and veganism, the negative views of them, and the lack of vegan options only compounded this problem, acting in conjunction with the French meat-based gastronomic tradition to prevent animal rights activists from being able to effectively use food as a cultural resource in their work.

Promoting Veganism in the United States

Activists in the United States faced far fewer challenges than French activists when using food as a cultural resource. U.S. activists did not report that people widely believed vegetarians ate fish and chicken, or that vegans were in a cult. In comparison to France, few such misconceptions existed. Any complaints revolved around people's ignorance of butter being an animal product, or thinking that just one egg in a cake would make it "mostly vegan" and therefore acceptable for consumption by vegans. Thus it was not such outlandish misconceptions as cult membership that provided challenges to U.S. activists' use of vegan food as a cultural resource. Rather, they faced negative stereotypes that were, in a way, brought on by their own success. Jack Norris, one of the co-founders of Vegan Outreach, discussed his group's creation of new literature because of "anti-vegan" reactions to their main flyer, entitled "Why Vegan?" Jack said, "At one time there was no one that was anti-vegan because they didn't even know what it was. And then over time that changed." He continued:

> We used to leaflet exclusively with our pamphlet "Why Vegan?" And I think that at a certain point, on college campuses in particular, people got an idea of what a vegan was and they created sort of a negative opinion of it. And so it became a problem to promote the brochure with that word in bold on the front [. . .] They may have met a vegan who was very uptight about their veganism and made a big deal about animal products, small amounts of animal products in everything. And once again, gave the person the impression that being vegan is impossible.

Because of this, and because of people viewing veganism as "an all or nothing thing," Jack said that Vegan Outreach took the word "vegan" off the pamphlets and created a booklet called "Even if You Like Meat." This new pamphlet promoted the idea, Jack said, that "any amount of animal products you withdraw your support from reduces the amount of cruelty you're supporting." Since then, Vegan Outreach has developed two new pamphlets called "Your Choice" and "Compassionate Choices" that likewise avoid the word "vegan" and emphasize consumer agency in food choices. Thus, like many French activists, Jack saw the negative reactions to the word "vegan," and he decided to also promote a step-by-step approach with the "Even if You Like Meat" pamphlet.

People in both countries reacted to vegan activism by claiming that veganism was too difficult. But in the U.S., some of these negative reactions stemmed from people's previous experience with vegans. Jenna (VO) described negative vegan stereotypes that mirrored the outdated stereotypes of vegetarians in France. Her reaction to such stereotypes, though, represents animal rights activists' attempts to make veganism more mainstream than marginal:

> The words that come to mind when people think of vegans are "deprived" and "angry" and "on the margins of society." And I think Jon and myself and other leafleters who are out there every day, we look pretty mainstream.

We're always smiling. We're polite. We're friendly. And when we are engaged in conversation we know our stuff and we're never defensive. We're never offensive either. And it's very important to me to show the general public that it's okay to be vegan. I don't go to restaurants with my friends and insist that I can't eat anything. I'm engaged in a variety of activities, community activities. I try to maintain a healthy social life. I've looked into going back to school. Just trying to not marginalize us because we care about animal cruelty. And I think that may be the biggest obstacle that people, is that the idea that they're going to isolate themselves from everything they know and love. And if I can show them that I'm still a functioning member of society—and a happy one at that—I think that makes a compelling case that they too can go vegan.

Jenna responded to the stereotype of the "angry vegan" by showing she was a happy, "functioning member of society" who also cared about animal cruelty and was vegan. Just as the ethical vegans in sociologist Jessica Greenebaum's (2012) study altered their public behavior to present themselves as vegans, these activists went a step further to present themselves as "happy vegans." While veganism did not suffer the intensely negative stereotypes that it did in France, people still saw it as some-what "extreme," as in France. And, like French activists, U.S. activists reacted to this charge of extremism by trying to make veganism look mainstream and normal, as Stephanie explained: "We are trying to make vegetarian eating seem so mainstream and common, that anyone can do it. Which is true, you can get vegetarian food almost anywhere now. So we try to keep everything along the popular and mainstream."

How did U.S. activists make vegetarianism and veganism look popular and main-stream? They were able to avail themselves of celebrity support, a resource I discuss in Chapter 6 on the media. U.S. and French activists also tried to show that one could eat vegan or vegetarian food anywhere—Association Végétarienne de France had the "Mention V," which they gave to vegan- and vegetarian-friendly restaurants, and U.S. organizations such as Compassion Over Killing and Mercy for Animals created vegan guides to various cities and promoted vegan-friendly restaurants. Many groups engaged in vegan outreach to restaurants in order to get restaurants to offer more specifically vegan options. Dawn described her experience with restaurant outreach, saying that she brings in vegan products for the restaurateurs to try:

It is just interesting to see that it is very exciting for them. It's something new. It's like a new product. And so a lot of people in the food industry, they like to try different things. So it's been very popular, it's had a very positive reception. It's a matter of finding out what they are interested in offering, finding the price that they want to offer, going through their, the menu and trying to tailor the menu according to that restaurant. Because obviously every restaurant has got a different, they don't want to be like everybody else.

While French chefs and servers viewed vegetarianism and veganism as insults to their culinary heritage, these U.S. restaurateurs saw new vegan products as a way to differentiate themselves from their competition. The mere fact that such vegan products existed and were readily and commercially available set the U.S. movement apart from the French movement in a major way. While one of the main drawbacks to vegan outreach in France was the lack of vegan foods, a major boon for U.S. activists was the widespread availability of such foods. Fast food restaurants like Burger King and Subway carry vegan burgers, and most mainstream supermarkets carry a variety of vegan products. Even in my small hometown in eastern North Carolina, a center for industrialized hog farming and barbeque, one can find more vegan products in the supermarket than one can in a mainstream supermarket in Paris. Stewart (Vegan Outreach), who at the age of 44 was one of the older activists I interviewed, noted the historical change in vegan food availability in the U.S. He said there were more vegans and vegetarians in the U.S., and that "one place you'll notice that is in your local grocery store." He went on to describe these changes:

> Even at Wal-Mart and Target and Costco they have more and more vegetarian and vegan products. All these different brands of veggie burgers, and vegan meatballs, and different forms of Tofurky, and Smart Dogs, and all that stuff. You're seeing more and more and more of these products pop up. As they pop up you're seeing that makes it easier for people to go vegetarian. And it also makes it more mainstream. It used to be that if you were a vegetarian you were a little weird. "You're a vegan, what is that? What does that mean?" They used to call it "*vay*-guhn." And now vegan is a household word and vegetarianism is getting more middle-of-the-road than weird.

All of the U.S. activists I interviewed spoke of how easy it was to become vegan, and that a lack of vegan foodstuffs was no longer a sufficient excuse to not do so.

Thus, despite French people's great interest in food and cuisine, French activists were less able than U.S. activists to use food as a cultural resource for their activism. In fact, it was precisely because of the French interest in food and cuisine that food served as an ineffective cultural resource for promoting veganism. The French gastronomic tradition, written into law as *patrimoine culturel* (cultural heritage) in the case of foie gras, posed a significant constraint to French animal rights activists. Further, whereas U.S. activists could point to the facility with which one could become vegan, because of the vast amount of vegan foods available, French activists did not have such resources at their disposal. Finally, there was a bit of congruence between the two movements—both movements sometimes shied away from using the term "vegan." In France, this was due to a lack of understanding, but in the United States, it was due to conceptions based on previous exposure to the term.

6 Media and Terrorism

Nearly all activists attempt to garner media attention for their work. This is because, as journalism scholar Michael Meadows notes, mass media not only disseminate information, they create meaning by "making sense of the here and now" (1998: 2). In this sense, Meadows argues, media can act as a cultural resource for social movements because they play a role in the formation of culture. Some organizations, such as Greenpeace and PETA, make media a core aspect of their overarching strategic orientation. But such media strategies do not always succeed because of what sociologists William Carroll and R.S. Ratner (1999) call the "asymmetrical" relationship that social movements have with media—social movements need media more than media need them.

I found movement–media relationships even more asymmetrical in France than in the United States. While activists in both countries tried to use media, U.S. groups achieved more positive press and vastly more media coverage than the French movement. However, activists in both countries faced negative publicity in the media. Further, U.S. activists enlisted the aid of celebrities in their work, a tactic hardly used in France. French activists critiqued the celebrity- and media-focused approaches of U.S. groups, preferring to use their own independent sources to disseminate knowledge about animal rights. Thus mainstream media was a cultural resource primarily available to, and employed by, U.S. activists.

The one cultural resource that harmed U.S. activists more than it did French activists was the charge of terrorism. Shortly after September 11, 2001, the FBI called the Animal Liberation Front (alongside the Earth Liberation Front) the country's top domestic terror threat, thus cementing the idea of animal activists as "ecoterrorists." With the passing of the Animal Enterprise Terrorist Act in early 2006, animal rights activists could legally be charged as terrorists by the government. In France no such legislation exists, and the French government and popular culture do not view animal rights activists as terrorists. Some French activists saw the U.S. government's crackdown on animal activists as a sign of success for the movement, in that it garnered such backlash, and others used militant imagery as a way to recruit young activists into their movement. Thus terrorism was the one cultural tool that worked for French activists but against U.S. activists. I end this chapter, concluding the section on Cultural Resources, by re-examining the six cultural tools and placing them in theoretical context.

Media Mastery in the United States

At the October 2007 Becoming the Change conference on animal rights, Captain Paul Watson of the Sea Shepherd Conservation Society declared in his keynote speech that "Legislation gets us nowhere—the answer is the media. That's what Greenpeace and PETA do." One of the original founders of Greenpeace, Watson now takes to the open seas on his all-vegan flagship, the *Sea Shepherd*, to engage in direct action, such as physically blocking or ramming whaling ships, to protect sea creatures. While Watson certainly does his part to help enact and enforce legislation, he has moved out of the realm of legal action and into "piracy" and media stunts to promote animal rights. He also entered into popular culture, when, in November 2008, the series *Whale Wars* began screening on the cable channel Animal Planet. Over seven seasons, *Whale Wars* brought Watson's animal rights message to millions and millions of viewers. However, not all animal rights organizations enjoyed such vast amounts of positive media attention. They had to strategize to get the attention of the media and of their target audiences.

If animal rights organizations had as much money as their opponents, they would not need to spend as much time strategizing how to combat them. They could simply engage in widespread advertising campaigns, like meat and dairy producers do. But given their limited budgets, activists often try to use media like an advertising outlet. That is, they engage in media stunts to get attention for the cause, often with a goal of getting their targets to visit a particular website or to learn about how to participate in a specific campaign (e.g., boycotting a particular store). Sean described his organization's reliance on media in this cost-effective manner:

> We may meet 500 people during an hour during a demonstration, but if the newspaper comes and covers the event, then you've reached maybe 100,000 people, with the same amount of time and money. And then, of course, we advertise, we do put up billboards. We've put up a number of billboards across the United States about this campaign, just letting people know. But as a nonprofit organization, we're a little bit limited on the amount of money that we spend. We've found that oftentimes it's much more cost-effective to simply try to get the media attention and let them cover the event. So it's a form of free advertisement, if you will.

Sean's group tried to use the mainstream media to help disseminate their message. While his group paid for billboards, a form of traditional advertising, they also used media for "free advertising," thus placing them in an even more asymmetrical relationship with media. Carroll and Ratner (1998) note that the asymmetry of the movement–media relationship can be reduced in two ways. The first is through the universality of a movement's appeal, but this is not applicable in the case of the animal rights movement. Rather, animal rights activists engage the second tactic, staging "dramatic events that command media attention," to reduce this asymmetrical relationship (Carroll and Ratner 1999: 28). PETA is by far the best-known organization working in this category, with their arsenal of nearly naked protesters and people wearing animal suits. Their guerilla theater tactics have yet to grow old in the eyes of the mainstream media, though they have in the eyes of many activists.

These activists' use of media boiled down to disseminating their message to their target audience. While Sean spoke of "free advertising," one of the dangers of seeking media coverage as a tactic was that activists never know how media will portray their movement (Smith et al. 2001). Sociologist Erin Evans (2015a) found that the more transgressive an organization or a protest is, the less likely it is that media coverage will include any substantive arguments from the protest. Further, the more transgressive an organization or protest is, the more likely it is that media will give space to the movement's opponents. At the same time, organizations face the dilemma that non-transgressive protest tactics do not garner as much media coverage. Organizations that succeeded in breaking this mold included PETA and ALF (Animal Liberation Front). Evans (2015a) found that their organizational reputations, built over time, allowed them to use transgressive protest tactics and earn positive media coverage. Thus, to stave off some of the negative publicity that could come of such media stunts, some groups paid for their own advertising as a way to not only control the message, but to also target a specific audience. Stephanie's group focused on young females, so they ran ads on MTV and in teen magazines and college newspapers:

> In terms of getting our message out there, the avenues that we use include youth-oriented markets because of polls that showed that the most likely demographic to translate our message into action for animals is the young age bracket. The teen girls or the young adults. So that's where we again want to narrow down even further by focusing on that specific demographic, and we believe that portraying animal cruelty as it is, like just focusing on what happens to the animals is usually enough to compel people to want to remove their support for it [. . .] That's our main strategy, is getting our message out there. We want to reach the general public, obviously, we want everyone to know about this, but that same message doesn't generally work for everyone, because we're such a diverse society, and we need to create an appealing message to a specific audience to become effective. So right now we're focusing on our specific targeted audiences, the young adult age bracket.

Using market research, Stephanie and her group found that young women were most likely to support animal rights and to become vegetarian, so they targeted that specific group in their advertising. If activists cannot control media coverage of their movement, they can purchase positive coverage through advertising, or create positive coverage through social media.

Also in this market research, Stephanie learned that that "polls show that you need to get—any message, not just animal rights but any message—you need to get it out there seven to ten times, before someone really gets that message."

Thus Stephanie's group focused on sending out positive messages, because, as she said, "We want to make sure that they have positive experiences along the way, so that hopefully by the tenth time they get the message, they will want to make that change."

Celebrities in the United States

Another significant way animal rights groups used media was through the use of celebrity endorsements. Animal rights organizations enjoyed widespread support from celebrities, many of whom make their vegetarianism or veganism known in their media-saturated lives, and not just on the pages of animal rights organizations' magazines. Celebrities talk about animal rights and vegetarianism on talk shows, and a December 2006 television commercial for Macy's inserted veganism into the message, even though Macy's was not attempting to promote animal rights. In this commercial, a number of celebrities decorate Macy's department store in time for the holidays. Martha Stewart organizes everyone, Jessica Simpson helps trim the tree, Usher DJs the impromptu party, and Rocco DiSpirito provides food and hot chocolate for everyone. When Russell Simmons, a music mogul and vegan, approaches the table, DiSpirito says, with great emphasis, "And the world's best *soy* hot chocolate for you." This small example shows how veganism and animal rights are entering the public consciousness in the United States through media in ways unseen in France.

Again, PETA is the best-known organization for acquiring a diverse array of such celebrity supporters. Alicia Silverstone, film actress and vegan, has graced the cover of PETA's *Animal Times* magazine. Musician Rob Zombie and actor James Cromwell have recorded PSAs promoting vegetarianism, and actors Tom Hardy and Dominic Monaghan have appeared in print ads promoting the adoption of animals and the protection of wildlife. PETA counts so many celebrity supporters among their ranks that they even hold a contest each year where people can vote for their favorites. (I always vote for "Weird Al" Yankovic, who has yet to win.)

Of course, PETA is not the only organization with celebrity supporters—it is simply the largest one. At Farm Sanctuary's twentieth anniversary party, held in Hollywood, numerous celebrities came out to show their support, including actresses Emily Deschanel and Loretta Swit, among many others. Actor Joachim Phoenix wore non-leather cowboy boots to portray Johnny Cash in the film *Walk the Line*, in a widely reported example of celebrity veganism in the mainstream media. Phoenix narrated the acclaimed animal rights film *Earthlings*, and he also lends his talents to many animal rights organizations' endeavors.

Perhaps the best-known of all celebrity animal rights supporters is Pamela Anderson. This model became famous as an actress on the television show *Baywatch*, and she supported PETA even as a nascent star. As a vegan, Anderson has lent her likeness to many PETA campaigns, most recently in a vegetarian advertisement in which she was clad in nothing more than a few strategically placed lettuce leaves (Figure 6.1).

Figure 6.1 Pamela Anderson's vegetarian ad for PETA

Celebrities can help sustain a movement's momentum, but at the same time, celebrity involvement has also been shown to make movements seem less controversial, or less politically disruptive. In this case, we also see how a particular celebrity's image can affect how audiences perceive the movement (Meyer and Gamson 1995). While Sir Paul McCartney, another famous vegetarian who works for animal rights causes, commands respect, activists reported mixed feelings on the use of celebrities like Pamela Anderson for animal rights causes. On the one hand, attractive people enjoy the "halo effect," where others assume they are inherently good and have something to offer (Berry 2008). On the other hand, Pamela Anderson's slightly less than regal image caused some activists, like Grant, to question the efficacy of such celebrity endorsements:

Pamela Anderson, man [Laughs]. I don't know, she is kind of a ridiculous character, but that kind of exposure, it's alright. I guess in some aspects, that's bad, because then it's like, "Well, this idiot signed on to this cause, so it can't really be that worthwhile." Also, it's just more celebrity exposure to it, which is good, because Americans do what their celebrities tell them to do [. . .] I still don't think the media has a very positive outlook on animal rights, but I think it's more so than it used to be, as it gets more popular with the media, then American culture will be more influenced by that, because, I think even more than celebrities, I think American culture is influenced by the media.

Despite the potential negative consequences from using such celebrities, Grant acknowledged the power of media as a cultural tool for activists. Media play a part in producing consent and influencing public opinion (Gramsci 1988), and activists sought to be a part of that production to sway public opinion in their favor (Meadows 1998).

Celebrity endorsements of animal rights did not comprise the sole relationship between celebrities and the animal rights movement—activists sometimes capitalized upon animal abuse by celebrities to bring attention to a particular cause. Animal rights organizations often chastise singers and movie stars for wearing fur, as well as fashion designers who use it. One of the most prominent recent examples of this was the 2007 arrest and prosecution of professional football player Michael Vick for dogfighting. Officials seized 66 dogs from Vick's Virginia property where he and two friends ran a dogfighting ring, and where they killed "underperforming" dogs by drowning, hanging, electrocution, and slamming them against the ground. HSUS and PETA ramped up their anti-dogfighting campaigns, and reached out to educate Vick and the public on the issue. Vick pleaded guilty to the Virginia state charges of dogfighting, and he struck a plea bargain with the federal prosecutors. Vick ultimately spent 18 months in prison. And while he was initially suspended without pay from the NFL, Vick resumed his NFL career in 2009. In better news for animal advocates, the attention to dogfighting from Vick's case brought increased attention to the issue, and the remaining few states that had yet to pass legislation against dogfighting finally did so. By 2008, dogfighting became a felony in all 50 states.

Negative Media Coverage in the United States

As scholars and activists have frequently noted, mainstream media are not always friendly to social movements, and they often portray animal rights activists in a negative light. In the United States, the most damning accusation was that of "terrorism," which I discuss further below. Given the widespread negative portrayals, activists faced a dilemma when using media, as animal rights philosopher Tom Regan articulated in our interview:

I think that animal rights activists tend to be viewed by the public in the way the media represents who they are. And the dilemma of activism is that the media likes a scandal and something outlandish. The media loves a plane crash.

The media's not interested in safe landings; that's not a story. The challenge then becomes how you get the media to cover what we're doing. Well, you do something illegal or outlandish, then they'll cover it. With that, the downside of that, is that then the public's perception of animal rights activists is that they are people who do things that are outlandish and illegal because that's how they're represented in the media. The great challenge then is how you have animal rights values and beliefs and ideals represented in the media without doing things that are illegal and outlandish.

It is difficult to obtain coverage for animal rights activism without having a "catch" for media, as Regan noted. Given that dilemma, media cover the more "outlandish" aspects of animal rights activism, not the daily letter-writing or tabling events. Both activists and media are knowledgeable and strategic agents, working to create different versions of reality (Barker-Plummer 1995). Thus, even when activists specified they did not engage in any illegal activities, newspapers continued to define animal rights activists as dangerous, and still reported on "other activists" who presumably used illegal tactics. In an article in *Red and Black*, the student newspaper at the University of Georgia, a reporter contacted a SOS activist to ask her group's position on a new research center at the university, which would engage in animal testing. Although the activist interviewed specified that SOS would not protest against the center, the article nonetheless mentioned the threat of break-ins by activists:

> Regardless of her group's strong opposition to the animal experimentation that will occur in the Coverdell Center, she said they have no plans to protest. "We don't really use protest as a way to educate the UGA community about issues we feel passionate about. We're more about education and advocacy in a positive manner," she said. King said he does not expect outright protests to occur in front of the Coverdell Center, but he explained the steps the University took to keep radical animal rights activists from breaking into the building. Employees must use a keycard to enter the facility. This is a standard feature in labs where animal experiments are done, due to the threat of animal rights activists, he said. The mouse lab or vivarium is completely underground, so there are no windows – partly to keep activists out and partly to help preserve the hyper-clean environment of the lab, King said. (Attebury 2006)

While King mentioned the need to maintain the sterility of the labs, both King and the reporter gave more credence to the "threat" of animal rights activists in necessitating the security system. They de-emphasized the scientific reasons for such security while emphasizing the purported threat from animal rights activists. This negative portrayal exemplifies the belief among non-activists that all, if not most, activists engage in illegal activities. Here media "imagined" (Meadows 1998) our society for us, positing animal rights activists as dangerous threats, just as media created the idea that crime and mugging were out of control (Hall et al. 1978, McCormick 1995).

On such negative portrayals in media, sociologist Todd Gitlin (1980) specified a number of media framing devices media use against movements, using the New Left as his case study. Gitlin differentiated between early and later framing devices, specifying the later framing devices came about when the New Left started to use more militant tactics. These frames also emerged against the U.S. animal rights movement, though the early–later divide was not nearly as clear-cut as in Gitlin's study.

A 1974 article in *The New York Times* (Johnston 1974), demonstrates a number of early and later framing devices used to disparage animal rights activists. The author used a mocking tone, beginning the article with the sentence: "The Central Park Zoo was not a peaceable kingdom yesterday, but it was mainly members of the human species who were roaring, screaming, and snapping at one another." The article then emphasized internal dissention, by contrasting protesters who stayed outside the zoo with placards with those who entered the zoo to protest and talk to zoo visitors. The author used the framing device of delegitimization when he put quotation marks around the word "responsible" to describe the leaders of the peaceful protest outside the zoo, and he used trivialization by making light of movement language, dress, age, style, and goals, describing one protester as "a thin, impassioned woman."

Later articles showed more sympathy, or at least less direct antipathy, to activists by using more subtle framing devices to disparage animal rights activists. A 1990 article on wildlife pitted the organization Friends of Animals against scientists, trivializing activists by portraying their interests as solely emotional (Hamilton 1990). Quoting the Executive Director of the Council on Environmental Quality, the author claimed that swans were a nuisance, and that "if they were black and warty, people wouldn't care." The author moved on to describe Priscilla Feral, long-time vegan animal rights activist, as caring about the swan population because she liked to feed the swans with her daughter.

Before animal rights activists became "terrorists," opponents created the myth of the fake-blood-throwing fur protester. In a 1990 *The New York Times* article on fur coats, the author quoted a woman who opined:

> "Normally, my mink coat is out of storage by now, but I have been hesitating," said Judi Ellen, a travel consultant. "I am a little nervous about walking down a street and being pelted with eggs or paint by these groups. I will wear my mink coat, but I will be careful about where I wear it. I will probably take cabs and not walk around the streets." (Lawson 1990)

This later framing device, emphasizing violence in demonstrations, resembles the mistaken collective memory of Vietnam War protesters as being "anti-troop" (Beamish et al. 1995). Just as the myth of protesters spitting on returning war veterans came to be believed as a fact, so did the myth of animal rights protesters throwing fake blood or red paint on fur coats. While activists may wear donated fur coats covered in fake blood to protests, or throw flour on fur-wearing celebrities, animal rights organizations never promoted vandalizing coats in stores or coats that people were wearing. To do so, many activists acknowledged, would often result in more fur coats produced or purchased to replace the ruined ones.

Activists found numerous problems with stories such as those that characterized activists as throwing fake blood on fur coats. One main problem was people not having the time or inclination to verify whether the information reported was true or false in the first place. Lorena (an activist affiliated with multiple groups) gave the benefit of the doubt to people who believed what they read or heard in media, but she also saw part of her task as an activist as being to debunk these media myths and to provide information the media omits:

> I think it's so hard in this kind of society to go against what the media says. The media bombards us every single day with ads and information that can be completely biased. But people, with their hectic lifestyles, they don't have the time to really check their sources. And that's where we are. As an example, how many times I tell my friends, or a person I just knew, if they order veal at a restaurant, I say, "Have you ever heard about how veal is raised, and the cruelty involved in it?" And they say, "That's not true, no human would do that." And why doesn't the industry say that? Well, because then you wouldn't eat veal. But they have a hard time believing that I hold the truth, and not the media.

Lorena's friends believed media accounts (or omissions) of veal production to be "the truth," part of the unquestioned and unquestionable "common sense" (Gramsci 1988) facts created and promoted by animal industries and media. Given these threats of negative or uninformed media portrayals, some activists eschewed a media-based approach. Jack Norris, one of the founders of Vegan Outreach, said his group prefers to focus on individual interaction rather than media outreach:

> We take a one-on-one approach of individuals. One person handing a brochure to one other person, versus a mass-media stuff; we're not very mass-media oriented. We like people to see that another real person is doing something and cares about this issue. We feel like that makes an impression on people versus them seeing something on the TV. TV has been successful in persuading a lot of people to change but that's just not a tactic we use.

While Vegan Outreach did not necessarily seek media coverage, media sometimes sought them out. Given the great variety of cultural resources available to U.S. activists, not every group needed to avail themselves of every type of resource or strategy.

Meager Media Coverage in France

In France, animal rights activism received very little media coverage, especially compared to the coverage in the United States. In *The New York Times* alone,

3,179 articles on animal rights appeared between 1990 and 2014. In France, only 206 articles appeared during the same time period, in not just one but *nine* national daily newspapers combined.[1] Even if French animal rights activists achieved little media coverage, many of them saw the benefits to using media to disseminate their message, even if that meant facing the dangers of negative media portrayals. Elsa (Le Glaive) noted that media was not "conciliatory" towards activists and depicted negative images of them, "but at least people would hear about us. At least they'd hear about us. Take us out of the underground a bit."

Even if media were not the preferred cultural resource of activists, activists still saw benefits to using media to cover events such as protests. I attended an anti-*corrida* protest organized by CRAC, held on a side street in the outskirts of Paris in front of a youth hostel where, for some reason, *corrida* organizers and promoters held a meeting. During the protest, where the only passersby were the meeting attendees and some hostelers, activists lamented the lack of media attention. Virginie noted that no one from media was present, to which Tali asked, "What is the point of this protest, then? We're on a side street, no one can see us, so what is the point?" She then went on to compare this event to a recent protest against Jean-Paul Gaultier, where many bystanders and media observed the protest. Tali, Rob, and Virginie all said they thought the protest was pointless because no media attended, and there were no passersby to whom they could distribute leaflets.

Some French animal rights organizations attempted to use media in their tactics. Animal Amnistie in Toulouse began incorporating a "media event," usually a piece of guerilla theater, in all of their large tabling events. But even before the group started this strategy, Carol, one of the members, saw the use of media as part of a long-term strategy:

> I have always thought of education as being the most important aspect, really. Educating the public, well, we call it educating, but it's really informing the public. It's really informing them. To be able to inform the public you need to have the support of the media. Which is what PETA have understood, that they well understand, and they have their tactics to get media coverage. And in France not everyone agrees with these tactics, but I can see, I know, in many cases the ends justify the means [. . .] What matters is that those uneducated, uninformed people receive a message. And they have to get this message as often as possible, because once, twice, three times is not enough. They have got to hear it over and over again before it begins to register and before they begin to even think about it. Just over and over again. So that's long-term, that's a long-term strategy.

1 These articles appeared in a Proquest search for "animal rights" or "droits des animaux" in the body of any newspaper articles from January 1, 1990 to December 31, 2014. The U.S. search only included *The New York Times*. The nine French newspapers were the top nine in circulation in all of France, and included *Enjeux-Les Echos*, *L'Humanité*, *La Croix*, *La Tribune*, *Le Figaro*, *Le Figaro Economie*, *Le Monde*, *Les Echos*, and *Libération*.

Carol's remarks mirror those of the U.S. activist Stephanie, citing the need to get a message out numerous times, because people will not change their behavior after hearing about a problem one time. Carol also referred to the dilemma many U.S. activists described when working with media, saying media is only willing to cover an event "if someone is walking around naked on the streets," as she put it.

If activists were not naked, they successfully gained media attention by dressing as animals or engaging in guerilla theater. In Animal Amnistie's first "media event," Xavier dressed as a rabbit, and Carol, Daniel, Fabrice, and Laura all dressed as scientists. They pantomimed conducting cosmetic tests on Xavier the rabbit, and earned a write-up and photo in the *Dépêche du Midi*, a widely read regional paper based in Toulouse. And at the General Assembly of AVF, Isabelle recounted participating in a PMAF campaign that toured France, in which she dressed in a chicken suit to bring attention to the plight of hens in battery cages. She described it as a very easy stunt, because she did not need much help, but she got good coverage in the press. These responses echoed the U.S. responses on cost-effectiveness and media events. French activists also characterized gaining the most media coverage with the least amount of activists as successful.

By far, the French group that most often used media as a cultural resource was PETA France. Jérôme Bernard-Pellet, the main organizer for PETA France, proclaimed in our interview, "If you wanted to summarize PETA France's activities in one word, that would be 'media.' That's the specialty of PETA France." Indeed, PETA France had getting media coverage down to a fine science, and some of their actions have been picked up by Reuters and CNN. Jérôme's description of why PETA France used media echoed U.S. activists' description of free advertising:

> Even on a worldwide level, you could simplify and say that PETA is an advertising agency for animals. PETA uses the same techniques as advertising, but the big difference is that it's not to make money—it's to defend a good cause.

Such attention did not come easily, though. PETA France often used nudity to attract media, as Jérôme noted that "if we did the same action with clothes on, there would be four to five times less media there." Jérôme said PETA's methods were "voluntarily shocking" and "politically incorrect," because it was the only way to attract media attention. However, he lamented that it was unfortunate that such methods engendered critiques within the animal rights movement. As I discuss further below, many activists critiqued PETA's frequent use of nude women, some criticizing it for being "too American" a style of activism. To this latter critique, Jérôme responded that such activism actually works:

> The strategy for that, to get in the media, is exactly the same as PETA U.S. It's to do things that are a bit shocking, politically incorrect, torrid, esthetic, and theatrical, with the sole intention of attracting attention. And it works well. Certain skeptics said a few years ago that there was such a difference

in cultures and mentalities that the Anglo-Saxon methods would never work in France. And in fact, it's the contrary. These Anglo-Saxon techniques work very well in France because they're new to France.

Jérôme correctly stated that garnering media attention worked in France. Media were very attentive—to *other* social movements. Conducting the same search of nine national daily newspapers, which only garnered 206 articles on the animal rights movement, one finds 1,779 articles on the environmental movement, and 2,513 on the labor movement. Thus it was not so much that the French media did not report on social movements as that they were particularly uninterested in the animal rights movement.

Given this lack of mainstream media coverage, even for PETA France, a group that put most of its efforts into media attention, French activists not asso-ciated with PETA France sought alternative media outlets or created their own media. Such strategies represented two main ways that movement organizations could escape the typically asymmetrical relationship with mainstream media (Carroll and Ratner 1999). Social media and the internet became ways activists could create more balance in media coverage. In addition to creating and main-taining their own websites, activists used the internet to create and disseminate their own media, or to use alternative and social media sources to spread infor-mation about their work. Nathalie (CAP) said it was "good to create your own media," as well as putting videos on Dailymotion or YouTube. Virginie (CAP) echoed this:

> Really reporting, having activists use this tool to communicate between themselves, and to get attention to their actions, and then knowing the alter-native medias a bit more, like Indymedia, to see there are other ways of com-municating, to get the information out there. There is really a whole field to invest in.

Just as the women's liberationists eschewed the media approach of the National Organization of Women because they saw media as part of the patriarchal prob-lem they were fighting (Barker-Plummer 1995), these French activists resisted mainstream media interaction.

Celebrities in France

Most French activists rejected the mainstream media approach that the U.S. movement and PETA France used. Only 7 of the 37 French activists I interviewed spoke positively about using celebrities, saying they would like to use celebrity endorsements, and naming celebrities who supported animal rights or vegetarianism. Besides Brigitte Bardot, one of the better-known celebrity supporters was the singer Renaud. A politically-charged singer born of the May 1968 revolution, Renaud has spoken out against *corrida* and inserted his anti-*corrida* stance into his public life, as Bernadette described:

He's very, very much against bullfighting. He's brilliant, he does loads of stuff. He works with CRAC, you know, Comité Radicalement Anti-Corrida. And he does stuff like, every concert there will be a stall against bullfighting. And once he was doing a thing where people can get his signature on a photo, like an autograph, and if they wanted an autograph they had to sign a petition against bullfighting to get it, that kind of thing. And whenever he's invited on a television program, or something like that, he'll wear a t-shirt saying "I'm against bullfighting," that kind of thing.

Renaud is actually the exception to the rule, as Bernadette later noted that few celebrities actually involved themselves in animal rights or vegetarian activism. AVF devoted a section of their website to famous vegetarians and vegans, but most of them are British or American (Association Végétarienne de France 2015). To add more French celebrities to the list, they included a disclaimer that says that not everyone on the list is a strict vegetarian, and "some of them cheat." Thus, even if French activists wanted to use celebrity endorsements, they often could not because of the lack of celebrities who would support them. I asked many French activists what they thought of the popular U.S. tactic of using celebrity endorsements, to which Frédéric (AVF) replied:

> Here in France, we'd love to! I think it's good to do that, but we have a hard time getting celebrity support [. . .] Here in France, there are no stars. That's not because I think it's a bad idea, it's because we can't do it!

In addition to the widespread disapproval of such a tactic, using celebrities was also simply not an option for the French animal rights movement. Many activists noted that there were not enough famous French vegetarians to use them in an advertising campaign—or not enough famous people willing to admit they were vegetarian. One activist I interviewed said:

> Vegetarianism is still very poorly viewed in France, because people think that if you are vegetarian you are in a cult. So there are famous people who are vegetarian, but it's still very hush-hush. There are a lot of stars who are vegetarian, but they don't say it. I know they are, though, because I see them on the list of donors for [my organization].

Nathalie (CAP) went a step further and said that given the negative image of vegetarians in France, it might hurt a star to come out as a vegetarian. She said, "it's too bad for their image," and continued:

> It's not marketable, so it's not in the interest of stars to promote vegetarianism. And, there are very few vegetarian stars. Even when a celebrity is vegetarian in France, she doesn't say it because it's not good for her image. There are some who say they want to go further, I think, but most of them don't say it. Here in France, the only stars we see actually come from the United States and England.

Although these French activists saw celebrity endorsements as currently impossible because celebrities would never admit to being vegetarian, Sara (Lyon Antispécistes) saw the possibility of some positive outcomes for the movement. However, she also noted that this tactic probably worked better in the United States than in France, because of people's obsession with celebrities in the U.S.:

> I think that using stars isn't completely idiotic, when people have an image of vegetarians and think that they're completely starved. But at the same time, using a star isn't, well, since she's a star she'll more easily get on television, but that's all. If one must use a celebrity, I understand that, but you have to choose well. In the United States, maybe I'm mistaken, but I think that people are more interested over there with what stars do, that's more important. So maybe it's more useful over there. Here, the media, everyone doesn't care.

Sara noted that people in the U.S. were more interested in celebrities' lives than were people in France. This obsession was also reflected in media and in the news, where in the U.S. one sees more reporting on stars' lives than in France. Sara also warned that even if one were to use celebrities, the organizations should choose wisely. This points to the final problem of celebrity use in France—of the few celebrities who support vegetarianism and animal rights, many have bad reputations, or at least do not command much respect.

For example, PETA France recently hired Ève Angeli, a singer, and Zara Whites, a porn actress, as spokespeople. Whites was vegetarian, but Angeli was not. Many activists were chagrined at the use of a non-vegetarian as a spokesperson for a vegetarian organization, but moreover, they were concerned because Angeli, as one activist put it, "[is] as dumb as a post. She's very well known for her stupidity." In contrast to these two, many activists said they preferred Pamela Anderson, because at least she was vegetarian.

By far the best-known French celebrity to support animal rights was Brigitte Bardot, the actress-singer-model who founded her own animal protection organization in 1986. Many French activists critiqued Bardot for not being vegetarian (she eats fish), but more so, they critiqued her far-right politics. While French activists appreciated the attention Bardot brought to animal rights when no movement existed in France, they bristled at the thought that the best-known French animal rights activist was associated with the National Front and held many far-right political views. Activists such as Philippe (AVIS) complained of being viewed as right-wing or fascist because of the conservative reputation Bardot had cultivated since becoming an animal rights activist:

> She's the only one who's really in the media as a well-known person, there's just her. What comes to mind to the average French person, is Brigitte Bardot. She's the only one who gets in the mainstream media, who is known by her name. At the protest yesterday, there was just a few journalists, and they only mentioned her, they didn't mention other people who were there. But then again, reactionary people, that's not my thing. She's married to a right-winger,

in the National Front, and she's always been close to the National Front. That doesn't give the movement a good image or incite the public to join us. Even though it's typically a movement that came from a progressive milieu, in France, this isn't the case.

Again, as Meyer and Gamson (1995) note, the use of celebrities can be a double-edged sword. On the one hand, Bardot's fame as a French cultural icon provides more attention to the issue of animal rights. But on the other hand, her infamy as someone associated with the National Front can create negative associations for the movement as a whole.

French Media Coverage

Just as in the United States, French media often portrayed activists in a negative light. But unlike the U.S. movement, which mitigated such negative portrayals with more sympathetic media images, the French movement endured predominately negative media depictions. French activist organizations did not have the money to purchase advertisements in major newspapers or on television networks, and those organizations who may have had the money did not do so. Given the paltry, and mostly negative, reporting on the movement, French activists saw media as a major challenge to their work, and not as a cultural resource they could use. As Elsa put it: "The media says, 'animal rights activists are crazy, they're dangerous,' and the French believe it. They believe it. So us, with our little flyers, it's difficult to work against that. We're not equal, in the face of the media."

Indeed, of the few newspaper articles that focused on animal rights, the vast majority focused on three specific subjects, two of which portrayed animal rights activists as "crazy" and "dangerous," as Elsa put it, by focusing on death at the hands of animal rights activists. The only one of these three main topics that actually focused on French activists described various anti-fur protests at fashion events. I attended one such event, organized by PETA France, at Jean-Paul Gaultier's thirtieth anniversary party. PETA had recently stepped up their anti-fur campaign aimed at the designer, resorting to protests since he would not engage in discussion with PETA France on the issue of his continued use of fur in his fashion line. A dozen activists swarmed the gala opening of Gaultier's party, held at a famous nightclub near the Paris Opera. As the security guards tried to push the activists away, a young woman in the crowd waiting to get into the club fainted. When security asked for a doctor, one of the activists came to the rescue: Jérôme, the main organizer for PETA France, is also a medical doctor. After the protest, as I walked to the metro with Tali and Rob, two of the activists, I said I thought it was good that it was Jérôme who went to help the young woman, because that could only look good in the media. Tali said she disagreed, because the media would simply blame whatever happened on the protesters. Even when such a fortuitous event occurred, activists still feared the media would turn it against them.

The second major animal rights topic covered by the French media was the hunger strikes and death of Barry Horne. Horne was an English animal rights activist serving an 18-year sentence for planting incendiary devices in stores profiting from animal exploitation, such as leather goods stores and stores that tested their products on animals. Horne went on two hunger strikes in 1997 and 1998 and, after a series of subsequent hunger strikes, he died from liver failure. Media reports were not sympathetic, calling Horne a "terrorist" in articles such as "The Terrorist Delirium of the Friends of the Beasts" (Revol 1998).

The final major animal rights topic covered in the French press was Volkert van der Graff's 2002 murder of the Dutch politician Pim Fortuyn. While van der Graff admitted to killing Fortuyn for political reasons, fearing his right-wing party's rise to power, media seized upon the fact that van der Graff was a vegan and animal rights supporter who worked for an environmental organization. Headlines such as "Presumed Murderer of Pim Fortuyn Protector of Animals" did little to debunk ideas that van der Graff killed Fortuyn for animal rights reasons (*Libération* 2002).

Braced for such negative press, some activists tried to proactively avoid certain media framing devices as described by sociologist Todd Gitlin (1980), such as disparagement by numbers, or undercounting. At the post-Veggie Pride meeting, where activists began to plan the following year's events, one activist said, "We need a way to count how many people are in the protest, because the media will always say there were less of us." Another cautioned against using numbers, though, saying, "But we don't want to look stupid. To an omnivore, for us to say, 'Yeah! We had 500 people!', that's not so impressive. Five hundred people from all over France?" Media accounts of Veggie Pride in fact rarely reported the number of participants, except for a (fairly accurate) 2003 article: "In 2001, there were 200 of them, last year, 500" (*Libération* 2003).

More often, media engaged in framing devices that emphasized violence and radical flanks. Concerning the New Left and SDS, Gitlin (1980) found that later framing devices emphasized the presence of communists and violence in demonstrations. With animal rights, such media framing often centered around the ALF. Though the ALF specifically avoids violence towards all living creatures, media often framed them as violent. Just as radical flanks (Haines 1988) often served as "martyrs" for the mainstream flanks of the movement, so did the ALF for mainstream animal rights activists and organizations. While Bernadette said she supported the ALF, she pretended not to in order to make her and other animal rights activists look more mainstream to the public:

> When you tell someone that you're an animal rights activist, they'll look at you a bit weirdly, thinking, "Does she blow things up?" That kind of thing. Right away, they'll think, "Ooh, extremist" [. . .] It's like this article that the *Radio Times*, an English magazine, published, describing antivivisectionist activists as terrorists. And you know, it was, "All people who are against vivisection are burning things up and attacking people," that kind of thing. That's deliberate misinformation, when you know that the ALF

is against attacking people, and is against physical violence towards any living being, human or non-human. So I think that's mainly why. They try and scare people away from us and what we're trying to do by giving us this false image. Because it's kind of incredible that we end up being the people who are dangerous and aggressive and violent, when the only vague violence that we do, or some people do, is burning a building where animals are tortured. How violent is that? Whereas vivisectionists and people working in labs cut open live animals every day. But no, they're not violent, they're fine. They're the good ones. They're trying to reverse the situation, and they've managed quite well, I think. Sadly. Which is why on the stall, if anyone says, "What do you think about these people who burn labs," I say, "Ooh, no, that's too much."

Bernadette called such depictions of the ALF, and of animal rights activists in general, "deliberate misinformation." These framing devices, such as when media relied on statements by government officials or other authorities, or when they paid more attention to movement opposition than the movement itself (Gitlin 1980), emerged in numerous media–movement encounters. For example, in a debate between Stephanie Rebato of PETA and Yves Salomon, a furrier, on the television show *T'Empêches Tout le Monde de Dormir*, the show helped spread rumors that animal rights organizations were funded by oil companies.

Fogiel [host]: So you are for a complete ban of fur?
Rebato: Absolutely. Why does Mr. Salomon not use fake fur?
Salomon: I'm very pleased that we are discussing this subject tonight, because we are wondering, and we would love for you to clarify this for us, this would be a huge discovery for all of us: who is financing you? Who finances these huge publicity campaigns? Every time you talk about fake fur, you know, fake fur, it's petrol, there are huge petrol companies, and we all wonder, who is behind you?
Rebato: Fake fur, look . . .
Salomon: [interrupts] Fake fur is a petrol product, it's a synthetic product. I think this would interest all of the viewers [smirking].
Rebato: Me, personally, I don't even wear fake fur. I personally do not even wear fake fur, because it's too close to the image of real fur.
Salomon: You defend it, you brought it up here tonight, in front of everyone, and I think this is a huge piece of evidence that you, that you . . .
Rebato: [interrupts] No, no, no, I'm not here to give publicity for fake fur. I'm here to denounce the barbarism that goes on each day.

Before Rebato could continue, Fogiel interrupted again and changed the subject. Effectively, Rebato never had a chance to correct this charge, thus leaving viewers to wonder whether PETA is indeed a subsidiary of Exxon Mobil.

French Activists' "War of Position"

Most French activists I interviewed actively critiqued a media-based approach. These critiques centered on the idea that media stunts were often misunderstood, or ignored, in the media-saturated world in which we live. They also reflected the French activists' preference for longer-term processes of changing societal structures, rather than quick-fire media blitzes. Media sociologists Carroll and Ratner (1999), in analyzing Greenpeace media strategies, describe this as the difference between Antonio Gramsci's war of maneuver and his war of position. For the animal rights movement, PETA's Running of the Nudes, and other media stunts, exemplify Gramsci's war of maneuver, in that they deploy demonstrations and direct action to attack specific institutions.

Such media blitzes can backfire and ultimately work against the movement's short- and long-term goals. For example, René described a PETA protest in front of a KFC, where passersby thought the demonstration was actually an advertisement for KFC. Tali critiqued PETA's Running of the Nudes, an anti-bullfighting protest where nude activists run through the streets of Pamplona, for not accomplishing what she believed it should do—stopping bullfighting:

> The running in Pamplona, I think that's horrible. It doesn't stop corrida, it makes the Spanish people laugh at us. It makes one more spectacle, but no one cares. It makes people laugh more than anything. And there's one thing that I don't understand, is why nudity is used for animal rights and not for human rights. To go defend people dying of hunger, or people with illnesses, you would never see people getting naked. So why this carnival, this circus, why is that only for animals?

While Tali looked to the end goal of ending bullfighting, PETA's stated goals for the event are much lower-scale. Rather, PETA viewed the event as a way to reach out to the public:

> Running nude through the streets of Pamplona attracts media attention and provides a tremendous opportunity to spread the word about how animals suffer during bullfights. It gives us a way to reach people who aren't aware of the cruelty involved in the Running of the Bulls. Tourists need to know that bulls suffer a slow, painful death in the bullring, and the "Running of the Nudes" is a fantastic way to get that message out to the international public. (PETA 2015a)

Instead of these media blitzes, many French activists preferred a media strategy that resembled Gramsci's war of position, which is a longer-term process of changing societal structures. It was difficult to combine a war of position and a war of maneuver when engaging media, as Agnèse (Lyon Antispécistes) described:

> It's a banality to say that media influence people and public opinion. But evidently, the movement has a very tiny amount of influence over the media.

It's an unequal battle. I think that either we try to use the media, thus enter into the media game, like PETA does, and that's something that I don't like. Or either we refuse this logic of the media and we work on the ground, you know what I mean? Work in the streets, to establish a concrete presence in town, in universities. That's what I prefer [. . .] I think we have to keep our independence, keep this hope that it is possible to live differently.

It was this long-term view that many French activists took, preferring to engage in a long-term war of position in which they built a counter-hegemonic force through education and consciousness-raising. But taking such a long-term view sometimes meant sacrificing smaller achievements along the way, as I will show in Chapter 8.

U.S. Activists as "Ecoterrorists"

The one cultural resource that harmed U.S. activists more than it did French activists was the charge of terrorism. As early as 1987, animal rights opponents called activists "terrorists" because of their direct action methods against hunting and fur trapping.[2] Around the same time, the term "ecoterrorism" came into use by opponents of environmental and animal rights organizations. But after the September 11, 2001 attacks in the United States, the charge of "terrorism" became more onerous, and much more powerful. Thus it came as a blow to animal rights activists when, just five months after the attacks, James F. Jarboe, the Domestic Terrorism Section Chief of the Counterterrorism Division of the FBI, called the Animal Liberation Front "a serious terrorist threat" in a congressional testimony on February 12, 2002 (Federal Bureau of Investigation 2002).

While I did not interview any ALF activists, the fact that any animal rights activists were being called "terrorists" affected everyone involved in the movement. This was not a case where the radical flanks martyred themselves for the mainstream flanks. In this case, the radical flank of the ALF being called terrorists made all animal rights activists fear the same charge. Because of these threats, activists saw the government as a primary challenge to their work. When I asked Justice what challenges she faced in her activism, she immediately responded:

The current administration. Labeling us as terrorists, spying on us and our groups. Painting that portrait in the American mind, in the American public that animal rights activists, and activists in general, being terrorists and being unpatriotic and un-American.

2 The earliest such charge I found came from a January 4, 1987 article in *The New York Times*, entitled "Trap Law Stirs Debate on Fur," in which the head of a group of furriers says of animal rights activists in Western Europe (notably England, West Germany, and the Netherlands): "They virtually destroyed the market for furs in those countries. It got very violent and vicious. We were dealing with a brand of terrorism."

Just as antiwar activists became "unpatriotic" and "un-American" simply by virtue of protesting war, animal rights activists became unpatriotic, un-American terrorists simply by virtue of being active for animals. Even activists in small, grassroots, mainstream organizations felt the public they were trying to reach saw only the radical flanks, and only thought of terrorists, when they thought of animal rights, as Grant explained:

> I would say, most people probably—and this is judging from my past experience as being a meat-eater and part of the average American public in this regard—that when most people think of animal rights activism, they think of the negative, or what I consider the negative, personification of it. Which is "acts of terrorism." Which is ridiculous, because it's not really terrorism.

Grant had only recently become a vegetarian and an animal rights activist a little over a year before our interview. Coming from a traditional, religious, Southern upbringing, Grant said he himself had seen animal rights in a negative light until he started exploring the issues in his philosophy courses.

This cultural trend towards calling animal rights activists terrorists affected even the most mainstream of organizations. When I interviewed Heidi in the summer of 2005, she described how her group, the Humane Society of the United States, arguably one of the most mainstream animal protection organizations in the U.S., actively tried to avoid being called terrorists:

Heidi: Well I've had, I would say, tactics proposed that were so wacky or that would look so bad that we would take repercussions for the activity. So I want to say usually, it's the more wacky or questionable, certainly HSUS has taken a stand against any kind of violent tactics or intimidation or threats. Because of the backlash. And I would say certainly that everything is much more scrutinized since September 11th. So we have to be very aware of how societal events affect our strategies as well.

Elizabeth: Do you mean more scrutiny since September 11th . . .

Heidi: Yeah, over the word "terrorism," or any kind of intimidation, or you know, like things that weren't looked at before are looked at a lot more harshly now.

Heidi's statement was also interesting in that, as we spoke in the summer of 2005, she seemed to foresee the coming attack from animal rights opponents in the private sector.

Later on, against this anti-animal rights backlash from the government, HSUS and many other animal rights and animal protection groups came out publicly to remind people that they did not employ or promote any violent tactics. On the one hand, this shows the ideological diversity within the U.S. movement, with activists targeting other activists, and mainstream organizations seeking to distance themselves from the radical flank. But on the other hand, in doing so, these organizations may have helped to reify the image of animal rights activists as terrorists, as journalist Will Potter (2008) and sociologist David Naguib Pellow (2014) both argue. For example, after a 2008 fire at the house of an animal researcher at the University of California Santa Cruz, the FBI immediately accused animal rights activists of the attack. Amidst the suspicion of animal rights activists, the Humane Society of the United States contributed $2,500 towards a reward for information leading to the capture and arrest of those involved in the attack (Pacelle 2008). As of the latest updates on this case, from 2012, the FBI continues to target animal activists, subpoenaing them for Grand Juries, and yet neither the Animal Liberation Front nor any other animal liberation organization has ever claimed responsibility for the attack (Potter 2012a, 2012b, 2013, Animal Liberation Frontline 2012).

U.S. Counter-Movements and the "Terrorist" Frame

Once the frame of "animal activists as terrorists" became salient, counter-movements in the United States began to use it as well. Counter-movements and opponents such as the National Rifle Association and the Center for Consumer Freedom recognized the salience of the frame and the power it had to damage the radical flank of the animal rights movement, and thus they used this frame to their advantage. The Center for Consumer Freedom, founded in 1995, and dedicated to "promoting personal responsibility and protecting consumer choice," is widely known to be a front for the tobacco and meat lobbies. Run by Richard Berman, a Washington lobbyist who represents the alcohol, tobacco, restaurant, and hospitality industries, the CCF was founded with $600,000 from the Phillip Morris corporation. A Long-time opponent of animal rights, the CCF runs many anti-animal rights websites, such as petakillsanimals.com and activistfacts.com, where it tells readers "the truth about animal rights extremists."

When antivivisection activists decided to turn their battle against Huntington Life Sciences to the New York Stock Exchange, an ad appeared in *The New York Times* in April 2006, funded by an anonymous group called "NYSE Hostage." When activists succeeded in blocking HLS's stock from moving from the Pink Sheets (a lower-tier market) to the Over the Counter Bulletin Board (a more exclusive stock market), "NYSE Hostage" began the ad campaign. The ad depicted a man wearing a balaclava and it claimed: "A domestic terror group with a single-issue focus—the 'rights' of laboratory animals—trained its sights on the New York Stock Exchange."

In December 2006, a graphic novel called *Freedom in Peril*, purportedly created by the National Rifle Association, leaked onto the internet. The comic was a reaction to the Democrats' recent win in the congressional elections, and in it, NRA leaders Wayne LaPierre and Chris W. Cox wrote a letter in which they warn NRA supporters that the "anti-gun" lobby will try to disguise their anti-gun mission as anti-terrorist legislation. The graphic novel attacked government leaders as well as celebrities affiliated with the Democratic Party, gangs, and "animal rights terrorists." The NRA did not provide copyright permission to reproduce the image here, but it can easily be found on the internet. The cover image includes a running man and a woman (with visibly unshaven legs and sensible shoes) carrying torches, bats, and gasoline. Alongside them are an angry dog, pig, bull, and chicken. There is even an owl carrying sticks of dynamite, and a lobster running alongside the group. Primarily attacking PETA and HSUS, the pamphlet claimed:

> PETA's tax filings reveal contributions to violent terrorist cells like the Animal Liberation Front (ALF) and the Earth Liberation Front (ELF), who have committed countless firebomb attacks and caused more than $110 million in destruction. This eco-terrorism movement is so dangerous, the FBI has declared it America's number one domestic terrorist threat. They've upstaged al-Qaeda as the greatest terrorist threat on American soil.

They also alleged that anti-hunting groups poison hunters' dogs, a highly doubtful claim. When this pamphlet was leaked onto the internet in late December 2006, many NRA supporters cried foul, claiming it was a hoax. However, NRA spokesperson Andrew Arulanadnam confirmed it was indeed an NRA publication, but only a working draft they had not yet approved (Baram 2006).

How did activists respond to these claims? While some activists reacted as HSUS did, by distancing themselves from any violent activities, others tried to respond with a bit of humor, as Paul Watson of the *Sea Shepherd* did at the October 2007 Becoming the Change animal rights conference. He told the audience that animal rights and conservation groups have never harmed anyone, but we are called terrorists. Why was that, he asked? "Because we terrify the meat-eating bastards." But the animal rights movement was dealt a major blow in November 2006 with the passing of the Animal Enterprise Terrorism Act.

The Animal Enterprise Terrorism Act (AETA) is a bill created to amend the Animal Enterprise Protection Act of 1992 (AEPA-PL 102-346), making it stronger, expanding its purview, and giving federal authorities the ability to increase penalties for offenders. For example, the AETA expanded the term "terrorism" to include not only acts that interfere with, but also acts that *promote* interfering with, any animal enterprise. Activists worried about the broadness and vagueness of the new bill, such as its open-ended description of an animal enterprise as nearly any enterprise that uses or sells animal products. In the 1992 AEPA, an animal enterprise was defined as:

(A) a commercial or academic enterprise that uses animals for food or fiber production, agriculture, research, or testing;

(B) a zoo, aquarium, circus, rodeo, or lawful competitive animal event; or

(C) any fair or similar event intended to advance agricultural arts and sciences;

And in the 2006 AETA, its definition was expanded to include what could describe nearly any business in the United States:

(A) a commercial or academic enterprise that uses or sells animals or animal products for profit, food or fiber production, agriculture, education, research, or testing;

(B) a zoo, aquarium, animal shelter, pet store, breeder, furrier, circus, or rodeo, or other lawful competitive animal event; or

(C) any fair or similar event intended to advance agricultural arts and sciences;

Furthermore, the definition of the offense expanded greatly as well. The 1992 AEPA described the offenses under the bill as follows:

(a) OFFENSE.–Whoever–

(1) travels in interstate or foreign commerce, or uses or causes to be used the mail or any facility in interstate or foreign commerce, for the purpose of causing physical disruption to the functioning of an animal enterprise; and

(2) intentionally causes physical disruption to the functioning of an animal enterprise by intentionally stealing, damaging, or causing the loss of, any property (including animals or records) used by the animal enterprise, and thereby causes economic damage exceeding $10,000 to that enterprise, or conspires to do so; shall be fined under this title or imprisoned not more than one year, or both.

The 2006 AETA expanded that definition to include nearly any person who has any sort of relationship with such a broadly defined animal enterprise (italics added):

(a) Offense- Whoever travels in interstate or foreign commerce, or uses or causes to be used the mail or any facility of interstate or foreign commerce–

(1) for the purpose of damaging or interfering with the operations of an animal enterprise; and

(2) in connection with such purpose–

(A) intentionally damages or causes the loss of any real or personal property (including animals or records) used by an animal enterprise, or any real or personal property of *a person or entity having a connection to, relationship with, or transactions with* an animal enterprise;

(B) intentionally places a person in reasonable fear of the death of, or serious bodily injury to that person, a member of the immediate family (as defined in section 115) of that person, or a spouse or intimate partner of that person by a course of conduct involving threats, acts of vandalism, property damage, criminal trespass, harassment, or intimidation; or

(C) conspires or attempts to do so;

Even if actions did not incur any bodily harm or economic damage, an offender can be fined and imprisoned for up to one year. Numerous opponents, not just animal rights activists, balked at this expansion of the definition, contending that the severely increased fines and branding of nonviolent civil disobedience as "terrorism" would have a "chilling effect" on activism. The bill passed in the House on a voice vote with only six members of the house present, and Project Censored called it one of the top 25 under-reported news stories of 2006 (Project Censored 2010).

As journalist Will Potter (2006) first reported on his blog Green is the New Red, The National Association for Biomedical Research took out a full-page ad in *Roll Call*, a daily Capitol Hill newspaper widely read by Congress members and staffers. The NABR did not provide copyright permission for the image, but it is easily found on the internet. The black and white image in the ad depicts a vandalized laboratory. Menacing words stand out in red, on the wall: "Your home is next." On animal rights activists, the ad reported:

> The threat is growing and is so serious the FBI has classified these extremists as one of the most serious domestic terrorist threats in the U.S. today. That's why we urge you to support legislation designed to counteract the increasingly violent activity aimed at shutting down research in this country.

Since the passing of the 2006 AETA, a coalition of 240 animal protection and social justice organizations banded together to raise awareness of AETA and other similar pending state bills. At the October 2007 Becoming the Change conference, journalist Will Potter and lawyer Lauren Regan spoke on the AETA. Regan, of the Civil Liberties Defense Center, gave a history of the concept of ecoterrorism as it applied to animal rights activists. Potter, author of the blog and book *Green is the New Red* (2011), spoke of the current "Green Scare" of ecological and animal rights activism, akin to the anti-communist Red Scare. Both speakers assured the audience the AETA would likely never apply to them, but that its point was to instill fear in activists. If the government could make mainstream, above-ground activists scared, the movement would die. Potter encouraged the activists to continue their work, because "the threat of you existing is a cultural threat."

The Ambivalence of Militant Imagery in France

In France, animal rights opponents did not denounce activists as "terrorists" as they did in the United States. When French activists spoke of the threat of being called terrorists, it was usually in reference to the Animal Liberation Front in the U.S. or the U.K. For example, in response to a question on how French people viewed animal rights activists, Christine (AVF) cited "extremists" and "cult members," and then went on to a depiction that has more to do with U.S. problems than French ones:

> I read in the newspaper that there was a television show talking about the ALF, and saying they were classed like Al Qaeda. So, in fact, they were taken to be terrorists, even though the ALF has never killed anyone. It's people who save animals at the price of liberty. But given the price that people accord to

animals, if you attack corporations you put the economic health of the country in peril! I'm not a part of the ALF, but because of this vision, people in the ALF are treated and considered as being outside the law.

The image of animal liberationists as terrorists emerged at the animal rights conference Les Estivales de la Question Animale, in August 2006. Patrick Sacco, a convicted member of the group Greystoke, who was arrested for liberating monkeys from a government lab in the early 1980s, said he had friends in the ALF in England, but he did not like their violent tactics. During the discussion period after his presentation, I said that activists in the U.S. were being called "terrorists," and asked if this was the same in France. Patrick replied, "No, because there aren't any liberationists left to call terrorists." At the same time that Patrick decried terrorist images and actions, saying they were not positive or valorized, he also deplored the fact that there were no such activists in France that could even be called terrorists.

This ambivalence characterized French activists' view of the threat of being called terrorists. While no one said they wanted to go to jail or have the government follow their every move, a few activists saw such government threats as a sign of success. They believed if activists were that threatening to the government, they must be doing something right. Others viewed the masked animal liberator image as a tool to attract young, militant activists, as one activist described:

ALF, things like that, I think more at the university, there are quite a few political things, people do things for political prisoners, so why not get people interested by that? I think that ALF, that's a powerful, people are going to put on masks to go save animals, that's a little, I think that could attract young people. It's the image of people wearing hoods, going to save animals, and I think that's rather impressive to people. It's a little bit of marketing, you see these photos and, I think that a younger public is more receptive to that. They see that side, and they might go liberate some cats, that's great. I think it's not a bad way to get people on your side. But, I don't know what kind of impression that would give.

Another activist spoke of the "mythical side" of animal liberationists with face masks, which this activist claimed to be a source of admiration from non-activists, and which was an image that this activist's group tried to incorporate in their actions. In this sense, "terrorism" became a cultural tool that worked in favor of the French movement because it garnered new activists, and it was not (yet) used against the movement by the French government, counter-movements, or other opponents. Since France's new social movements are characterized by more radicalism and militancy than in other countries (Duyvendak 1995), some activists took this as an opportunity to win more young militant activists to the cause of animal rights.

Perhaps the strongest example of such ambivalence was the idea that government threats and surveillance signaled a certain level of success for a social movement. To some activists, it indicated a sort of legitimacy. When I first met

Gilberte, a seasoned activist, she offered to give me information on the movement in France, so I gave her my notebook to write her contact information. Gilberte turned to me and cautioned me to keep this notebook safe. "You've got a lot of contact information for people in the movement in here, and if this falls into the wrong hands, it could turn out badly." I said I understood completely, that no one sees the notebook but me, and that it is always in my possession. She then told me I should keep everyone's identity confidential, and never to say that a specific person said something. I responded that I never do that, unless the activist chooses public participation, and even then, I let them see what I have written before publishing it.

Gilberte said the French government watches animal rights activists, and "if they got a hold of this book, it could be very bad for the movement." I said I understood that as well, especially since in the United States the government viewed animal rights activists as terrorists. I said the U.S. government even listened to phone calls and put spies in the movement to infiltrate it. I told her about some examples of police pretending to be activists, and about the SHAC 7 trial. To this, Gilberte responded, "We aren't there yet," but that the government still watched animal rights activists. Saying "we aren't there yet" implies that this is where she sees the movement going.

The French movement did start to attract more interest from the government. When I returned to the conference Les Estivales de la Question Animale to present my research in July 2010, there was a stranger in the audience. No one seemed to know him, and this was a small crowd of about 40 people, all of whom knew one another. His leather boots and military haircut certainly made him stand out in a crowd of anarchist animal rights activists. He stayed for my presentation, and when he left, rumors started flying that he was part of the Renseignements Généraux, the intelligence wing of the French government that investigates political radicals.[3] There was a mixture of fear and excitement at the prospect of the French government spying on the group. Luckily, he never returned, and the government did not attempt to shut down the conference or the activists who organized it.

Cultural Resources in Context

In the four chapters in this section on Cultural Resources, I examined six specific cultural resources available to animal rights activists—and their opponents. These cultural resources differ from structural resources because they are contextual and publicly available (Williams 1995). Public availability means that symbols that primarily hold internal meaning for a movement will not have much impact in a wider political arena. This also means that cultural resources are constructed at the social level and are wielded by specific actors, but their power and effectiveness depends upon their interpretation by others, namely, their targets.

---

3 Although the Renseignements Généraux wing was folded into a different agency in 2008, French activists still referred to the organization, sometimes as just R.G.

This leads to the importance of contextuality. Sociologist Rhys Williams (1995) argued that the contextuality of cultural resources implies that one cannot simply exchange one symbol or ideology for another. For Williams, that cultural resources are contextual meant that a coalition of Catholic priests would carry more political weight in Boston than in Salt Lake City. But this implies that religion might be a cultural resource for challengers in nearly any arena, and challengers should just find the appropriate religion to use in their various contexts. As Williams works within the sociology of religion as well as social movements, he has demonstrated how very different social movements—Civil Rights and the Religious Right—used religion for very different purposes (Williams 2002). Williams notes that the form of American Protestantism both movements used was culturally resonant in the United States, leaving us to ponder how cultural resources such as religion might resonate in other cultures. In these chapters I attempted to answer some of those questions by showing how religion, as well as five other cultural resources, varied in resonance between the French and U.S. contexts.

By demonstrating how culture variably "works" in these different contexts, I do not wish to imply that the meanings behind such cultural tools are static, overly powerful, or simply recreate the structure which gives them meaning, in a classical Marxist hegemonic sense. Likewise, I do not claim that these cultural resources are weak and susceptible to constant construction and reconstruction by agentic individuals, in a Birmingham School or feminist cultural studies sense. Rather, I view the meaning of such cultural tools and symbols as a process, emerging from various forms of interaction between their producers, their receivers, and the cultural contexts in which they exist. In this sense, cultural contexts act as a structuring force, but not an all-powerful one. The cultural context itself is also structured by these interactions.

These chapters improve upon overly agentic studies by demonstrating that culture is not infinitely malleable (Hays 1994). Animal rights activists manipulated various cultural symbols to achieve not just political goals, but also cultural goals. However, as I have shown with the variability of these cultural resources, shared symbols and beliefs on the environment, religion, health, food, media, or terrorism cannot always be manipulated to achieve activists' desired goals. Just as culture is not infinitely malleable, it is also not purely strategic. Since culture is a relatively understudied aspect of social movements, scholars have a tendency to characterize activists' use of culture as strategic more than anything else. Jeff Goodwin and James Jasper (1999: 49) soundly critique this tendency, taking as an example Doug McAdam's (1996) analysis of Dr. Martin Luther King Jr.'s use of Christian rhetoric in his speeches:

> But does McAdam believe that King made a calculated decision to employ Christian themes in his speeches as part of a "strategic effort" to legitimate the civil rights movement? That is like saying that King made a strategic choice to speak English, rather than seeing English as part of the culture shared by King and his audiences [. . .] Nor does he mention the possibility

that King employed Christian themes because, as a Baptist minister with a doctorate in theology, he actually believed that those "themes" were true or valuable for their own sake.

By highlighting the duality of culture at various levels, I attempt to exemplify this means/ends distinction in social movement actors' strategic choices. Simply because a cultural resource resonates (or does not), that does not mean that an activist will (or will not) choose to use it. In these chapters I have focused on how the dominant culture shapes the broad cultural strategies available to animal rights activists, demonstrating shared opportunities and constraints as well as the variable resonance of specific cultural resources. While this approach shows which paths may be the most or least fruitful for activists to take, it does not explain why they make the strategic and tactical choices they do. It could be that French activists did not make health arguments because dominant cultural beliefs constrained their ability to do so. However, I found it more the case that activists did not make such claims because they did not resonate with their own beliefs. The macro-level analysis presented in this section on Cultural Resources cannot explain activists' actual strategic choices. In the next section on Strategic Choices, I move to a meso-level analysis, to show how the culture of the animal rights movements in France and the United States influenced activists' strategic and tactical choices.

Part III
Strategic Choices

7 American Pragmatism

Social movement organizations function within a broader social and cultural context, including the region or country in which they work. I examined this dominant culture in detail in the previous section on Cultural Resources, showing how existing culture provided similar constraints and variable cultural resources to the animal rights movements in both the United States and France. The previous section showed how each movement's toolkit was expanded, or contracted, by virtue of the cultural tools available in their culture. But how do activists then choose among those tools? To understand the strategic and tactical choices of individual social movement organizations, we must examine how they function alongside other organizations within the social movement of which they are a part. Group cultures, identities, and the symbolic boundaries surrounding them are not only formed through individual tastes in tactics or as challenges to mainstream culture; they are also formed through internal debates within a movement. In this section on Strategic Choices, I will demonstrate how we can best understand such decision-making by examining social movement organizations' strategic orientations, which are shaped by the social movement in which they work.

Making Strategic Choices

How do social movement organizations make strategic choices? Social movement scholars have employed the work of organizational sociologists to understand the isomorphism of organizational forms (DiMaggio and Powell 1983) as well as why organizations might differ between fields (Oliver 1991). The dialogue between social movement and organizational studies needs to be extended to include what happens within organizations—the process of strategic decision-making. In this section on Strategic Choices, Chapters 7 and 8 address why strategic and tactical choices cohere in an organizational field within a country, but differ between countries. I draw upon organizational and cultural theory to understand strategic decision-making in animal rights organizations in France and the United States.

Social movement organizations (henceforth abbreviated SMOs), as well as other ideologically-driven organizations such as nonprofits (Ward 2000), do not always conform to traditional explanations of organizational behavior. The rational systems (Thompson 1967) and natural systems (Selznick 1957) perspectives view organizations as calculating behavior to achieve specific goals. While some SMOs engage in "tactical innovation," as Douglas McAdam (1983) termed it, or "strategic adaptation," as Holly McCammon and her colleagues (McCammon et al. 2008) did, to effectively adapt and achieve their goals, many do not (Beckwith 2009), as I show in the French case.

Social movement scholars have offered explanations of strategic decision-making that rely less upon a systemic organizational perspective than do organizational theorists. Earlier, rationalist theories of resource mobilization or political opportunities argue that SMOs make decisions based on a cost–benefit analysis of deploying resources (McCarthy and Zald 1977) or by exploiting openings in the political opportunity structure (Gamson and Meyer 1996). Moreover, these rationalists did not examine "costs" or "benefits" as cultural constructs in themselves, such as understanding the ways in which activists come to see something as a cost or a benefit. Instead, as Jeff Larson (2013) argues, they treat such understandings as a given. After the cultural turn, others argued that activists make choices based on symbolic associations with their personal "tastes in tactics" (Jasper 1997) or with a group's belief system or ideology (Meyer 2004), sometimes through what Mayer Zald (2000) termed "ideologically structured action." These rationalist and individualist explanations cannot explain decisions made at the group level, especially decisions that contradict activists' or SMOs' ideologies, as I show in the U.S. case.

A field approach (Downey and Rohlinger 2008, Jasper 2006a) is a necessary complement for understanding how SMOs make strategic and tactical choices because it acknowledges that these choices do not take place in a vacuum. SMOs function not only in relation to their opponents, but also in relation to other organizations within their movement—in their social movement "family" (della Porta and Rucht 1995) or the "social movement industry" (McCarthy and Zald 1977). By taking a field approach, I also delineate movement fields at the national level.

In addition to taking a field approach, we also need to understand how culture affects strategic decision-making. Social movement scholars now use more organizational approaches to study social movements (see Davis et al. 2005 for a good overview), but they tend to focus on organizational models as forms of culture (Haveman and Rao 1997, Ruef and Scott 1998, Thornton and Ocasio 1999), and not on how culture might impede or enable organizational processes like strategic and tactical decision-making. Further, many scholars tend to characterize activists' and others' use of culture as purely agentic, rather than as a structuring force itself (Archer 1988). Finally, these approaches typically study strategic choices after the fact, and they miss the process of decision-making. By analyzing how SMOs function within a social movement field, and how the culture of the field structures strategic choices, my approach brings together disparate theories of culture and action in social movements, organizations, and culture.

In Chapters 7 and 8, I address the question of how activists in SMOs make strategic choices. I take a meso-level approach and place SMOs within the larger field in which they work. Using a similar meso-level approach, Liam Downey and Deana Rohlinger (2008) explain strategic choices of SMOs based on their relations to a variety of actors, including allies, opponents, authorities, and audiences. I echo their method but add cultural and neoinstitutional theories. I examine how the culture of the social movement field structures SMOs' strategic and tactical choices, influencing such decisions more than individual reasons or factors external to the movements.

In this chapter, I first explain my approach to institutional logics and strategic choices from a cultural and meso-level perspective. I then show how the U.S. movement developed a logic of "pragmatism" that emphasized efficiency and effectiveness. Chapter 8 demonstrates how the French movement promoted a logic of "consistency" that valued the internal coherence of thought and action. These logics guided strategic decision-making, enabling certain decisions while impeding others. Organizational theory can help explain the existence of such cultural logics, but not how and why different logics developed within the same social movement. Thus Chapter 8 concludes by delineating the limits of diffusion and isomorphism within the movement field.

Strategy, Tactics, and Decision-Making

Before looking at research on the decision-making processes for choosing strategies and tactics, it will help to clarify the two and their relationship to one another. According to social movements scholar James Jasper (2006a: 5), strategy includes five components: a movement (1) declares goals, (2) employs means to achieve those goals, (3) recognizes and/or encounters resistance, (4) which makes strategy inherently social and interactive, and (5) is oriented towards the future. These components may or may not be explicit or conscious. The means–ends relationship is the cornerstone of strategy (Smithey 2009). The means, in these cases, are a movement's tactics, and these tactics exist within a broader strategy. Thus, while inherently related, the difference between strategy and tactics can be teased apart by viewing tactics as the specific actions implemented to achieve a movement's goals. However, as Jasper (2006a: 70) reminds us, "The distinction depends on your perspective." I use Jeff Larson's (2013: 1) definition of tactics as "forms of collective action publicly deployed, whether in-person or via audio, visual, or written media, in service of a sustained campaign of claims making."

When considering activists or SMOs within a single social movement, different groups choose different strategies and tactics (Crossley 2002). In the foundational resource mobilization and political opportunities theories of social movements, strategic and tactical choice was based on a rationalist logic, with activists choosing the most efficient method to achieve their goals (McCarthy and Zald 1977, Tilly 1978). The political context can shape tactical opportunities and constraints, or even entire tactical repertoires (Tilly 1979). As tactical repertoires became more routinized and familiar to activists, it seemed that the choices of activists and organizations became more synonymous with their structural position than with any sort of "artful" decision (Jasper 1997).

After the cultural turn, social movement scholars began to incorporate identities and individual and organizational values to understand strategic and tactical preferences. Activists and SMOs might have different "tastes in tactics" (Jasper 1997), which implies that tactics are directly related to identities (Polletta and Jasper 2001), or how social actors see themselves (Smithey 2009). Or, engaging in "ideologically structured action" (Zald 2000), activists' behavior is shaped by ideological concerns and belief systems. As activists' political and lifestyle practices reflect their ideological concerns, their tactics would necessarily follow those belief systems as well. However, as we will see in Part 3, ideological commitments cannot fully explain strategic and tactical choices. These gaps between theory and data result from the lack of empirical studies on how social movement actors engage in strategic decision-making (as noted by Jasper 1997, 2005, 2006a). This makes it difficult to assess the usefulness of these theories, much less create new ones. Moreover, much of what we do know describes individual explanations of such choices, and we need to better understand how groups of activists arrive at these decisions.

A Meso-Level Approach to Strategic Choices

Our understanding of strategic choices is also hampered by a theoretical and empirical focus on individual-level explanations of past or future behavior (Emirbayer and Mische 1998, Hitlin and Elder 2007). Such individual-level approaches obscure the relationship between actors in the broader social movement field. Scholars have been calling for studies of relational approaches to tactical choice (Smithey 2009: 661), as well as studies of institutional fields (Larson 2013, Larson and Lizardo 2015) for better understanding tactical choices. Recent scholarship on social movements and organizations paves the way for researchers to take a meso-level approach to analyze decisions made and enacted at the SMO level.

Organizational theorists Roger Friedland and Robert Alford (1991) originally based their definition of institutional logics on anthropological definitions of culture, where culture was equated with social structure. Institutional logics affect the creation of new organizational forms (Haveman and Rao 1997) and enhance organizational legitimacy (Ruef and Scott 1998). They also influence power in organizations (Thornton and Ocasio 1999), a finding that shows institutional logics might also affect internal processes like strategic action. To strengthen this link between culture and organizational studies, and to show how institutional logics affect strategic action, social movement scholars must rethink institutional logics using theories that view culture as structured (Bourdieu 1977, Giddens 1984, Sewell 1992).

Much of this work, though, has focused on external culture and its impact on movement emergence, taking a new eye to what were previously thought to be "objective," structural, political opportunities (Polletta 1999). We still know little of how culture affects the everyday work of these movements once they emerge. SMOs function within a broader social and cultural context, including the region or country in which they work, and this extant culture has been shown to influence movement culture (Moody and Thévenot 2000), organizational form (Crozier 1964), and the effectiveness of a movement's symbolic repertoires (Williams 1995). But to understand the strategic and tactical choices of individual SMOs, one must also examine how they function alongside other SMOs in their social movement—their movement culture.

We already know quite a bit about movement cultures, such as the culture of the labor movement (Fantasia 1988), or the culture of certain feminist movements (Taylor and Whittier 1992, Martin 1990). What we do not yet fully understand is how these movement cultures might also act as structures. Just as the extant culture in which a movement works affects a movement's emergence, organization, or effectiveness, how might internal movement cultures constrain or enable SMOs to choose certain forms of action? I view movement culture as the shared meanings that arise from interactions between SMOs, and between individual activists and their SMOs. This approach furthers our understandings of the internal dynamics of movement cultures, and it helps us move beyond the assumption that most intra-movement interaction occurs between mainstream groups and radical flanks (Haines 1988).

Movement cultures are related to institutional logics. Combining organizational, cultural, and social movement theory, I view institutional logics as movement-wide guidelines for creating, choosing, implementing, and evaluating strategic action. Institutional logics provide rules legitimating certain actions or solutions (March and Olsen 1989), and they determine the issues decision-makers privilege (Ocasio 1999). These unwritten rules also shape activists' and SMOs' strategic orientations, thus guiding how they choose their strategies and tactics. Institutional logics emerge from interaction between SMOs and individual activists within a social movement field. While they may be informed by extant culture, they do not come from "metasocial warrants," as political sociologist Alain Touraine (1977) described them. And like the constitutive rules that come from what Ann Swidler (2001) calls "anchoring practices," these institutional logics become stronger and more embedded in the movement precisely because they inform antagonistic social relationships. Like conflicting religious congregations (Edgell Becker 1999), these movement-wide interpretive frameworks defined appropriate practices in the field. In my cases, the field equated to the animal rights movement at the national level.

The idea that organizations influence each other within a broader infrastructure is nothing new to organizational sociologists. Such interdependence, including symbiotic or competitive relationships, has been cited as a primary factor in organizational habits (Pfeffer and Salancik 1978). Much of the work in this area focuses on the emergence of new organizational forms (Haveman et al. 2007; Rao et al. 2000; Schneiberg et al. 2008), such as how the antihierarchical culture of the women's movement influenced the creation of new organizational forms (Martin 1990). It also highlights the institutionalization of organizational forms as expressions of movement culture (Schneiberg and Soule 2005). Thus in Chapters 7 and 8, I look at how field conditions affect innovations—or stagnations—in SMOs' strategic and tactical choices.

My approach borrows from Downey and Rohlinger's (2008) meso-level theory of strategic orientation, but I add the necessity of looking to the interaction between SMOs in an organizational field that is structured by institutional logics. Downey and Rohlinger take a relational approach to understand SMOs' strategic choices within movements as a whole. By examining what they term the "strategic articulation" of a movement—the nature and extent of cooperative or competitive links between SMOs—one can better sense the shape of a social movement and thus the different possibilities for action in differentially articulated movements. Downey and Rohlinger used SMOs' previous choices to create their theory, but I seek to explain why SMOs made those choices in the first place. More than cooperative or competitive dynamics, I look at the culture of a social movement in order to understand why SMOs make strategic and tactical choices.

I similarly borrow from Jeff Larson and Omar Lizardo's research on institutional movement logics, which they define as, "A cultural template embedded in the practices and relations of social movement actors that provide them with a focus of attention, source of meaning and identity, and how to 'do' contention" (2015: 62). To Larson and Lizardo, such logics influence strategic action in a number of ways. I am particularly interested in how they denote a restricted set of choices for action and deliberation, as well as how such logics become "public knowledge" for activists and others. That is, SMOs develop, and become committed to, identities related to how they organize. As discussed in Chapter 6 on the media, Erin Evans (2015a) found that such identities helped SMOs garner more and better media attention. Here, I seek to understand how these institutional logics, including their identities and field of choices, affect SMOs' strategic and tactical decision-making.

Larson and Lizardo (2015) found three types of logics in the movements they studied. First, "public crusaders" described small, non-bureaucratic organizations, that typically held a local focus, and whose goals primarily included changing public opinion. "Professional insiders" included larger, more bureaucratic and professional organizations, most interested in state and federal policy-making. Finally, "urban activists" also included large and professional organizations, but described those with more of a local scope, interested in the local political economy. Larson and Lizardo observed the outcomes of decisions, whereas I focus on the processes of decision-making. The organizations in my study included a mix of all of the types of organizations they studied. But what bounded them together was not so much their focus, size, or hierarchy. Rather, I found that all of these organizations resembled one another in terms of the institutional logics that guided their decision-making, and this cohered by country. That is, organizations in the United States made decisions based on an institutional logic of pragmatism, whereas organizations in France did so based on a logic of consistency. In describing these logics and how they manifested themselves in strategic and tactical decisions, I answer Larson and Lizardo's questions about the extent to which an organization's issues–tactics–targets combination influences their relations with others, and vice versa. This also addresses the bigger question in this section on Strategic Choices, of how social movement organizations choose from among their strategic and tactical toolkits.

The Paradox of American Pragmatism

In the first wave animal rights movement in the United States, much of activists' activity centered on fur, vivisection, and hunting. One of the centerpieces of the anti-hunting campaigns of the 1980s and 1990s was a pigeon shoot in Hegins, Pennsylvania. Every Labor Day since the early 1930s, hunters from across Pennsylvania, and even other states, came to the small town to participate in the pigeon shoot. Hundreds of pigeons were kept in cages, released one by one, as the hunters shot them. Children, called "trapper boys" and "trapper girls," then collected the pigeons and discarded them into trash cans. If the pigeons were not killed instantly, the trapper boys and girls would kill them by ripping their heads off, banging them against the garbage cans, or stomping on them.

The nature of the hunt—that the pigeons were trapped and released with no chance to escape, and that children killed the maimed pigeons in such egregious ways—drew the ire of animal rights activists. A grassroots movement, led by the Fund for Animals, gathered support from animal rights activists all over the country. Going to Hegins to protest on Labor Day weekend became a rite of passage for many activists of the time. However, just as the grassroots movement was gaining momentum, when thousands of protesters would convene upon Hegins over the Labor Day weekend, the Fund for Animals pulled out of the protest, and decided to boycott Hegins protest events. Heidi (HSUS, formerly Fund for Animals) described this decision:

> That was actually, it was a really rough decision because there was so much energy around this in the grassroots and it really was this thing that people started coming to every Labor Day. And it was because we had built it up. But a lot of activists got their start there, a lot of them participated in their first civil disobedience, and it was a place they could, because there were other activists doing it. We had lawyers who watched the backs of the activists and bailed them out and took them through the court system, everything that a young activist would start their protest career in. So there was a lot of grassroots energy around this. And a lot of people believed that's how we were going to stop it. So when the Fund for Animals made the decision to withdraw from the protest, and to actually boycott the event, and we set up some other events around the state, like at tourism destinations where people would leaflet and say this is what is going on, we took a lot of heat from the grassroots movement. A lot of people felt like we were pulling back, they felt like we were giving up, and that we were not expending resources on this anymore.

Why would the flagship organization of the largest anti-hunting protest decide to pull its support from this event, especially when it seemed that support from animal rights activists was reaching a critical mass? And if the Hegins protest appealed to so many activists, why would the Fund for Animals encourage them to stop protesting this event? Since building this type of support from grassroots activists takes so much time and energy, one might think that the Fund for Animals would continue the protest, to maintain that momentum and support. We cannot under-stand this decision from an individual point of view—individual activists' tastes in tactics cannot explain the decision to withdraw, since the individual activists clearly wanted to continue. We must instead look to the burgeoning pragmatic approach of the second wave animal rights movement in the United States. Rather than relying on a critical mass of angry activists to effect change, more social movement organizations had begun moving towards legislative goals, to effect change from the top down. Heidi went on to describe what influenced the decision, and how the Fund for Animals explained it to the protesters:

> That probably was for me the most difficult area, was making this conscious choice to say, look, the birds are getting lost in this. The focus is now on the clash between the townspeople and the protesters. There's nothing about animal cruelty in here anymore, and people aren't thinking about that any-more. They're thinking about these big, bad activists coming into this little bucolic town that is just trying to raise money and telling them what to do. So it was a really conscious decision [. . .] We had to do a lot of explaining and spend a lot of time on the phone with activists telling them this was strategic, this is why we are doing this, because some people just didn't understand. They were just, "We have to protest, we have to witness, and we have to be there." They didn't quite get what we were trying to do. But once we explained it and once we put out press releases, and they started seeing things change, they understood. And when they saw that we were putting resources into legal battles and legislative battles. And we made sure that they were included, and they knew what we were doing, I think it swayed it back again in a positive direction. But that was a little struggle during that period of time.

The Fund for Animals, along with other organizations that had joined the cause, saw that their efforts to stop the hunt through the townspeople would not be suc-cessful. As the protest had galvanized both sides into a fierce "us versus them" battle, the focus became on the protesters and the townspeople, and not on the birds. In her research on the Hegins protests, Courtney Dillard (2002) found that the nonviolent forms of protest garnered more sympathy from the media than the more hostile forms, such as taunting, name-calling, and harassment of the hunters. Animal rights organizations thus pulled out of the protests in order to focus on lobbying state legislators to enforce animal cruelty laws to protect the pigeons. After this change in strategy, and after pursuing change in the courts and the state legislature, activists succeeded in ending the pigeon shoot in 1999.

Understanding why activists made this strategic change does not mean that we should conclude that legislative activism is more successful than protests. This is clearly not always the case. We also cannot understand it by pointing to the preferences of individual activists. To understand this decision, we must place it in the larger context of the culture of the second wave U.S. animal rights move-ment, which had come to define itself with a logic of *pragmatism*, or practicality.

The Hegins case is just one example among many that happened during the shift from the first wave to the second wave animal rights movement, during which time the institutional logic of pragmatism began to emerge. Activists began changing their focus to farmed animals because they represented the largest number of animals killed, changing their tactics to more efficiently using resources, and they began evaluating their methods to devise the most effective strategies and tactics to achieve their goals.

The U.S. animal rights movement developed an institutional logic of pragmatism that influenced SMOs' strategic and tactical decision-making. This logic of pragmatism referred to more than just weighing the costs and benefits of engaging in an action. Being practical and pragmatic in one's decisions became a value that activists used to judge themselves and others. Seen through a resource dependency or contingency theory lens, this culture of pragmatism could be read as SMOs merely striving for rational action and efficiency in their organizational environments (Binder 2002). Taking a new institutional approach, I argue that rationality, efficiency, and pragmatism *themselves* can be cultural tropes, and U.S. animal rights SMOs emphasized their pragmatic decision-making to signal their legitimacy in the broader cultural meaning system in which they worked. While influenced by the pragmatic culture of the U.S., societal-level logics are not transposed directly into movement fields (Thornton et al. 2012). Rather, pragmatism became a movement-wide institutional logic because it came from interactions between individuals and between SMOs.

The U.S. animal rights movement did not always value such practicality; during what I call the "first wave" of animal rights activism, from the late 1970s to the late 1980s, activists primarily focused their attention on fur, hunting, and animal testing, presenting the most visually disturbing forms of animal abuse, and relying primarily on emotions for mobilization. Many activists were initially drawn to animal rights for emotional reasons, such as through moral shocks (Jasper and Poulsen 1995).

But once what I call the "second wave" of animal rights activism began in the early 1990s, activists began focusing on industrialized animal agriculture and veganism in an attempt to center their efforts on the largest number of animal deaths. Thus as Heidi (Humane Society of the United States, or HSUS) noted when describing the current state of this second wave U.S. movement, "In many ways, you are seeing a loss of the idealism, and a move towards practicality." This institutional logic of pragmatism manifested itself in U.S. animal rights SMOs' strategic choices in three main ways: activists made decisions based on a consideration of resources, through a learning process, and by evaluating effectiveness.

Resources

Although resource mobilization theories largely explain initial mobilization, recognizing one's capacities may also guide action by influencing the type of action in which one chooses to engage, as well as whether a group would even choose to initiate or react with strategic action at all (Jasper 2006a).

Early resource mobilization theorists saw resources primarily as monetary (McCarthy and Zald 1977). Since then, resources have come to mean physical materials, activists themselves, networks, knowledge, symbols, and other cultural meanings (Cress and Snow 1996, Edwards and McCarthy 2004). To U.S. activists, the primary resources they considered in their decision-making processes were time and money.

Money proved a real constraint to many activists already mobilized at the local level in small grassroots organizations. A lack of resources could be the determining factor in choosing a strategy or tactic, as Justice, a student activist, described: "If it is too time- or money-consuming, then we might try to use the idea in another way, or we might just nix it altogether." At the same time, a lack of money could enable activists to engage in more creative forms of activism. Dawn, who worked with a large grassroots organization at the time of our interview, described how she encouraged independent activists and activists in small grassroots organizations to find cheap or free ways of engaging in activism:

> When I did activism before, the main argument I would get against people being involved was they don't have a lot of money. And I would say, "But it doesn't take a lot of money, there are a lot of things you can do for free." Like placing [an SMO's] website in the city paper here, and you can get requests from that. There are so many free things that you can do, that doesn't require, if you don't have a lot of money and you are a smaller group. Like designing a website for restaurants, vegetarian restaurants in the area, leafleting, you can get leaflets from other groups, and there are a lot of groups that will provide them for free. So even if you don't have any money, which I didn't when I was in Charlotte—at all—I still found ways to still get the message out there.

Dawn described a lack of monetary resources as a primary constraint on individuals who might want to get involved in activism. Thus she offered specific tactics, mostly free, that those individuals could do. Time and monetary considerations did not only apply to activists in grassroots or student organizations. Activists in large, bureaucratic organizations saw time and money as a constraint to micromobilization—getting individuals involved in activism in the first place—and thus they devised quick, free ways for individuals to engage in activism. For example, PETA's "activism guides" specify down to the minute how much time one can contribute—"Make a difference in 5 minutes or less!"—and they highlight that interested activists can receive the literature they suggest distributing for free. These same large SMOs also put out "calls to action" to their members, offering all of the materials and organization, if the members can simply show up to help provide more people in the protest or event.

Within a theoretically limited tactical repertoire, there still exist more tactics than any one person or group can use (Tilly 1995). Lack of time as a resource not only influenced strategic and tactical decision-making; it could be the catalyst for an entire organization's strategic orientation. Jon described Vegan Outreach's evolution from "doing anything and everything" to a more refined approach:

One weekend, for example, they [the founders] did nine different fur demos, and I think they just started to get really burned out, and started to really question why, what is the result of all this backbreaking work? And then they started to, I think, just question how they could get more bang per hour spent for the animals. And they started to really think about the number of farmed animals killed, versus animals killed for vivisection or circus or fur industries. So they came to realize that far more animals were killed for food than other forms of exploitation, and also that each individual person contributes, for the most part, to farmed animals suffering. Whereas your "average Joe" might not contribute to animals suffering for fur or even vivisection, for that matter.

Many other activists I interviewed said they, too, immediately responded by doing anything and everything when they originally became active for animals, but they learned that was not the best way to use their time. Jon said the Vegan Outreach founders wanted to get "more bang per hour," a very resource-efficient way of looking at activism. Other interviewees said their organizations chose to focus on chickens, because numerically they represented the largest numbers of animal deaths in the world. For example, Jon (Vegan Outreach) said: "We want to always have campaigns that will reduce animal, to the best of our knowledge, reduce animal suffering. And do our part to curb the number of animals raised and slaughtered."

Using an institutional logics perspective helps us to understand how and why these activists determined what they believed to be the most pragmatic ways of mobilizing for animals. A resource mobilization approach misses the distinction between objective, monetary-based measures of pragmatism, and activists' perceptions of pragmatism. For example, Animal Charity Evaluators is a nonprofit group devoted to measuring the most effective ways of advocating and donating to animal causes. Their research clearly shows that most people are motivated to donate money to companion animal organizations (ACE 2015a). And yet, their perception of pragmatism in animal advocacy is that organizations and individuals should pursue whatever saves the largest numbers of animals. An objective, resource mobilization definition of pragmatism in this case might indicate a need to focus on companion animal issues, since that brings in the most money. Instead, the definition of pragmatism developed by Animal Charity Evaluators and other activists means donating money to farmed animal issues, because that affects the largest number of animals killed (ACE 2015a). Within that, Animal Charity Evaluators recommends focusing attention on chickens and fish over cattle and pigs, because numerically chickens and fish represent the largest numbers of animals killed for food (ACE 2015b).

The institutional logic of pragmatism also led activists to favor more collaboration with other organizations, such as how Talia described her group's using the work of other activists rather than "reinventing the wheel":

We don't believe in reinventing the wheel or pouring energy into things that other people are doing perfectly well. If we want to do vegan outreach, perfect. We'll just take "Why Vegan" and distribute it. We're not going to waste our energy reprinting, or making up our own "why you should be vegan" pub-lication, when there's a perfectly good one that exists [. . .] We support the efforts of other movements, we do anything they ask us to do to support them.

Talia said she did not want to her group to "waste our energy" creating their own leaflets on issues that were already covered by other groups. If her group wanted to promote veganism, they would simply use materials from Vegan Outreach. Instead of seeing such liberal use of other groups' materials as laziness, a lack of individuality, or as promoting their competitors, Talia saw it as a way of sharing strengths. Activists cited this need to not "waste" resources on creating their own materials when there were already plenty of good materials in the movement, materials they believed to already work, as Amber explained:

> There is a lot of good information already out there. There are tons of good vegetarian starter kits. I personally wanted to create [our own] vegetarian starter kit, but our president said, "Why should we invest all that time and money into doing that, when there's already these great ones out there?" So he didn't see a value in having one that is specifically from us with our name on it. So what we do is we purchase them at pretty much cost. If they make anything off of that, it's not much. They basically let us have them for cost and then we send them with a letter from [our organization] and some addi-tional materials that we might want to include. It works out for everybody because Compassion Over Killing, for instance, their goal is to get vegetarian starter guides out to people. They don't care, they're sending them out for free. So at least we are covering the cost of that. But they are not trying to make money off of them, they don't have some kind of sense that, "Oh, well, [that organization] is just trying to profit off of our vegetarian starter kit." They are just happy to get the information out there because our goals are the same, even though as organizations, we might do things slightly different.

Although Amber proposed creating a vegetarian starter guide for her own group, the practicality of using other, already existing, guides won out. Many activists and organizations shared their resources and expertise in such a way, even if it meant promoting competitor organizations.

Learning Process

As strategic and tactical repertoires are limited (Tilly 1995), activists sometimes develop new tactics in order to reach their goals, or even to sustain the move-ment. Activists engage in "tactical innovation," creatively devising new tactical forms in order to offset their institutional powerlessness, to counter their oppo-nents' tactical moves, and in order to keep up the "pace of insurgency" (McAdam 1983). One of the best examples of this process comes from the U.S. Civil Rights movement. While collective memory represents the tactical innovations of sit-ins as spontaneous eruptions of collective action, sociologist Aldon Morris (1984) demonstrated these tactics were learned, studied, deliberate tactical choices. Such "hinges" in collective action are conscious, practiced, and determined to be successful before activists implement them (Beckwith 2000).

At the beginning of the second wave animal rights movement in the United States, and as described above, many organizations evaluated strategies and tactics through a process of trial and error more than a studied deliberation of best practices and effectiveness. But as the second wave movement grew, animal rights organizations began to self-evaluate to see which of their specific tactics were most effective. Several interviewees said they evaluated their own actions by sending follow-up surveys to people who received their vegetarian starter kits.

Perhaps the strongest embodiment of this logic of practicality in activists' learning processes comes from Faunalytics (known as the Humane Research Council until 2015). Informed by corporate-driven market research, Faunalytics conducts focus groups with non-activists to find the best ways for animal rights SMOs to reach their target audiences. Demonstrating this move towards practicality, Heidi described the importance of Faunalytics's work:

> We historically as a movement, have been, I want to say, intuition based. Like the things that resonate with us are often what we make our campaigns about. And it isn't us. Who cares what we think, because we are already sensitive to the issue. It's what the public thinks and what is going to reach them. Like with vegetarianism—is it going to be compassion towards animals, is it going to be your own personal health? Is it going to be the fact that it is better for the environment? What's going to resonate to change people's behavior? Because frankly, not everybody cares about animals. It's not even on the radar screen of people.

Heidi described a move away from what interests activists to a focus on what interests and what will change activists' target audience. But not necessarily all activists were immediately convinced that market research for animal rights organizations is the way to go. Faunalytics addresses such worries in a section of their website, where they answer the question, "Why research?" Their number one response takes the focus away from individual activists' preferences, and places it on the audience:

> You are not your own target audience. Animal advocates are different than "normal" people, and this is crucial when communicating with non-advocates (i.e., your target audience). Don't assume you know what they're thinking or how they'll react; all campaigns could benefit from a little research. As nonprofit consultancy Fenton Communications says: "Go with what is most effective in reaching your key audience, not what most appeals to those within your organization." (Faunalytics 2015)

Several of the activists I interviewed had used Faunalytics's services. Steven described how this market research helped his group to develop a new anti-fur campaign:

The Humane Research Council, really all that they do is study animal rights organizations and evaluate their materials and things. Through that resource we've been able to help craft our messages. One example is our anti-fur poster that we recently created. What the Humane Research Council found was that images of baby foxes or other animals that more closely resemble domestic dogs had more of a sympathy factor with the public, as opposed to images of chinchillas and other species that the general public sees more as pests or rodents. So by taking advantage of this already conducted research, we were able to more effectively craft our message and the images that we used.

Here, Steven's group made the strategic decision to appeal to their targets' sympathy towards dogs, and to avoid their antipathy towards rodents. While the overall evolution of the U.S. animal rights movement would predict more of a focus on farmed animals and less on emotions and fur, the empirical, consumer-based research helped Steven's group make this decision. More importantly, this marks a change from using instinct or intuition to guide strategic and tactical decision-making. Instead, Steven's group turned to social scientists and market researchers, to base their decisions on "evidence" and "scientific methods."

Activists in many organizations began to move towards empirical social science to understand all sorts of aspects of their work. Such marketing research also helped organizations decide even the minutiae of using direct mail versus email, as Amber described: "They have seminars on direct-mail and development [. . .] Whether it is effective to use stamps. That is one of the things with direct-mail, if you use a stamp you get a better response than if you have the preprinted insignia on the envelope."

As the animal rights movement grew into a larger, more established movement, activists found new ways to test which strategies and tactics worked best. Once organizations had enough money to engage in expensive campaigns, they wanted to make certain those campaigns would be successful, in a process that more resembles studied methods of tactical innovation than mere trial and error (Morris 1984, Beckwith 2000). The pragmatism of the U.S. movement led to the creation of organizations like Faunalytics and Animal Charity Evaluators, who help organizations hone the tactical options in their respective repertoires. Thus the pragmatic institutional logic of the U.S. movement encouraged organizations to use empirical social science research in their decision-making processes.

Effectiveness

The institutional logic of pragmatism also cultivated an interest in effectiveness. This sense of effectiveness, however, proved so broad and all-encompassing that some activists seemed to not feel a need to elaborate on any other factors, nor on what effectiveness specified. For example, Erin's (HSUS) entire response to a question about factors influencing a certain decision was: "The bottom line is how is this going to be effective, and whether it's going to be the most efficient way to improve the lives of animals." Here we can see why some scholars say strategy must often be inferred rather than directly studied (Ganz 2004, Larson and Lizardo 2015)—that a strategy or tactic would be chosen for its effectiveness seemed so obvious to these respondents that it did not merit further explanation. Activists understood effectiveness in two ways: first, in terms of cost-effectiveness, and second, in terms of efficiently choosing and achieving their goals.

While many of the activists who cited effectiveness as their primary interest did not define the concept, other activists retained clear expectations of what effectiveness meant. Effectiveness meant, first and foremost, cost-effectiveness. All social movement organizations are interested in cost-effectiveness. They are also interested in proclaiming their cost-effectiveness, especially to donors. Anyone who has ever donated to a social movement or a nonprofit organization has likely received statements from that organization specifically outlining how they use the money. All of my respondents who cited "cost-effectiveness" worked with large grassroots organizations who had just enough money to engage in costly tactics such as television commercials, but not enough money to do so if they were not absolutely certain that such tactics were the best use of their money, as Stephanie described her organization's use of commercials:

> That campaign offers a pretty clear way of evaluating the success in terms of cost–benefit analysis. We pay so much for a commercial, we get so many hits to our website, or so many impressions per ad. So there's a pretty clear way of identifying that.

Stephanie's response represents a common confusion between the terms "effectiveness" and "efficiency" (Pfeffer and Salancik 1978), and it also indicates a potential conflating of means and ends. This conflation occurred in most of my interviews with U.S. activists. Efficiency and effectiveness actually describe two different standards. What Stephanie described might better be termed efficiency, or "how well an organization accomplishes its stated, or implied, objectives given the resources used" (Pfeffer and Salancik 1978: 33). While effectiveness may be judged by efficiency, it is not limited to such economic motivations. Effectiveness describes achieving one's goals (Pfeffer and Salancik 1978, Seijts et al. 2004), or even satisfying one's stakeholders (Scott and Lane 2000) or maintaining organizational values (Quinn and Rohrbaugh 1981). Some could see this as confusing means and ends, or activists measuring the efficiency of their tactics as a proxy for how well they are working towards their ultimate goals of persuading someone to become vegan, decreasing the number of animals killed, passing laws, and so on. In a movement where the ultimate goal of total animal liberation seems so far into the future, it is easy to understand the desire to focus on measuring the number of media outlets that covered an event, the number of hits on a website, or the number of leaflets distributed.

This emphasis on efficiency and effectiveness pervaded the entire U.S. animal rights movement through its institutional logic of pragmatism. Rather than have activists engage in potentially ineffective activism, many organizations and animal rights conferences focused on training activists in "effective advocacy."

PETA created a guide entitled "Effective Advocacy: Planning for Success," in which they espouse principles from the self-help and business books *How to Win Friends and Influence People* (Carnegie 1990) and *The Seven Habits of Highly Effective People* (Covey 1989). Similarly, at national animal rights conferences, the speeches sound like they came out of a business training seminar. At the 2004 Animal Rights conference, nearly every speaker presented a "how-to" guide to various issues in activism: Waging Effective Campaigns, Effective Investigations, Effective Visuals, Effective Writing, Effective Publications, Effective Presentations, Effective Broadcasting, Effective Advertising, and Effective Negotiating. This activist training in "effective" methods featured prominently at many other national animal rights conferences. At the Taking Action for Animals conference, for example, activists were trained to lobby through a series of workshops and presentations, and then put their newfound skills to use on "Lobby Day," the last day of the conference.

Activists also understood effectiveness in its more traditional sense, of efficiently achieving their goals (Pfeffer and Salancik 1978, Seijts et al. 2004). This form of effectiveness also extended to the choice of goals in the first place. This shift is best exemplified by the burgeoning "effective altruism" movement. Philosopher Peter Singer, best known to animal rights activists for his book *Animal Liberation* (1975), pioneered the effective altruism movement with his books *The Life You Can Save* (2009) and *The Most Good You Can Do* (2015). Effective altruists seek to create the most change by choosing causes that will affect the most people or animals, by funding the most cost-effective groups working in these areas, who are using the most measurably effective tactics.

The organization Animal Charity Evaluators (formerly Effective Animal Activism) exemplifies effective altruism in the animal rights movement. They describe their work as follows: "ACE's goal in evaluating animal charities is to find and promote the charities which work most efficiently to help animals" (ACE 2015c). As noted above, Animal Charity Evaluators argue that the most effective way to help animals is to focus on farmed animals, as they represent the largest number of animals killed. Within that, they argue that if a person does not become a complete vegan or vegetarian, the next best choice would be to avoid chicken and fish, because that would affect the most animals. ACE also evaluates the effectiveness of the different tactics of organizations, arguing that, for example, leafleting is more effective than engaging in direct animal care through farmed animal sanctuaries, because leafleting to encourage people to become vegetarian will affect more animals for a smaller cost. ACE has already evaluated a number of tactics for their cost-effectiveness and goal-effectiveness (e.g., corporate outreach, leafleting, and humane education), and they plan to study many more (e.g., advertising, boycotts, demonstrations, and the creation of meat substitutes) (ACE 2015d). As more and more activists turn to Faunalytics and market research to understand how to best reach their audiences, and to Animal Charity Evaluators to understand how to do so in the most efficient ways, the institutional logic of pragmatism will become further entrenched in the U.S. movement.

How do individual activists figure into all of this objective research? What happens if an organization finds a particular tactic to be the most effective, but activists in the organization disagree with that tactic? I found the institutional logic of effectiveness to be so strong that it overshadowed all other considerations. U.S. activists chose the most effective strategies and tactics, even if they personally disagreed with them. For example, Megan described the backlash her organization faced from supporters when they decided to work with Rick Santorum, a well-known conservative politician: "They question our values as an organization and why we work with him." In addition to her organization potentially alienating their constituents, Megan stated she personally disagreed with Santorum's politics. If her organization's members and employees disagreed with him, why would they choose to work with him? Megan explained further:

> We always say animal rights is not a Democratic or a Republican position. And while he may hold other positions that are antithetical to my personal beliefs, he is fighting against these puppy mills. And so we support him in that and we do what we can to make sure that the bill is successful.

Megan depicted a situation in which nearly everyone involved in the issue, from organization employees to supporters, personally disagreed with Santorum on many issues, and yet they supported him on this issue because they thought he would be successful in passing this specific piece of legislation. (Ultimately, he was not.) Santorum has enjoyed public support from PETA and from HSUS, precisely—and solely—because of his support for legislation against puppy mills (*USA Today* 2005).

Many other U.S. activists reported that they decided to participate in, organize, or otherwise support campaigns or tactics that did not always align with their personal belief systems, if they thought those campaigns or efforts would be successful. For example, many college-based animal rights organizations participated in the Humane Society of the United States campaign to replace their college cafeterias' conventional, battery-cage eggs with cage-free eggs, even though many of their members were vegans who did not support eating eggs at all.

Thus here we can see how the institutional logic of the U.S. movement enabled pragmatic choices by activists, emphasizing their concern for resources, learning processes, and effectiveness. Rather than basing their strategic and tactical choices solely on their personal preferences, on their opponents, or on other external factors, U.S. activists primarily sought to optimize resources in order to achieve their short-term goals.

As U.S. activists expected practicality in themselves, so did they in others. They critiqued other activists or groups if they thought they were "wasting" resources or being impractical, such as asking for unattainable goals, or putting too many resources into small goals. Second wave activists who favored farmed animal issues often critiqued the tendency to focus one's efforts on one type of animal, or on a small group of animals, when farmed animals comprised the vast majority of all animals killed in the United States. More broadly, though, activists critiqued philosophical in-fighting among activists, preferring instead to focus on common goals and practical ways to achieve those goals, as did Joe (Vegan Outreach):

> I said a long time ago, I don't want to fight with other animal people. Whatever it is that they can offer, I'll appreciate. I know that privately, and sometimes publicly, I'll criticize because I know that it could be so much more, it could be so much better. But I guess that quote I was speaking to a minute ago, the whole dividing line along philosophy, whatever you want to call it, is really just kind of a waste of time, alienating to ourselves, to the public at large. They're watching this group of wackos argue with each other over welfare versus—but the bottom line is, we're trying to reduce suffering, right? I don't really want a label for myself. It's just what's happening is wrong. What's happening is unjust. And I would like to stop it to the greatest degree that I can.

Joe was speaking of the welfare versus abolition debate, which is currently widespread in the U.S. animal rights movement and has existed since its inception (Jasper and Nelkin 1992). To him, and to many U.S. activists, philosophical differences may be important, but not so important that they would take him away from his practical work for animals. Such a pragmatic culture does not define the animal rights movement in every country, however. The power of movement culture stands out more clearly in France, where activists avoided successful tactics in order to maintain their logic of consistency.

8 French Consistency and Cross-Cultural Choices

When I first met Fergus, leader of the animal rights group l'Armée des Douze Singes ("Army of Twelve Monkeys," or ADS), he said French people were more sensitive to animal testing than to meat-eating, which was why ADS tries to use animal testing as an entry point to vegetarianism and animal rights. I asked him why he thought French people were so sensitive to animal testing, and he replied, "Because it doesn't touch their plate." A reasonable response, since the meat-based French gastronomic tradition would likely be a difficult practice to topple by itself. Further, polls show that 64–68 percent of the French are opposed to animal testing, at rates higher than all 15 other industrialized countries included in the studies, including the U.S. (Pifer et al. 1994). A One Voice poll showed 72 percent French opposition to animal testing (One Voice 2014). Whereas many U.S. groups began with vegetarianism, then moved to veganism, which opposes all uses of animals (including vivisection), ADS took the opposite direction. Given the French attitudes towards traditional cuisine and against animal testing, this sounded like a rational decision that would lead to successful outcomes.

However, Fergus also told me he did not think that French people were ready to give up meat, and that ADS's strategy of creating vegetarians through anti-vivisection activism would ultimately fail. He and other ADS activists continued in this defeatist tone to passersby at their information tables, sometimes discouraging them from signing petitions against vivisection, stating that petitions "don't get anything accomplished." Since ADS's goal was to promote animal rights and to create more vegetarians in France, why not take a broader focus in their activism? Why focus on vivisection, especially when they claimed it was a fruitless endeavor?

Scholars who study social movements would try to answer this question by arguing that perhaps Fergus simply did not like petition-signing as a tactic (Jasper 1997), or that his group decided upon petitions as a relatively low-cost way of getting their message out (McCarthy and Zald 1977). I believe this decision has to do with more than a simple cost–benefit analysis, and rather than looking at Fergus as an individual activist, I want to understand how his group came to this seemingly contradictory decision. Following Downey and Rohlinger (2008), I take a "field approach" and look at how ADS, and other social movement organizations, function in relation to their opponents as well as to other organizations within the same movement.

I argue that the interaction of organizations within a social movement field creates a movement-wide culture, and this culture provides guidelines for the various individual organizations' strategic and tactical choices.

In France, this movement culture valued consistency, meaning activists expected, in others as in themselves, a consistency of thought and action. I use the English term "consistent" for the French term *cohérent*, which I heard throughout my interviews and fieldwork sites. French activists continually described their actions, decisions, tactics, and so on as being either *cohérent*, meaning consistent with their values, or as *incohérent*, meaning inconsistent with those values. Consistency became a guiding logic as well as a value to activists, used to judge themselves and others both in and outside the movement. This logic of consistency meant not only that individuals' actions should be consistent with their beliefs, but that organizations' strategic and tactical decisions should be consistent with the philosophies upon which they are based. New institutional theorists focus on these constraining aspects of a field when explaining decision-making. Institutional actors often choose to act in familiar ways, or in ways intended to appease powerful outsiders, without consideration to increasing outcomes for smaller costs (Edgell 2006).

To this focus on value-rational action I add the important factor of those values coming from the institutional logic developed through interaction between activists and between organizations, within a particular social movement field. The institutional logic of consistency guided French animal rights organizations' strategic choices in three main ways—activists sought to maintain a consistency of personal practices, a consistency of organizational ideology and tactics, and a consistency of individual activists' actions with the ideology of their organization.

Consistency of Personal Practices

One of the primary ways in which people participate in lifestyle movements is by changing aspects of their daily lives to better align with their belief system. Sociologist Ross Haenfler and his colleagues (Haenfler et al. 2012) term this a part of "lifestyle movements." Environmentalists recycle, straight edge youth avoid drugs and alcohol, simple living advocates avoid overconsumption, and people interested in animal rights avoid eating animals or using them in other ways. In France, this consistency between one's practices and one's beliefs became a central aspect of the French animal rights movement. The nascent quality of this institutional logic can be seen in activists who became vegetarian as a result of judging themselves as "inconsistent," or acting in ways that contradicted their own beliefs, as Sebastien (Stop Gavage) described:

> That was the "click" moment, when I was reading a graphic novel about a historical saga on the Buddhist movement. Then, I realized there were civilizations, societies who didn't eat meat. And me, I was against hunting, against bullfighting, and I remember when I read this graphic novel I was eating sausage, or bacon—which I loved, because I loved meat. And then, I had

a click moment about the level of my inconsistency. The inconsistency of being against bullfighting and hunting, and recognizing animals as sentient individuals, and continuing to eat them even though it wasn't necessary. So that gave me my click moment.

Many French activists, including Sebastien, said they opposed bullfighting and hunting before they were vegetarian, and they saw such difference between thought and action as "inconsistent." Similarly, Hervé (Collectif Antispéciste de Paris) saw such inconsistency in himself, but he did not want to become vegetarian yet. So, rather than going vegetarian, he said he stopped doing the things that made him inconsistent:

> I went to a meeting with a bunch of different organizations. There were traditional animal defense organizations, punks, a little bit of everything. And this is where I bought this t-shirt. It says "tauromachie, bucherie!" (bullfighting, butchery!) But I still ate meat. My shirt said, "tauromachie, bucherie!" but I ate meat. That isn't right. So what I did, was I stopped wearing my shirt.

Hervé, of course, eventually became vegetarian. But his valuing the consistency of thought and action was so strong that it first led him to avoid the things in his life, like his anti-bullfighting shirt, that made his non-vegetarianism inconsistent.

Animal rights activists frequently played upon this logic of consistency of personal practices when talking to their target audiences. For many, the inconsistency came from the act of loving companion animals while eating farm animals. Activists often pointed out this inconsistency in others in an attempt to get them to become vegetarian, as Sophie (Animale Amnistie and Association Végétarienne de France) explained:

> Our goal is to diminish—we won't say stop, because that's impossible—but to diminish animal suffering. To make people reflect upon their relationships with animals. I'm speaking of any animal, not just their dog or their cat, who is babied at the house, and treated well, because that's rather normal. But to make them reflect globally on the respect that they should have towards animals, on the fact that animals merit as much dignity as humans. So that's our goal, to get people to reflect on that. Because, there's lots of people who tell us, "Yes, I love animals," and then we see them eating their chicken sandwiches. So you want to tell them, "Sure, you love animals, but not by eating them." Does eating animals mean you love them? For us, that's completely inconsistent.

While at tabling events, activists often muttered about women wearing fur coats who were also carrying dogs, wondering why they pampered their dog and yet wore the skin of another animal. Working from the assumption that the value of consistency worked for them, activists also used this value to motivate their targets to become vegetarian. While I was at a tabling event with the group International

Campaigns in Paris, one activist described his decision behind which flyers he gives to people who pass by the table. Comparing all the flyers on fur, vivisection, and vegetarianism, I said that I prefer to give out the flyers from the group Association Végétarienne de France, because the food issue is closest to my heart. Going further, though, he said, "I think if you can get people to go vegetarian, then they will see that all of their other actions, like if they wear fur, would be inconsistent with their other actions." This activist believed that if he could convince people to become vegetarian, they, too, would eventually become vegan because of the inconsistency of their actions.

"Consistency" would not be considered a guiding logic of the French animal rights movement if it merely resided in the minds of a few activists who judged themselves inconsistent for not being vegetarian while supporting animal protection efforts. Nor would it necessarily be considered a movement-wide logic if activists only used it against their non-vegetarian target audiences. In myriad settings, I saw vegan and vegetarian animal rights activists invoke this logic of consistency to judge other activists. In this sense, consistency served as a boundary marker to make certain that those in the movement maintained their consistency of thought and action.

For example, when I attended a dine-out at a vegetarian restaurant with the Paris-based group International Campaigns, Gilberte said I should also attend some of the dine-outs of the Association Végétarienne de France. I asked if she ever attended them, and she said she did sometimes but she did not really like to because

> They're a bunch of people who are vegetarian for their health. Maybe half of them would be vegetarian for the animals, but if I attended a dine-out, I'd hear half of them talking about their digestive problems and not about animal rights.

What she really found hypocritical, she said, was that if she attended the dinner and then stepped outside for a cigarette, they would all yell, "How can you do that? That's so bad for your health!" Meanwhile, she said, some of them would come to the dine-outs wearing fur. After Gilberte critiqued fur- and leather-wearing vegetarians, we all got ready to pay. When Gilberte got out her pocketbook, Estelle, another activist, said it was cute and picked it up. She then put the purse to her nose to smell and see if it was made of leather. Gilberte looked at her and said, "No, it's fake, definitely." One might assume that Gilberte's stated outrage at vegetarians who wear fur or leather would preclude her using fur or leather herself, but Estelle wanted to verify that Gilberte's actions were consistent with her values. This consistency of personal practices and beliefs is a cornerstone of cultural movements that focus on lifestyle and consumption choices (Cherry et al. 2011, Haenfler et al. 2012, Cherry 2015). Thus, while this phenomenon is not relegated to only French activists, the movement-wide interest in maintaining a consistency of personal practices constituted an institutional logic particular to the French movement.

Consistency of Individuals with Organizational Ideology

The institutional logic of consistency also manifested itself in the French movement by encouraging an alignment between individuals and their organization's declared ideology. In contrast to how U.S. activists chose to employ strategies or tactics with which they personally disagreed because of their institutional logic of pragmatism, here French activists chose strategies and tactics that fit best with their organizational ideology regardless of whether activists personally thought they would be successful.

One of the main ideologies in the French animal rights movement is antispeciesism. Antispeciesists seek to abolish speciesism, an oppression they see as linked to racism and sexism. Thus it was hardly surprising that many antispeciesist activists took issue with the U.S. organization PETA (People for the Ethical Treatment of Animals) and their tactics involving naked women. Unlike many U.S. organizations, which constructed a more mainstream identity in relation to PETA, French activists, especially antispeciesist groups, constructed an even more radical identity than PETA. To them, PETA represented the mainstream, especially because of their use of sexist tactics.

These philosophical differences proved problematic for antispeciesists, who did not necessarily find PETA's tactics ineffective. For example, the Collectif Antispéciste de Paris's antisexist stance proved problematic when Collectif members wanted to attempt a PETA campaign because they found the action innovative and the message compelling. At a planning meeting, someone brought up PETA, after which Virginie said she did not like PETA because of their sexist tactics, and that only once had she ever seen a PETA protest that did not involve a woman in a bikini. Hervé then brought up PETA's "meat tray" action, which Nathalie explained to be a protest where people lie in a package and are wrapped up in plastic, like meat in a butcher shop. Virginie said that ultimately she liked this protest, she liked the idea it puts forth, that human flesh is also meat, but she did not want to participate in a PETA action because of their sexism. She said if anyone wanted to participate in this action, they would be selected by PETA "only because they were sexy."

Here we can see how the institutional logic of consistency constrained antispeciesists' strategic and tactical decision-making. Even though all the individual activists I observed and interviewed thought the meat tray action to be effective, and the action did not violate their personal tastes in tactics (Jasper 1997), only activists in groups with an expressed antispeciesist philosophy avoided such tactics. James Jasper (2006b, 2011) has discussed moral emotions as encouraging action, but these moral emotions do not include moral evaluations of particular tactics. I found these moral judgments of tactics to be the primary factor in French activists' strategic and tactical decision-making. Even when all the individuals in a group believed a tactic to be potentially useful, the institutional logic of coherence proved powerful enough to hinder its use. In this sense, French activists also exhibit elements of lifestyle movement activists who seek "morally coherent" personal identities (Haenfler et al. 2012: 9) in their own personal lives and actions. But here, French activists extend this sense of coherence or consistency further, to the strategies and tactics they use with their SMOs.

Many other French activists, even those who considered themselves antisexist, did not problematize PETA's tactics. These animal rights activists believed that the ends justified the means. Fabrice (Animale Amnistie) said that although he understood the critiques, he thought it was wrong to criticize PETA because they do so much good for animals. Similarly, Diana (Association Végétarienne de France) heaped praise upon these PETA tactics:

Elizabeth: Now I wanted to ask you about your personal opinion on some of the tactics and strategies that are used in the States.
Diana: [*Interrupts and answers before I ask a question*] PETA. Adore it. Anything they do, I adore it […]
Elizabeth: Some feminists have critiqued the use of nude or scantily clad women in advertisements for animal rights.
Diana: [Again, interrupts before I ask the question] In theory, I approve of that disapproval. I agree with them. But in practice, whatever works, go for it. I'm willing to put my, to me, getting, I'm more key on getting animal progress than I am for getting female rights, because I think use your body if you have to. But I wouldn't want, in our work, we've made the important point of using, matching two men and two women. Always male and female. But that's only lip service, really. As far as I understand. If we didn't have any men, I'd want to use the women, anyway, because we need to get the media attention. But I acknowledge that theoretically, one should be not using women's bodies. And if you have to use them, at least use male and females equally.

The fact that Diana mentioned the link between theory and practice further shows the strength of the institutional logic of consistency in the French movement, this link between a pattern of thought and a corresponding pattern of action. We can see how this logic of consistency acted as a cultural structure, as Diana admitted that "in theory" she also disapproved of these tactics. Mere theory was not strong enough to keep her and other French activists from engaging in these tactics, though. Only activists in groups who specifically claimed an antispeciesist (and thus antiracist and antisexist) philosophical identity were constrained by the logic of coherence to such an extent that they avoided these tactics.

These examples serve to demonstrate how the institutional logic of consistency created barriers for individual activists' strategic and tactical decision-making. Even though all the individual activists I observed and interviewed thought the meat tray action to be effective, only activists in groups with an expressed antispeciesist philosophy avoided such tactics. Even when all of the individuals in a group believed a tactic to be potentially useful, the power of the logic of consistency proved strong enough to hinder their use.

Consistency of Organizational Ideology and Tactics

Max Weber's (1978) theory of value-rationality and new institutional theorists argue that people can act rationally in accordance to their beliefs, even if those actions seem to counteract their goals. Neoinstititutional theory allows us to understand individuals' preferences and actions while at the same time theorizing how culture structures their preferences (Edgell 2006). When French activists decided to use strategies and tactics that did not offer the best chances of attaining their short-term goals, they were not simply cultural dupes; rather, they were acting rationally according to their beliefs. As the environment constrains organizational actors to change further in later years, and as goal-oriented behavior may be reinforced without it serving to achieve that goal (DiMaggio and Powell 1983), so the culture of the French animal rights movement constrained activists from making strategic choices that would effectively help them attain their goals.

One of the primary ways in which the institutional logic of consistency manifested itself in the French movement was through individual movement organizations ensuring their tactics corresponded with their group's ideology. This aspect was particularly strong in France, where the movement is divided among different ideologies. Of course, every movement says it is divided, but in France, this was the first time I viscerally felt this at every moment I was there. Whenever I met a new group of activists, the first questions they asked me were about which side I was on, which theorist I preferred, or which groups I supported or did not support. These experiences never occurred in my U.S. fieldwork.

The three ideological divides in the French movement were welfarism, animal rights, and antispeciesism. Welfarists seek animal protection, but they do not question the underlying conception of animals as property. Animal rights activists in France primarily take an abolitionist approach and wish to abolish all human uses of animals. And "antispeciesist" refers to activists who fight discrimination based on species, seeing the issue as linked to other forms of oppression like racism and sexism. When each type of organization considered their strategies, tactics, or mere participation in an event, they based it upon their organizational ideology. Thus welfarist groups engaged in welfarist actions, animal rights groups in abolitionist actions, antispeciesists in antisexist and antiracist actions, and so on. Unlike the rest the book, where I use the term "animal rights" to refer to a number of different philosophical orientations, here I use the precise terms welfarism, animal rights, and antispeciesism to describe the specific, and sometimes contrasting, philosophies within the larger movement.

The logic of consistency puts the vast in-fighting in the French movement into perspective. The fact that such internal debates exist is nothing new—probably every social movement has factions according to ideological differences. What is important to understand, though, is how these ideological differences manifested themselves in strategic and tactical differences, and how they led to what might be mistaken for simple tactical blunders had they not been contextualized within the movement's culture of consistency. Looking at each organization individually cannot explain their strategic and tactical decision-making. Instead, seeing how these organizations interact, understanding their competitive relationships within their broader social movement field (Pfeffer and Salancik 1978), and evaluating their decisions with the institutional logic of coherence, can explain these organizations' strategic and tactical decisions.

One of the largest welfarist organizations in France is One Voice. This group epitomized the welfarist ideology that French animal rights and antispeciesist groups critiqued, especially since One Voice's primary campaigns centered on protecting companion animals (dogs and cats) from uses such as animal testing and fur. When One Voice announced a protest against companion animal testing in front of the Ministry of Research, a debate soon began as to whether animal rights advocates and antispeciesists should attend the protest or not. Yann, an antispeciesist, said he would attend the One Voice protest, but he wanted to bring a banner that said, "Stop experimenting on all animals." Victoria, an animal rights activist, said she thought it was "stupid" to mobilize activists against dog and cat testing, because, she told me, "Of course everyone is against testing on companion animals. I don't need to wear any kind of sticker that says I'm against testing on companion animals, because everyone is against that."

Victoria was correct, at least in part. By mobilizing the French people's love for pets, One Voice managed to gather over 350,000 signatures, in what they claimed to be the most-signed petition ever in France. If this strategy proved so effective, why did animal rights and antispeciesist groups avoid it? Animal rights and antispeciesist activists do not support harming companion animals, to be certain. But they did want to maintain their logic of consistency and thus distanced themselves from welfarist strategies. Simply because French people love companion animals did not mean that animal rights or antispeciesist activists wanted to use that tactic: the existence of a potentially effective tactic in their tactical repertoire (Tilly 1986) did not mean antispeciesist and animal rights activists were bound to choose it. These French organizations chose their tactics based on how they corresponded with their underlying group ideology, not on whether an available tactic was potentially successful or resonated with their targets' beliefs (Snow et al. 1986) as U.S. activists did.

Nathalie (Collectif Antispéciste de Paris) perfectly summarized why her group rejected ideas they knew were effective:

> I don't know if we reason in terms of functioning. It's clear that there are things we don't want to do, but not so much because it won't work, but because we don't want to do them. Because sometimes, in order to push people, people do things we don't agree with. It's not because they might not affect our audience, it's because it's against our convictions.

Nathalie explained that her group rejected potentially effective ideas for ideological reasons. For example, the strategy of promoting vegetarianism by linking companion animals to farm animals has proven successful in the U.S. movement. The U.S. animal rights group Compassion Over Killing exemplifies this tactic in one of their t-shirt designs. The shirt depicts a dog on a plate, and the caption asks,

"Why not? You eat other animals, don't you? Go vegetarian." The society-wide cultural constraints of this rhetorical tactic are obvious. The image of the dog on the plate would only resonate in countries where humans typically do not eat animals like dogs and cats. Thus this image could be successfully used in France. However, this did not happen, and distancing one's group from welfarism only partially explains the avoidance of this tactic.

Nathalie's group, the Collectif Antispéciste de Paris, encountered this issue when discussing a flyer for an upcoming event. The discussion centered on a phrase in the flyer that described eating companion animals. Everyone agreed that the argument they were trying to make was, "How can you love your companion animal and feel shock at people eating companion animals, but eat other animals yourself?" The activists liked the dog-on-a-plate image and thought it made a good statement, but they recanted when Ivora reminded the group of a woman who came to the last tabling event and who said, "I hate what the Chinese do to animals," referring to eating dogs. Virginie then noted that the image of the dog on the plate could be considered racist, so the group decided to omit the phrase and the image.

In discussing whether to use this tactic involving a companion animal or not, and why, no one cited a desire to avoid being labeled as a welfarist organization. Rather, these antispeciesists worried more about seeming racist, as antiracism is a core foundation of antispeciesist philosophy. As described above, since antispeciesists stand against racism philosophically, they also do so tactically. Although the image and tactic perfectly fit the argument they were trying to make, they avoided the tactic of the dog on a plate to maintain consistency with their antispeciesist beliefs.

Now we can return to the case of Fergus and l'Armée des Douzes Singes from the introduction to this chapter, who engaged in antivivisection activism as a path towards vegetarianism even though personally disagreed with the tactic, thought it would fail, and discouraged passersby from signing petitions against vivisection. To make sense of ADS's strong antivivisection focus within their animal rights activism, one must also understand ADS's ideological position within the French animal rights movement, which must be evaluated by the logic of consistency. ADS prided itself on being an abolitionist animal rights organization. But a belief in abolitionism, in itself, cannot explain their singular focus on vivisection. ADS chose to focus on abolishing animal experimentation as a consistent abolitionist challenge to what they saw as inconsistent antispeciesist activists. These animal rights activists based their critique of antispeciesists on philosophy, a critique compounded by the cultural logic of consistency. First, these animal rights activists opposed the utilitarian stance of philosopher-activist Peter Singer (1975), a position promoted by many (but not all) antispeciesists. A utilitarian approach to animal issues allows for some animal testing, for example—a subject often at the center of arguments between animal rights activists and antispeciesists. Antispeciesists following the logic of coherence would thus place less emphasis on antivivisection activism, and more on animal equality, a topic at the root of antispeciesism.

Second, and ironically, though philosophical differences provided the basis for most of the internal squabbling between activists, engaging directly in philosophical debate only engendered more critique. Many animal rights activists took issue with the simple fact that antispeciesists spent a large amount of time writing philosophical texts, such as those published in the journal *Les Cahiers Antispécistes*. To them, antispeciesists were all talk and no action. Antivivisection work was, as ADS activists agreed, not the best way to create a vegetarian France, but it was the strongest, most ideologically consistent challenge to utilitarian antispeciesists. Thus it is not factors external to movements such as movement–opponent interactions (McAdam 1983) that explain these strategic and tactical decisions; it is the interaction of organizations within a social movement field that best explains such choices.

In this chapter I have shown how the cultural context of a social movement can explain activists' and organizations' strategic and tactical choices. By undertaking a meso-level analysis to see how organizations function within the broader social movement field, this approach does not disentangle decisions from their contexts (Hickson 1987). Since strategic choices often do not seem like choices at all, it is easy to ignore the complexity behind actual decision-making (Jasper 2006a). My approach also represents a move from individual-level explanations of strategic and tactical decision-making to an analysis of actual decision-making processes in action. Movement-wide institutional logics acted as structures, enabling organizations to make certain choices while constraining them from making others. An organization's strategic or tactical choice had to conform to the values upheld by the social movement. Activists in the French animal rights movement believed in the consistency of thought and action. Thus French activists privileged the question of "Do I believe this to be true?" over asking whether a tactic or strategy might work in practice. The movement-wide logic of consistency of thought and action helps us to understand the varying strategic and tactical decisions made by different organizations, as well as the philosophical in-fighting that marred the movement. Activists avoided strategies and tactics that went against their philosophical convictions. Thus antispeciesists avoided tactics they found to be sexist, and animal rights activists favored tactics that highlighted vivisection, for example.

The approach developed here explains the specific strategic and tactical choices made by French organizations. The French focus on consistency, and its avoidance of successful tactics in order to maintain such consistency, may lead one to wonder whether the French movement, or any other animal rights movements, should simply take a pragmatic approach to their work. In the remainder of this chapter, I address this question by investigating the use of pragmatic approaches in France, and the use of philosophically consistent approaches in the United States.

Cross-Cultural Choices

In this section on Strategic Choices, I have explored the U.S. movement's institutional logic of pragmatism, and the French movement's logic of consistency. Here, I seek to compare the two logics, to see what happens when these two cultures collide. If movement logics, or movement cultures, act as constraining and enabling structures, influencing SMOs' strategic and tactical choices, how transferable are these logics? Could the seemingly more successful pragmatic logic of the U.S. movement work in France?

Analyses of institutional logics shed new light on isomorphism and diffusion processes because they show legitimacy, rationality, and technical demands to be themselves culturally constructed (Lounsbury 2005). My analysis furthers this claim by showing the limits of institutional isomorphism between countries, even when the organizations are all part of a larger movement field, and even when the institutional logics have been introduced into other fields. Isomorphism influences the movement internationally, in that iterations of the movement in different countries all share certain norms as regards goals, strategies, and tactics. They share long-term goals of animal liberation and of vegetarianism as a means and an end, and, although the media highlights illegal direct actions, legal, moderate tactics are the norm. In this sense, we can easily recognize the movements in both countries as animal rights movements. However, within that normative form, movements differ between countries. I showed how these two movements differed—the U.S. movement developed and employed a logic of pragmatism, and the French movement created and affirmed its logic of consistency. Here, I show what happens when these two logics collide—what happens when French activists attempt to use pragmatic logics, or when U.S. activists attempt to use consistency in their choices.

United States: Making Inconsistent Choices

The animal rights movement in the United States was governed by a logic of pragmatism. While this may make perfect sense to U.S. readers, who may want to call the French activists "irrational," it is important to look at the U.S. movement from other angles. If we were to evaluate the U.S. movement by French standards, U.S. activists would be seen as "inconsistent." Both U.S. SMOs and French SMOs with U.S. influences made strategic and tactical choices that followed this logic of pragmatism but that were inconsistent with their personal beliefs. Grant summarized this logical quandary perfectly in the following quote, in which he described how he made his strategic and tactical decisions based on what would be most successful:

> To me, I mean, that's based on not what I think is extreme, but what the audience would think is an extreme action, or event, or opinion. So I think it's, when I'm using the word "extreme," I'm using it relative to the audience. Like, if I'm talking to my parents, who are Baptists and very Southern, they were born in the South, raised in the South, it continues to bother my dad. My mom's a little more understanding. But it actually insults my dad that I don't eat meat. Sometimes. Sometimes he's like, "Why do you . . . ?" That's not uncommon. I have several friends that are actually sort of insulted or offended by these sorts of things. So when I talk to people like that, and I think when

you're engaged in activism, you need to have a thorough understanding of your audience. And if you present, even if you may be right, right in your opinion, if you present opinions that they would think are extreme, then it's automatically going to turn off your audience. And if you want to be successful, you are going to have to tone down, and, I guess compromise. I guess that's another example of compromising in animal rights activism. I think the goal is being successful. And you are going to have to make sacrifices.

Grant claimed that the goal was success, and that in order to achieve that goal, activists must make sacrifices and compromise their opinions. While Grant described the difference between presenting one's entire range of beliefs versus a more toned-down version, his belief in compromising and sacrificing in order to achieve success presents a perfect contrast between the French and U.S. movements' logics of action. Grant spoke of personal, internal inconsistency, but more often it was the SMOs and the activists within them which were inconsistent.

For example, while some groups may publicly present a welfarist identity, many of their employees and activists support animal rights. This philosophical mélange is perhaps best exemplified by PETA. On the "About Us" section of PETA's website, they explicitly base their philosophical position on Peter Singer's (1975) utilitarian work, *Animal Liberation*. This might lead one to believe that PETA is a utilitarian organization. However, from their presentation of their work in various campaigns, interviews, and even their mission statement, they claim to support abolition of all animal abuses: "Ingrid Newkirk's biography shows that she is an abolitionist who remains committed to the idea that animals are not ours to eat, wear, experiment on, or use for entertainment" (PETA 2015b). As noted in earlier chapters, strict followers of Singer's utilitarian philosophy argue that it is acceptable to allow certain forms of animal testing, provided they benefit more beings than they harm. PETA answers this exact question in the "Frequently Asked Questions" section of their website on animal testing:

Question: "Would you support an experiment that would sacrifice 10 animals to save 10,000 people?"

Response: Suppose the only way to save those 10,000 people was to experiment on one mentally challenged orphan. If saving people is the goal, wouldn't that be worth it? Most people will agree that it is wrong to sacrifice one human for the "greater good" of others because it would violate that individual's rights. There is no logical reason to deny animals the same rights that protect individual humans from being sacrificed for the common good. (PETA 2015c)

Which is it? Are PETA abolitionist or welfarist? PETA emulates abolitionist organizations in that many of their campaigns call for the end of cruel animal practices, and their actions to help farmed animals primarily center around veganism (PETA 2015d). Abolitionists, of course, would call PETA a welfarist organization. For example, PETA's "Shameway" campaign against Safeway successfully lobbied the grocery store chain to implement the following changes: (1) increase purchases of poultry killed using "controlled atmosphere killing," (2) increase purchases of pigs from suppliers that do not use gestation crates, and (3) double its purchases of cage-free eggs (PETA 2015e). These demands would certainly qualify "Shameway" as a welfarist campaign. No matter how one classifies PETA on the whole, their campaigns emulate both welfarist and abolitionist actions.

With these examples I mean to imply not that U.S. activists do not understand or care about philosophy, but that in many cases, including the largest animal rights organization in the world, the pragmatism of creating new activists superseded the desire to be philosophically consistent. U.S. activists drew boundaries between their SMOs and others based on the effectiveness of tactics and strategies, and not based on their underlying philosophical traditions, as in France.

The philosophical inconsistency of the U.S. movement afforded U.S. activists more leeway with their strategic and tactical choices. French SMOs, in contrast, had fewer choices, since they were constrained by philosophical consistency. U.S. activists took a more pragmatic approach to their activism, trying different tactics with different audiences, appealing to individual activists' personal tastes in tactics, or even waging campaigns that did not fit exactly with their philosophical beliefs. For example, Erin worked with a large animal rights organization in the U.S. whose ultimate goal was, as she said, "total animal liberation." This abolitionist goal, however, did not impede her organization from engaging in what she called "welfarist" campaigns:

> Success for the animal rights movement is success for the animals. That means no more cages, no more leg irons, no more of any of the institutions and implements that we use on a day-to-day basis to torture them and to take away from them every single thing that nature, or God, or whoever you believe in, designed for them to have. And that's what we're looking at, you know, a lot of [our] campaigns are basic welfare campaigns like the [fast food restaurant] campaign. Nobody is saying hey, you there, go vegan now, put that chicken down, and never eat another one for the rest of your life. All we're saying is hey, [fast food restaurant], you hold the purse strings. You have the power in this situation to change the behavior of your suppliers. If you are going to eat chicken, we are simply asking that you not boil them alive. Or that you not slit their throats while they are still fully conscious. Those are basic welfare strategies, but we certainly, although we are looking right now for improvements and changes that will benefit animals in the most minimal way, of course, we have our eye on the prize, and that is total animal liberation.

Although Erin's organization had an overarching abolitionist goal, this group did not only engage in abolitionist campaigns. According to Erin, they saw welfarist campaigns as a step towards "total animal liberation." Many other groups in the U.S. employed such a mix of welfarist campaigns within an abolitionist philosophical outlook, for the same reasons as Erin cited: they were working towards eliminating the practices that harm animals. Thus, we can see that U.S.

activists fully understood the logic of consistency, but they did not employ it in their actions. They saw "inconsistent" actions as working towards a long-term goal, because they viewed such inconsistent actions as being more effective.

French Organizations with U.S. Influences

Sociologist Marco Giugni (1998) argues that successful actions will be borrowed by other SMOs. To him, movement similarities can be explained by the diffusion of information and of models of action. I did find that two French SMOs employed the U.S. movement's logic of pragmatism: the Association Végétarienne de France (AVF) and PETA France. Though these organizations militated in France, PETA France and AVF took their institutional logics from the U.S. movement, since they were structurally and culturally connected to the U.S. organizational field.

Some theorists assume that if a successful practice is introduced into a movement field, it will be uncritically adopted (as critiqued by Campbell 2000: 54). Although these French SMOs took their pragmatic logic of action from the U.S. movement, their pragmatic institutional logics did not diffuse to other French SMOs. Moreover, the French animal rights movement as a whole did not institutionalize the logic of pragmatism *precisely because of* their logic of consistency. For ideological reasons, French activists did not borrow from what they considered to be a more successful U.S. movement. Nearly every French activist I met asked me to give examples of what activists did in the U.S. to become more successful, but they always decided against those strategies or tactics because they did not fit with their SMO ideology.

For example, while leafleting with the Collectif Antispéciste de Paris, I noticed that all the activists leafleted in the same way: they held out the flyers for passersby to see, become interested, and then take on their own. This reminded me of newspaper sellers, but without them yelling "read all about it!" I continued leafleting in my own way, handing tracts to individual passersby. Méryl noticed that I gave out four flyers in a row without rejection, and she smiled and nodded in an approving manner. Méryl said she was impressed that I could distribute tract after tract, but then chided me, saying, "Oh, this is your 'American efficiency.'" I laughed and said, "It's just like making a car," and pantomimed my leafleting technique over and over again, like I was doing it on an assembly line. Méryl then told me she had just noticed that I actually handed flyers to people, rather than just holding them out for the passersby to notice. When she said this, Nathalie noticed as well. Nathalie tried it and said, "Hey, it works!" However, my "American efficiency" was then ruled inappropriate for the organization, because Nathalie said it was too "violent" a method of leafleting. They continued with their previously approved method of holding up the flyers, and continued to pass out fewer flyers than with the "American efficiency" approach.

Similarly, Sebastien (Stop Gavage) described a failed protest he helped organize. The participating activists were pleased with the content, but the outcome left much to be desired:

We were happy because we were able to make a flyer that was really strong, from an ideological point of view. We saw ourselves in it 100 percent, as we did in the protest and in the slogans. But sure, there were only 150 of us at the protest in Paris. And at the end of it all, we didn't succeed in advancing anything because our discourse was too far gone. We need to put things into perspective.

Not only did AVF and PETA France's logic of pragmatism not diffuse to other French SMOs, its presence and use engendered further conflicts within the French movement. These conflicts denoted the limits of institutional isomorphism within this international movement field. While others have studied conflicts within organizations (Edgell Becker 1999), here I look to conflicts within an organizational field. Just as anchoring practices become more entrenched when employed in antagonistic relationships (Swidler 2001), looking at culturally informed institutional logics in interaction helps make the implicit rules of action explicit.

Diana, an organizer with AVF, said, "I do believe that we need to hit every angle. That's what AVF stands for more than anything else, is providing all the information, all the different motivations for becoming vegetarian." This approach echoes the pragmatic U.S. approach of trying all methods to be able to find the most effective one, regardless of philosophical consistency. Jérôme, an organizer for PETA France, similarly described his group's promotion of vegetarianism, but he then went further, to characterize PETA France's entire choice of campaigns as a pragmatic approach that takes the whole movement into account:

> PETA concentrates on things that we are the only ones capable of doing. We are the only ones, pretty much, who are able to fight against multinational corporations. This is why most of our campaigns have large targets. We're very well-adapted for international problems, but not so well-adapted for problems that are localized in one town. The role of PETA is not to promote, to regulate the problem of the overpopulation of dogs and cats, it's to work against huge multinational corporations.

Both of these groups used a pragmatic approach and, not coincidentally, both groups were heavily influenced by U.S. and U.K. organizations. The Association Végétarienne de France specifically modeled itself after Anglo-Saxon vegetarian organizations, and PETA France is the French arm of U.S.-based PETA, meaning they primarily engaged in PETA campaigns against international corporations, and they did not tailor their activism to animal issues in France. These Anglo-Saxon influences thus explain these groups' pragmatic strategic and tactical choices.

The differences between the U.S. logic of pragmatism (exemplified here by PETA France and AVF) and the French logic of coherence become clearer when the two logics collide. Diana (AVF) described such a conflict when her group tried to collaborate with the antispeciesists for Veggie Pride:

I think we need to hit vegetarianism and animal rights from all angles, and that's where we have come to, not come to blows with, but that's where we don't, are not totally compatible with the antispeciesists. But we have a, I would say we have a, now we have a happy coexistence. We had a little bit of a, teensy weensy bit of turbulence at the beginning of the Veggie Pride, when they wanted to restrict us to no, like we had on our stand, we had books on our stand on the health aspects of vegetarianism. And one of the organizers came and said that we had to take them off, that we were only allowed to deal with animal rights and recipes.

Indeed, an entire section of the Veggie Pride webpage was devoted to describing the types of signs and literature permitted at Veggie Pride protests:

Concerning banners, signs, and other visual messages: we ask that these messages not promote any other motive for vegetarianism and veganism than that of the rights of individual animals. In particular, this means that these messages do not make reference to the advantages of vegetarianism and veganism for human health, for the third world, for the environment, or for species protection. (Veggie Pride 2015)[1]

The Veggie Pride organizers did not object to the tactics, the acts of bringing flyers and banners to the protest. What they objected to was the pragmatic—but inconsistent—strategy of using multiple arguments for vegetarianism. Other French animal rights organizations also wrote disclaimers on their websites about what type of literature was acceptable or not on their tables, in an attempt to regulate the consistency of arguments. Thus while these institutional logics may be generalizable or transposable to other areas of activists' lives like cultural schemas (Sewell 1992), they did not easily diffuse to other organizations or integrate within an organizational field.

While this analysis favors explanations over predictions, this does not preclude predicting possible outcomes. When I received an email announcing the first ever Veggie Pride parade in NYC, I looked at the webpage and saw the description of marchers: "The parade will include animal-rights activists, environmentalists, and people simply concerned with their health" (Veggie Pride NYC 2015). I immediately thought the French organizers of Veggie Pride would dispute this, given their institutional logic of consistency. This thought proved correct, for when I forwarded the email to the French organizers, their organizational email list exploded with activists claiming it was a "shame" and an "unfortunate disfigurement" of Veggie Pride since it did not solely focus on animal rights. Although the French movement's tactic of Veggie Pride moved to the U.S. movement, its logic of consistency did not.

---

1 The specific quote comes from a previous version of the webpage. The current, cited version discusses the same issues in multiple areas.

Culture and Institutional Logics

Why did the French and U.S. movements develop different movement cultures and institutional logics, when they both take part in the same larger animal rights movement? Organizational theorists view institutional logics as nested logics, taking aspects of dominant, society-wide cultural logics and translating them to an individual level (Friedland and Alford 1991). While this may be true, organizational theory alone cannot tell us how that process happens. We need to look to comparative cultural sociologists to understand why these institutional logics differed between countries in the same movement field.

When speaking of how broader cultural beliefs vary between countries and translate into differing modes of action, Michèle Lamont (2000: 243) argues that such national cultural differences can be explained by viewing consistency and pragmatism as "institutionalized cultural repertoires or publicly available categorization systems." Lamont (1992) previously found that historical themes in France and the United States explained why upper-class men in the U.S. drew boundaries based on factualism, efficiency, expertise, and pragmatism, whereas in France, they drew them based on eloquence, general competence, *un sens critique*, and a strong capacity for abstraction. The repertoires of evaluation differed between the two countries because they drew upon differing historical themes. Historical national repertoires in the U.S. included ideas of pragmatism, populism, and an ideology of "Americanism," whereas historical French themes included republicanism, as well as aristocratic, socialist, and anarchist traditions.

These same historical national repertoires help explain the creation of differing institutional logics in the French and U.S. animal rights movements. Lamont (1992: 137) found the pragmatism and populism of the U.S. manifests itself in anti-intellectualism, which explains why U.S. activists placed more emphasis on pragmatic action and less emphasis on philosophically informed action. This can be seen in the U.S. movement's focus on "how-to" manuals and training sessions at conferences rather than philosophical debates. Lamont (1992: 138) also found the aristocratic tradition of France favors high culture and intellectualism, and thus French activists placed a higher importance on a knowledge of philosophy and a consistency of philosophy and action. This can be seen in the French movement's publication of philosophical journals and tracts and its discussion-based conferences rather than any emphasis on practical training of new activists.

The ways in which these historical national repertoires affected the institutional logics and modes of action can be seen in other social movements in France and the United States. Using a similar comparative cultural approach, Michael Moody and Laurent Thévenot (2000) found that activists in the French and U.S. environmental movements engaged different strategies because they had differing cultural understandings of "professionalism" and of which strategies were effective and acceptable. U.S. activists viewed professionalism as being versatile and knowing multiple arguments. French activists saw professionalism as demonstrating competency and commitment in a particular area. Further, demonstrations of U.S. modes of professional action in France raised suspicion about one's commitment.

These differing institutional logics found by Moody and Thévenot (2000) complement my findings. French environmental activists followed a consistency of thought and action by demonstrating competency and commitment in one area, whereas U.S. activists engaged a pragmatic logic of action by demonstrating their versatility and ability to use multiple arguments. Even in singular studies of U.S. movements without a comparative component, we can see hints of a pragmatic cultural logic. Gay rights activists strategically deployed different identities depending upon their audience or goals (Bernstein 1997). Civil Rights activists and labor unionists tested tactics before implementing them, trying out different modes of action before choosing what they found to be the most effective (Morris 1994, Beckwith 2000). Thus the animal rights movements in France and the United States developed different institutional logics not because they reflected individual values, but because individual activists translated historical cultural repertoires into action.

The meso-level analysis employed in this section also illuminates the concept of group style, from sociologists Paul Lichterman and Nina Eliasoph. Group style is the "recurrent patterns of interaction that arise from a group's shared assumptions about what constitutes good or adequate participation in the group setting" (Eliasoph and Lichterman 2003: 737). Group styles endure even when they threaten a group's survival, are inefficient, or are critiqued by other groups (Lichterman 2006). They may also, in the case of the U.S. movement, lead to greater success, though less internal consistency. The concept of group style primarily explains how individual agency may be constrained by group culture. It makes sense that individual actors can be constrained by the values of the group within which they work, as in the case of Ryan, who chose to leave the organization with which he was working because it was stifling his activism:

> I think if you're a part of an organization, it should be a progressive group of individuals that, like a group of individuals that want to progress within their, you know, move forward and evolve their praxis. If I was a vegetarian and I became part of an animal rights organization, I'd want the organization to be a positive group that made me want to become a vegan, or a raw foodist, or something. Or if I was a part of an animal rescue thing, I don't want to just raise ten dollars a month for spaying and neutering animals, I'd want to go break into a cow pasture and save things, you know? I'd want it to be a group of individuals that would progressively push me further and further and inspire me. And it just seemed like with that group I was like, I don't really feel like these kids are saying anything new, and in a way, I just feel like we're just trying to streamline a lot of our ideas so that we can reach a wider audience, but then again, it's like you dilute it so much that you alienate some of the more, I guess, radical community.

While such a micro-level perspective explains individual activists' dissatisfaction with organizations, it cannot explain SMOs' strategic and tactical choices. If we broaden the scope of group style from a micro–meso-level interaction to a meso–macro-level interaction, this better explains group-level actions and decisions. Paul Lichterman (2006) hints at such a broader utility, as he notes that group styles may occur in many settings across groups, in different organizations, and may belong to broader cultural repertoires.

On Making Strategic Choices

The animal rights movement in the United States was characterized by an institutional logic of pragmatism, where activists valued practicality in strategies and tactics. The question activists asked themselves was not so much "Do I believe this to be true?" but "Does research show this to be effective for my target audience?" Activists in the French animal rights movement believed in the consistency of thought and action. Thus French activists privileged the question of "Do I believe this to be true?" over asking whether a tactic or strategy might work in practice. These movement-wide logics help us to understand the varying strategic and tactical decisions made by different SMOs.

On this meso–macro interactional level, political scientist Lee Ann Banaszak (1996) found that external political influences on the women's suffrage movements in Switzerland and the United States shaped the movements' different strategic and tactical choices. Swiss activists failed to perceive certain political opportunities, whereas the U.S. suffrage movement better assessed their opportunities and better mobilized to take advantage of them. Likewise, the political values of the Swiss movement sometimes caused them to avoid options that would have been viable, and perhaps more successful. In these chapters I took a similar approach, but I looked at the external cultural influences on the animal rights movements in France and the United States to explain the same variables.

Also at this meso-level, though they did not specify an interest in political or cultural influences, Dennis Downey and Deana Rohlinger (2008) created the concept of social movement articulation to explain the level of competition or cooperation within a movement. Strategic articulation refers to the overall level of strategic interaction within a movement. Movements may be strongly articulated, as in the U.S. case, where there are relatively dense interactions and substantial strategic coordination among actors. This is seen in the U.S. through the sharing of activist materials, the formation of coalitions against the Animal Enterprise Terrorist Act, and through gatherings specifically for SMO interaction, such as the Summit for the Animals. Or, movements may be weakly articulated, as in the French case, where there is a widespread lack of coordination among SMOs, and predominantly competitive relationships.

In this section on Strategic Choices, I wanted to take this concept further, to see where such strategic articulation comes from in the first place. I argue that it does not come from the dominant culture, but rather from the culture of the social movement itself. Just as there are numerous different types of feminism, there are numerous schools of thought surrounding animal rights. The U.S. movement valued a logic of pragmatism, which put practice before philosophy, thus stifling many philosophical debates but enabling a stronger strategic articulation among SMOs.

The French movement valued a logic of consistency, which put philosophy before practice, thus encouraging philosophical debates at the expense of successful practices. This culture of consistency, when combined with the numerous philosophies of animal rights, enabled a weaker strategic articulation among French SMOs.

The approach developed in these chapters explains the strategic and tactical choices made by SMOs in the French and U.S. animal rights movements. These chapters can answer the question of how organizations make decisions, but they cannot explain the overall differential successes of the French and U.S. movements. In order to answer the primary question guiding this book, we must return to the findings from each of these analytic sections, and look at them as a whole. In the concluding chapter I will show how, when taken together, the analyses presented here can explain the differential successes of the French and U.S. animal rights movements.

Part IV

Movement Outcomes

9   Explaining Movement Success

In the introduction to this book, I asked why the animal rights movement in the United States enjoys more success than its French counterpart. U.S. activists have encouraged hundreds of companies to stop testing their products on animals, have successfully lobbied the government to outlaw animal fighting, and have convinced numerous clothing designers and stores to stop using and selling fur. French activists, in contrast, barely count dozens of such campaign successes in their work. These differential outcomes are even more puzzling given the similarities between the historical trajectories of the two movements. The animal protection, antivivisection, vegetarian, and first wave animal rights movements in both countries virtually mirrored one another, until the current second wave animal rights movement that centers on factory farming and veganism.

Given these historical similarities, explaining the differential successes of this second wave of the animal rights movement necessitates more than merely stating that the U.S. movement is older or more established, or that animal rights activists' claims resonate more in the United States than in France. Given the similarities in French and U.S. activists' goals, strategies, and tactics, and even the particular cultural claims they use to make them, the answer is not as simple as pointing to differences in longevity or the basic functions of the two movements.

My research points to two main analytic tools necessary to understand such variations in movement success. First, rather than conflating culture and agency, or culture and strategy, we need to conceive of culture as a structure. Culture may provide roadblocks to activists, but it also gives them building blocks for their work. I have shown how culture, at varying levels, shaped more opportunities for U.S. activists than it did for French activists, for whom culture played more of a constraining role.

Second, understanding movement success requires looking to a complex interplay of factors, rather than looking at solely whether and how activists attained their goals. We must look at the arguments targets use against activists, how those arguments emanate from culture, and how activists might combat the problem at its root by attacking those aspects of culture. Therefore, we must also look to how activists' arguments resonate within the dominant culture in which the movement works. Finally, we must look to how activists choose their strategies and tactics, and how they take into account these varying cultural constraints and opportunities.

The key to understanding social movement success through these myriad factors is to see how they fit together. To understand their interplay, I use the concept of repertoires. As defined by political sociologist Charles Tilly (2006), repertoires describe the range of strategies, tactics, or forms of contention available to protesters in a particular society and period. Much like cultural sociologist Ann Swidler's (1986) cultural toolkit, protesters choose from the strategies or tactics available to them in their repertoire. Repertoires also constrain activists' possibilities for action by limiting the number of strategic or tactical choices available in a given place or period. Though activists may choose certain tactics more often than others because of the "advantage of familiarity" (Tilly 1986: 390) it is not mere "dumb habit" (Tilly 2006) that can explain how people choose tactics from their repertoire.

Repertoires vary by political regimes, time periods, and social settings, and they are modified by various innovations that contribute to substantial changes in a given repertoire (Tilly 2006). Thus any one social movement that takes place in various settings may have different repertoires. Such is the case with the animal rights movements in France and the United States. But understanding movement success does not lie solely in explaining the differences in strategic and tactical repertoires. The fit between activists, tactics, and settings, which I have explored in this book, better explains effectiveness or success than simply evaluating what different activists hold in their respective bags of tricks, as Tilly explains:

> We should resist the temptation to label one of the two repertoires as more efficient, more political, or more revolutionary than the other. Nor does it help to call one repertoire "traditional" and the other "modern," any more than one can say that contemporary English is superior to that of Shakespeare, as if one were clearly more efficient or sophisticated than the other. We must recognize that repertoires of contention are sets of tools for the people involved. Backward/forward, prepolitical/political, and similar distinctions do not classify the tools but the particular circumstances for using them. The tools serve more than one end. Their relative efficacy depends on the match among tools, tasks, and users. (Tilly 2006: 54–55)

I do not wish to say that the U.S. movement's tactical repertoire was simply "better" in some way than that of the French movement. Rather, I strive to show not only how the "match among tools, tasks, and users" fit together differently in the U.S. than in France, but also how aspects of the external culture as well as the culture of the French and U.S. animal rights movements played a part in that fit. I draw my findings together in light of this concept of repertoires in order to demonstrate how activists' short- and long-term goals, cultural settings, and social movement fields all worked together such that the animal rights movement in the United States enjoyed more success relative to the movement in France.

Scholars have employed the concept of repertoires to a great extent to talk about culture. Culture can *be* the repertoire, as in Rhys Williams's (2002) concept of "symbolic repertoires." Symbolic repertoires are symbolic tools handed down from generation to generation, which people use to construct their social world. The repertoire of ideological and cultural expressions available to movements both constrains and enables movement activities (Williams and Kubal 1999).

Culture can also *shape* repertoires. When scholars look to what shapes a movement's activity, they typically analyze structural resources such as money, members, networks, or organizational power (Williams 1995). When used to explain strategic and tactical choices, such analyses reek of the "technological determinism" rejected by Tilly (2006). In his earlier work, Williams (1995) asked what were the strategic limitations of various types of cultural resources, and I attempted to answer such a question in Chapters 3–6 on Cultural Resources.

In Chapters 3–6, I demonstrated how cultural resources varied between France and the United States. While the environment worked in both countries, and terrorism worked against the U.S. movement, using health, religion, food, and the media resonated in U.S. culture but not in France. Thus dominant culture differentially shaped the repertoires of the two movements. The U.S. movement's repertoire expanded to include those four successful tools, while it contracted in France as those tools were rendered virtually useless. In each case, culture acted as a structure, placing an external effect on social movement activity.

Once repertoires are constructed, actors must choose from the strategies and tactics available to them in their given repertoire. Scholars have proposed a variety of explanations for how activists make such choices, such as familiarity (Tilly 2006), habit (Tilly 2006), learning processes (Koopmans 2005), or ideology (Meyer 2004). Others claim the habitus can explain individual or group choices. Individual life experiences shape an activist's habitus, and that habitus, in turn, influences strategic or tactical choices (Crossley 2002). Looking beyond such individual preferences, others place the emphasis on the tactics themselves. Some tactics cluster within the field of tactical repertoires, in such a way that they seem to go together. Tactics further apart in the field of tactical repertoires, in contrast, are less likely to be combined by activists (Ennis 1987).

In Chapters 7 and 8, the section on Strategic Choices, I showed how French and U.S. activists made their choices based upon the prevailing institutional logic of their social movement field. In Part 3, I demonstrated that activists in the French animal rights movement valued a logic of consistency of thought and action, whereas activists in the U.S. movement favored a logic of pragmatism and practicality. Different social movement organizations within the broader social movement field also favored different philosophies of animal rights, which can explain why different groups chose different strategies and tactics within one particular repertoire.

Thus threading my analysis together with the concept of repertoires can explain why the animal rights movement in the United States was more successful relative to the movement in France. While activists in both countries shared long-term goals of total animal liberation and veganism, in the shorter term the dominant culture in each country expanded the strategic and tactical repertoire of the U.S. movement, while constricting that of the French movement. Given these varying repertoires, U.S. activists chose from within them based upon a logic of pragmatism and practicality, which favored success over ideological consistency. In France, activists chose their strategies and tactics based upon a logic of consistency, favoring ideological purity over short-term practicality.

Validity and Activists' Perspectives

In congruence with the feminist values guiding my research, I wish to clarify my thoughts on the implications of this research for animal rights activists themselves. All of the participants in this study are engaged, informed cultural actors and I expect they will take their own conclusions from this research. But as I write not only *about* animal rights activists, but also *for* animal rights activists, a primary concern of mine is the extent to which my analysis represents the lived experience of the activists who participated in this study. This concern hits at validity not just for the activists, but also, selfishly, for the results of my analysis. If none, or few, of my participants saw themselves on these pages, I would feel that I let them down in some way, that I did not get at the meanings they gave to their animal rights activism. While this may be the case (and I hope it is not), I stand by the sociological analysis I presented in this book. I do not know to what extent my analysis represents the experience of the activists in my study, but I certainly understand it does not represent all animal rights activists.

My thoughts here are informed by extended conversations with activists before, during, and after my data collection and analysis. In addition to presenting this research at sociological conferences, I have also presented the results to activists at their individual groups' meetings and at movement-wide conferences. When I first returned to France to present my findings, at the 2010 gathering of activists at Les Estivales de la Question Animale, I spoke about my research to a woman I did not know. I told her I was nervous about my presentation, because I was afraid I would be telling the audience things they already knew. The woman looked at me, disappointed, and said, "I certainly hope I didn't come all this way to hear things I already knew!" After my presentation and the ensuing discussion, I approached the woman to ask her what she thought of my findings. Her initial disappointment turned to excitement as she told me that she found the research very informative for her own work, and that she saw new ways to approach different aspects of her group's activism.

I believe participants in this research appreciated the opportunity to discuss their work, as simply getting the word out about animal issues was of utter importance to them. Talking about animal rights not only helps the animals, but it also helps potential activists, as Stewart (Vegan Outreach) said:

> I think for people that are vegan and are very concerned about animal rights, it's sort of like, living in America is sort of like living in a dysfunctional family where there's this horrible, horrible thing going on but what we don't talk about it. There's like this pent-up energy and they can't talk about it, but it's happening. It's happening all the time. And all these animals, they're caged, they're given hormones, they're bleeding to death, they're beaten, all of these horrible things. Parts of them are being amputated without anesthetics. And

it's a horrible thing to live with. And so when they see someone out there telling people about it, it's a release and it feels really good to them to have somebody out there speaking about something that they care about so deeply.

Heidi (HSUS), too, recounted such experiences, as when she helped a person find his "click" moment:

He turned to me and he had tears in his eyes. And he said, 'Heidi, this has got to be stopped.' And I was like, I still get choked up, it was one of those pivotal moments where he actually saw what we saw.

As a vegan animal rights activist myself, I hope this work will help readers to better understand the plight of animals, and the aspirations of animal rights activists. Without meaning to imply that vegan and sociologist are mutually exclusive identities, as a sociologist, I also hope that my analysis will, in turn, help animal rights activists see their own work in a different light.

I believe the activists I interviewed would most agree with the chapters analyzing the variability of cultural resources. Again, as these activists are informed cultural actors, they are not blind to the constraints of the French gastronomic culture on the promotion of veganism, nor the U.S. legal system's views of activists as terrorists. No one likes to be told that certain paths of action are permanently "cut off" to them, but this is not what I am attempting to do in these chapters. Rather, I believe these chapters may bolster the beliefs of activists on the most and least fruitful paths for activism, and I hope that they provide a broader context in which to make their future strategic and tactical decisions.

On such decisions, I believe that activists in both countries will disagree most with my assessment of the social and cultural factors that inform their strategic and tactical choices in Chapters 7 and 8. I think that French activists would agree that they all value a consistency of thought and action, and I doubt any U.S. activists would disagree that the U.S. animal rights movement favors pragmatism, including research and activist training. However, I think activists might disagree that these cultural values in their respective movements were so strong that they influenced their strategic and tactical choices. Again, I stand by my analysis, no matter how disconcerting it may be. I believe that these chapters, as distressing as they may be for activists, would ultimately benefit the animal rights movement the most. If activists can acknowledge that certain beliefs guide their actions more than they might realize or admit, they might be able to work against such forces for the betterment of the movement. While I am not trying to change the entire culture of the French or U.S. animal rights movements, I am attempting to help activists see more clearly the social forces that inform their work, for better or for worse.

Limitations and Future Research

This project has contributed to many areas in the study of culture and social movements, while also highlighting paths for future research. At the same time, this research has its limitations. First, some might see my emphasis on the cultural aspects of the animal rights movement as incomplete, since I did not fully explore all of the political and institutional barriers and opportunities for the movement. This was a purposeful choice on my part, given that most studies only examine institutional and political structures, while ignoring culture or seeing culture as a free area that only contributes to strategy or agency. That being said, a more traditional political-institutional perspective would add much to this study. For one, it would allow us to see how social and cultural structures are intertwined, and a comparative perspective might be able to discern which one had more influence on the movement. Future studies of the animal rights movement could include an investigation of how institutions and businesses such as agriculture, for example, play a part in the movement and in the practices that challenge the movement. Lobbying, and other forms of political power, play a role in these processes as well.

Another limitation is that this research primarily focused on activists, and it did not devote equal attention to their targets. While I did interrogate passersby at tabling events, and I observed their interactions with activists, more in-depth investigation of targets and activist–target interactions would better illuminate the boundaries of cultural resonance of various strategies and tactics. Rachel Einwohner's (1999) work in this area provides one such example. While she focused on the effects of gender and identity on micro-level protester–target interactions, future studies could take a more macro-level focus, as I did in this research.

There are also limitations to my study as regards cultural change as a goal of the animal rights movement, and as a goal of social movements more generally. We would arrive at a more comprehensive understanding of this goal of cultural change if I gathered more data on the targets or opponents of this movement, and more long-term information on the movement. I approximated opponents' opinions from previous studies, from activists' interactions with their targets, and from media sources, but a specific study of animal rights opponents—at multiple points in time—would provide the necessary sources to evaluate the extent of the cultural change attained by the animal rights movement in this area.

Finally, as regards all qualitative research studies, there are limitations to my data. I only studied the animal rights movements in France and the United States. While this smaller sample allows for more in-depth comparisons, it lacks in breadth. Future studies could assess the validity and reliability of my findings by investigating similar processes in the animal rights movements in other countries, or with other social movements in France and the United States. As this type of study on the intersections of culture, structure, and agency emerges more often in social movement studies, I hope that my work, despite these limitations, provides a significant foundation for future research.

Policy Solutions and Implications for Activists

My research focuses on how culture affects the strategies and tactics that are available to activists, and how activists choose among them. How might this relate to the passing of specific policies? How might activists find some solutions to inform their work? First, we need to understand some of the existing research on policy reform. Studying the issue of marital rape legislation, criminologist Jennifer McMahon-Howard and her colleagues (McMahon-Howard et al. 2009) found that states that passed smaller reform laws did not subsequently pass larger, wider-reaching laws against marital rape. Similarly, on the issue of hate crime legislation, sociologists Sarah Soule and Jennifer Earl (2001) found that states may "shield themselves" from passing strong and/or controversial laws by enacting weaker ones, to avoid criticism and show that they are engaged on the issue. That is, states that pass weaker, or partial, laws against hate crimes are slower to adopt stronger laws criminalizing hate crimes than states that did not pass such earlier laws. The conclusions of these studies send a message that, at the state level, it is better to seek strong, wide-reaching laws as an end goal, rather than settling for smaller, weaker laws as an interim goal.

On this issue, sociologist Erin Evans (2015b) studied the effects of federal guidelines on animal testing, using the passing of the 1966 Animal Welfare Act and the subsequent 1985 amendment as her case study. She found that policy reform, specifically the 1985 amendment to the Animal Welfare Act, changed animal use in laboratories and created "stepping stones" for future activism. After the passing of the 1985 amendment to the Animal Welfare Act, using some species of animals in research became more expensive and impractical, and viewed as unethical. The number of regulations on animal use greatly increased, as did the cost per animal for some species. This, in turn, affected whether and how scientists chose to use certain animals in their research. The number of dogs, cats, and primates in NIH-funded research has decreased during this time. However, the total number of animals used for research has increased, specifically the use of rodents and pigs. Regulators came to see bioethicists as important consultants on animal use, and their inclusion in such policy-making decisions helped usher in the National Institute of Health's 2011 moratorium on research with chimpanzees.

Thus we see two competing visions of how to proceed with policy reforms for animal rights issues. On the one hand, the findings from McMahon-Howard et al. (2009) and Soule and Earl (2001) point towards only pursuing the most wide-sweeping legal changes. This equates to only pursuing the movement's ultimate goals—their desired outcome (Einwohner 1999) or a full response (Gamson 1990). On the other hand, the findings from Evans (2015b) point towards intermediate policy reforms as setting the stage for future reforms, and even the desired abolition of certain animal practices. These two competing visions perfectly mirror the major debate in animal rights surrounding welfare reforms versus the pursuit of total abolition. While there are many strong arguments for both sides of this debate, I do not believe there exists enough empirical data on this issue to be able to make a conclusive recommendation one way or the other. For now, we can see how the findings in this area might apply to animal rights issues.

Sociologists might be able to compare these legal case studies mentioned here to the animal rights movement by comparing the state-wide adoption of bans on dogfighting, for example. Laws against dogfighting developed state by state, culminating in the Animal Fighting Prohibition Enforcement Act of 2007. Future research could examine the passing of each individual state law, to see if they follow the same patterns as described in the findings from McMahon-Howard et al. (2009) and Soule and Earl (2001). Without any similar findings specific to the passing of animal laws, it would be difficult to take the policy reform findings from these studies and apply them wholesale to the myriad goals and issues taken up by animal advocates. Further, marital rape and hate crimes are not part of a larger, economic industry, as are most areas of focus for the animal rights movement.

Therefore, if we think about how these case studies might apply to animal rights, it might help for animal advocates to focus on abolishing certain specific practices, rather than attempting to abolish all animal practices at once. Consider the case of animals in entertainment, which includes bullfighting, dogfighting, cockfighting, circuses, and many other practices. U.S. activists have successfully banned dogfighting in all 50 states. Given these successes, it seems that conducting state-by-state campaigns to ban certain animal practices would be a successful strategy for U.S. activists. Given the size of the country, and the fact that France has created country-wide loopholes to European Union legislation, as well as regional loopholes to French legislation, it seems a similar strategy for France would necessitate targeting the state rather than smaller *départements*. Activists in both countries have been pursuing and continue to pursue such policy strategies.

Returning this discussion to the cultural contexts that I studied, my research should help activists better understand the tools in their strategic and tactical toolkit, the more or less useful times to deploy them, and how to be reflexive when making those decisions. I hope this will be true for animal rights activists, and I also hope my findings will be useful to activists in other movements. For example, groups fighting against institutionalized discrimination in the criminal justice system could look to the cultural tools available in the country in which they work, to see which tools might be most effective for their work. Given my findings, in the United States, such tools could include religion and the media. There are likely other cultural resources that would benefit this movement, such as the frame of human rights. Then, activists would seek to be reflexive about when and how to deploy them. Of course, activists in this and other movements are all informed cultural actors, ready to avail themselves of the resources available to them, or ready to create new ones.

When readers, both activist and academic, look at the findings from each of these chapters, they might conclude that the animal rights movements in France and the United States are simply on different paths. Many French activists to whom I spoke were disheartened by their progress in comparison to other animal rights movements, especially that of the U.K. But as French activists preferred to keep their eyes on the prize, on the end goal of animal liberation, perhaps by sticking to these goals they will achieve their end goal more quickly than movements who take smaller steps of reform. Perhaps the U.S. movement, with its multiple reformist and welfarist campaigns, will reach their end goal of animal liberation at a slower pace than the French movement. This, of course, is the burning question for all animal rights activists: whether to follow abolition or reform strategies. As noted above, I cannot definitively answer that question in this book, but I hope that sociological research can help answer it in the future. And, of course, my research will not stop activists from holding strong opinions on the subject. For now, I hope that this project has shed some light on the relationship between culture and activism, and that it will help inform activists' future work.

Appendix
List of Participants

United States

Name*	Organization	Years in animal rights movement**	Age,** profession
Eric Griffith	Speak Out for Species (SOS), Athens, GA	6	30s, librarian
Wendy Moore	SOS	6	30s, librarian
Carrie Mumah	SOS	2	21, student
Dylan Clark	SOS	1	22, student
Francesca Valente	SOS	3	21, English teacher in Italy
Jean Pembleton	SOS	4	22, English teacher in Martinique
Jack Norris	Vegan Outreach (VO)	17	40, President of VO, registered dietitian
Jon Camp	VO	5	29, Outreach Coordinator for VO
Jenna Calabrese	VO	5	21, Outreach Coordinator for VO
Jeff Boghosian	VO	8	36, software engineer
Joe Espinosa	VO and Mercy for Animals (MFA)	11	35, social worker
Stewart Solomon	VO	5	44, high school science teacher
Suzanne Haws	VO	5	28, homemaker
Eleni Vlachos	VO	6	20s, musician
Heidi Prescott	Humane Society of the United States (HSUS), Washington, D.C.	16	30s, Senior VP of Campaigns for HSUS, former Director of Fund for Animals (FFA)
Josh Balk	HSUS	3.5	25, Outreach Coordinator for the Factory Farming Campaign at HSUS
Erin Williams	HSUS	12	31, Communications Director for Factory Farming Campaign at HSUS

Bruce Friedrich	People for the Ethical Treatment of Animals (PETA), Norfolk, Virginia	10	36, Director of Vegan and Farm Animal Campaigns at PETA
Lorena Mucke	Multiple affiliations	4	34, humane educator
Dawn Ratcliffe	Unaffiliated (at time of the interview)	9	20s, activist
"Sean"	Anonymous SMO	5	20s, campaign coordinator in an animal rights SMO
"Diane"	Anonymous SMO	4	29, campaign coordinator in an animal rights SMO
"Stephanie"	Anonymous SMO		20s, director of an animal rights SMO
"Richard"	Anonymous SMO	10	26, campaign manager of an animal rights SMO
"Megan"	Anonymous SMO	2 months	31, employee of an animal rights SMO
"Amber"	Anonymous SMO	3	34, director of an animal rights SMO
"Steven"	Anonymous SMO	10	22, director of an animal rights SMO
"Talia"	Anonymous SMO	5	44, director of an animal rights SMO
"Austin"	Anonymous SMO	7	21, student
"Justice"	Anonymous SMO	4	26, student
"Grant"	Anonymous SMO	1	22, student
"Ryan"	unaffiliated	2.5	21, student

*Quotation marks around a name denote confidential participation. No quotation marks denote public participation.

**Age and years in the animal rights movement are based on information at the time of the interview.

France

Name*	Organization	Years in animal rights movement**	Age,** profession
Nathalie Cornevin	Collectif Antispéciste de Paris (CAP), Paris	10	35, secretary
Virginie Beaujouan	CAP	10	29, historian
Hervé Henry	CAP	7	30s, automotive engineer
Yann Zoldan	CAP	2	18, student
Ivora Cusack	CAP	2	31, film director and sound editor

(continued)

(continued)

Name*	Organization	Years in animal rights movement**	Age,** profession
Méryl Pinque	CAP	10	31, literary critic
André Méry	Association Végétarienne de France (AVF), Paris	12	57, President of AVF, retired from pharmaceutical industry
Diana Dunningham Chapotin	AVF, Paris	Most of her life	52, retired teacher
Emmanuel Bouvot	AVF, Paris	10	38, research and development
Christine Pruvost	AVF, Lyon	4	26, home worker for the aged
Frédéric Berthelet	AVF, Lyon	6	41, technician
Charles Notin	Welfarm (formerly Protection Mondiale des Animaux de Ferme), Metz	12	59, retired math teacher
Ghislain Zuccolo	Welfarm	19	36, Director of Welfarm
Dominic Hofbauer	Welfarm	5	37, Director of Education, Welfarm
Johanne Mielcarek	Welfarm	4	24, Development Assistant, Welfarm
Antoine Comiti	Stop Gavage, Bordeaux	4	39, electronic engineer
Sebastien Arsac	Welfarm, Stop Gavage, Cahiers Antispécistes, Metz	12	30s, worked at PMAF
Brigitte Gothière	Stop Gavage, Cahiers Antispécistes, Metz	12	30s, nonprofit sector
David Olivier	Cahiers Antispécistes, Veggie Pride, Les Estivales, Lyon	18	50, computer engineer
Yves Bonnardel	Cahiers Antispécistes, Veggie Pride, Lyon	20	40s, activist
Agnése Pignataro	Antispécistes, Lyon	10	29, doctoral student in philosophy
Sara Fergé	Veggie Pride, Les Estivales, AVELY, Lyon	3	24, French teacher
Fabrice Alvarez	Animale Amnistie, Toulouse	7	42, English teacher
Carol McNeill	Animale Amnistie, Toulouse	1	40s, English teacher
Sophie Pedon	Animale Amnistie, and AVF delegate, Toulouse	1	38, secretary
Daniel Lacourt	Animale Amnistie, Toulouse	2	49, photographer

Fanny Lacombe	Animale Amnistie, Toulouse	16	31, administrative assistant
Philippe	AVIS, Toulouse	10	37, mechanical technician
Jérôme Bernard-Pellet	PETA France, Paris	4	33, medical doctor
Elsa	Le Glaive, Lyon	6 months	21, student
"Bernadette"	Anonymous SMO	9 months	22, teacher
"Tali"	Anonymous SMO	6	28, teacher
"Rob"	Anonymous SMO	4	27, computer engineer
"Julie"	Anonymous SMO	1	23, sales
"René"	Anonymous SMO	9	25, sales
"Fergus"	L'Armée des Douze Singes	2	19, student
"Albert"	unaffiliated	2	23, storekeeper

References

ACE (Animal Charity Evaluators). 2015a. "Number of Animals vs. Amount of Donations." Retrieved October 15, 2015 (www.animalcharityevaluators.org/research/foundational-research/number-of-animals-vs-amount-of-donations/).

ACE (Animal Charity Evaluators). 2015b. "Effects of Diet Choices on Animals." Retrieved October 15, 2015 (www.animalcharityevaluators.org/research/foundational-research/effects-of-diet-choices-on-animals/).

ACE (Animal Charity Evaluators). 2015c. "General Recommendation Process." Retrieved October 15, 2015 (www.animalcharityevaluators.org/recommendations/about-our-recommendations/general-recommendation-process/).

ACE (Animal Charity Evaluators). 2015d. "Interventions." Retrieved October 15, 2015 (www.animalcharityevaluators.org/research/interventions/).

Adams, Carol J. 1990. *The Sexual Politics of Meat: A Feminist-Vegetarian Critical Theory.* New York: Continuum.

Agulhon, Maurice. 1981. "Le Sang des Bêtes: Le Problème de la Protection des Animaux en France aux XIXème Siècle." *Romantisme* 31: 81–109.

American Dietetic Association. 2003. "Position of the American Dietetic Association and Dietitians of Canada: Vegetarian Diets." *ADA Reports* 103(6): 748–765.

Animal Liberation Frontline. 2012. "New Grand Jury Subpoenas and Updates in Santa Cruz Arson Investigation." Retrieved September 15, 2015 (http://animalliberationfrontline.com/new-grand-jury-subpoena-informant-in-santa-cruz-arson-investigation/).

Animal Liberation Front. 2015. "The ALF Credo and Guidelines." Retrieved September 26, 2015 (www.animalliberationfront.com/ALFront/alf_credo.htm).

Archer, Margaret. 1988. *Culture and Agency.* Cambridge: Cambridge University Press.

Assemblée Nationale. 1995. "Report 'Au nom de la commission d'enquête sur les sectes.'" Retrieved October 6, 2015 (www.assemblee-nationale.fr/rap-enq/r2468.asp).

Association Végétarienne de France. 2015. "Célébrités végétariennes." Retrieved September 25, 2015 (www.vegetarisme.fr/pourquoi-etre-vegetarien/celebrites-vegetariennes/).

Attebury, Danee. 2006. "Controversial Animal Tests to be Conducted on Campus." *Red and Black.* April 11.

Banaszak, Lee Ann. 1996. *Why Movements Succeed or Fail: Opportunity, Culture, and the Struggle for Woman Suffrage.* Princeton, NJ: Princeton University Press.

Baram, Marcus. 2006. "NRA's Graphic Attack on Its Enemies Leaked Onto Internet." Retrieved September 25, 2015 (http://abcnews.go.com/US/story?id=2759754&page=1).

Barker-Plummer, Bernadette. 1995. "News as a Political Resource: Media Strategies and Political Identity in the U.S. Women's Movement, 1966–1975." *Critical Studies in Mass Communication* 12: 306–324.

Beamish, Thomas D., Harvey Molotch, and Richard Flacks. 1995. "Who Supports the Troops? Vietnam, the Gulf War, and the Making of Collective Memory." *Social Problems* 42(3): 344–360.

Becker, Howard. 1960. "Notes on the Concept of Commitment." *American Journal of Sociology* 66: 32–40.

Beckwith, Karen. 2000. "Hinges in Collective Action: Strategic Innovation in the Pittston Coal Strike." *Mobilization* 5(2): 179–199.

Bell Jr., Derrick A. 1980. "Brown v. Board of Education and the Interest-Convergence Dilemma." *Harvard Law Review* 93(3): 518–533.

Bernstein, Mary. 1997. "Celebration and Suppression: The Strategic Uses of Identity by the Lesbian and Gay Movement." *American Journal of Sociology* 103(3): 531–565.

Bernstein, Mary. 2003. "Nothing Ventured, Nothing Gained? Conceptualizing Social Movement 'Success' in the Lesbian and Gay Movement." *Sociological Perspectives* 46(3): 353–379.

Berry, Bonnie. 2008. "Interactionism and Animal Aesthetics: A Theory of Reflected Social Power." *Society & Animals* 16: 75–89.

Binder, Amy J. 2002. *Contentious Curricula: Afrocentrism and Creationism in American Public Schools*. Princeton, NJ: Princeton University Press.

Bless, Herbert, Klaus Fiedler, and Fritz Strack. 2004. *Social Cognition: How Individuals Construct Social Reality*. New York: Psychology Press.

Bourdieu, Pierre. 1977. *Outline of a Theory of Practice*. Cambridge: Cambridge University Press.

Bourdieu. Pierre. 1993. *The Field of Cultural Production*. New York: Columbia University Press.

Briet, Marie-Odile. 2010. "Végétarien, mais pas trop." *L'Express* September 20. Retrieved October 19, 2015 (www.lexpress.fr/styles/saveurs/vegetarien-mais-pas-trop_920752. html).

Brillat-Savarin, Jean-Anthèlme. 1994 [1825]. *The Physiology of Taste*. Translated by Anne Drayton. Harmondsworth, Middlesex, England: Penguin Books.

Brody, Jane E. 1998. "Final Advice from Dr. Spock: Eat Only All Your Vegetables." *The New York Times* June 20. Retrieved September 29, 2015 (www.nytimes. com/1998/06/20/us/final-advice-from-dr-spock-eat-only-all-your-vegetables.html).

Burawoy, Michael. 2000. "Introduction: Reaching for the Global." Pp.1–40 in *Global Ethnography: Forces, Connections, and Imaginations in a Postmodern World*, edited by Michael Burawoy, Joseph A. Blum, Sheba George, Zsuzsa Gille, Teresa Gowan, Lynne Haney, Maren Klawiter, Steven H. Lopez, Seán Ó Riain, and Millie Thayer. Berkeley: University of California Press.

Calverd, Alan. 2005. "A Radical Approach to Kyoto." *Physics World* July: 56.

Campbell, Donald J. 2000. "The Proactive Employee: Managing Workplace Initiative." *The Academy of Management Executive* 14(3): 52–66.

Carnegie, Dale. 1990. *How to Win Friends and Influence People*. New York: Pocket Books.

Carroll, William K. and R.S. Ratner. 1999. "Media Strategies and Political Projects: A Comparative Study of Social Movements." *Canadian Journal of Sociology* 24(1):1–34.

Cherry, Elizabeth. 2003. "It's Not Just a Diet: Identity, Commitment, and Social Networks in Vegans." MA Thesis, Department of Sociology, University of Georgia, Athens, GA.

Cherry, Elizabeth. 2006. "Veganism as a Cultural Movement: A Relational Approach." *Social Movement Studies* 5(2): 155–170.

Cherry, Elizabeth. 2010. "Shifting Symbolic Boundaries: Cultural Strategies of the Animal Rights Movement." *Sociological Forum* 25(3): 450–475.

Cherry, Elizabeth. 2015. "I Was a Teenage Vegan: Motivation and Maintenance of Lifestyle Movements." *Sociological Inquiry* 85(1): 55–74.

Cherry, Elizabeth, Colter Ellis, and Michaela De Soucey. 2011. "Food for Thought, Thought for Food: Consumption, Identity, and Ethnography." *Journal of Contemporary Ethnography* 40(2): 231–258.

Christian Vegetarian Association. 2015. "Compassionate Eating." Retrieved October 6, 2015 (www.all-creatures.org/cva/honoring.htm).

Clausen, John A. 1986. *The Life Course: A Sociological Perspective*. Englewood Cliffs, NJ: Prentice Hall.

Cole, Matthew and Karen Morgan. 2011. "Vegaphobia: Derogatory Discourses of Veganism and the Reproduction of Speciesism in UK National Newspapers." *The British Journal of Sociology* 62(1): 134–153.

Coleman, John C. and Leo Henry. 1990. *The Nature of Adolescence*, 2nd Edition. New York: Routledge.

Covey, Stephen R. 1989. *The Seven Habits of Highly Effective People: Powerful Lessons in Personal Change*. New York: Free Press.

Cress, Daniel M. and David A. Snow. 1996. "The Outcomes of Homeless Mobilization: The Influence of Organization, Disruption, Political Mediation, and Framing." *American Journal of Sociology* 105(4): 1063–1104.

Crossley, Nick. 2002. "Repertoires of Contention and Tactical Diversity in the UK Psychiatric Survivors Movement: The Question of Appropriation." *Social Movement Studies* 1(1):47–71.

Crozier, Michel. 1964. *The Bureaucractic Phenomenon*. Chicago: University of Chicago Press.

d'Anjou, Leo and John Van Male. 1998. "Between Old and New: Social Movements and Cultural Change." *Mobilization* 3(2): 141–161.

Davis, Gerald F., Doug McAdam, W. Richard Scott, and Mayer N. Zald. 2005. *Social Movements and Organization Theory*. Cambridge: Cambridge University Press.

de la Chesnais, Eric and Cyril Hofstein. 2013. "La chasse, deuxième sport en France après le foot." *Le Figaro*. October 9. Retrieved October 2, 2015 (www.lefigaro.fr/actualite-france/2013/09/08/01016–20130908ARTFIG00024–la-chasse-deuxieme-sport-en-france-apres-le-foot.php).

De Soucey, Michaela. 2010. "Gastronationalism: Food Traditions and Authenticity Politics in the European Union." *American Sociological Review* 75(3): 432–455.

Delgado, Christopher L. 2003. "Rising Consumption of Meat and Milk in Developing Countries Has Created a New Food Revolution." *The Journal of Nutrition* 133(11): 3907S–3910S.

della Porta, Donatella and Dieter Rucht. 1995. "Left-Libertarian Movements in Context: Comparing Italy and West Germany, 1965–1990." Pp.229–272 in *The Politics of Social Protest: Comparative Perspectives on States and Social Movements*, edited by J. Craig Jenkins and Bert Klandermans. Minneapolis: University of Minnesota Press.

Dillard, Courtney L. 2002. "Civil Disobedience: A Case Study in Factors of Effectiveness." *Society and Animals* 10(1): 47–62.

DiMaggio, Paul J. and Walter W. Powell. 1983. "The Iron Cage Revisited: Institutional Isomorphism and Collective Rationality in Organizational Fields." *American Sociological Review* 48(2): 147–160.

Downey, Dennis and Deana A. Rohlinger. 2008. "Linking Strategic Choice with Macro-Organizational Dynamics: Strategy and Social Movement Articulation." *Research in Social Movements, Conflicts, and Change* 28: 3–38.

Driscoll, Adam and Bob Edwards. 2014. "From Farms to Factories: The Social and Environmental Consequences of Industrial Swine Production in North Carolina." Pp. 209–230 in *Twenty Lessons in Environmental Sociology*, edited by Kenneth A. Gould and Tammy L. Lewis. New York: Oxford University Press.

Duyvendak, Jan Willem. 1995. *The Power of Politics: New Social Movements in France.* Boulder, CO: Westview Press.

Edgell Becker, Penny. 1999. *Congregations in Conflict: Cultural Models of Local Religious Life.* Cambridge: Cambridge University Press.

Edgell, Penny. 2006. *Religion and Family in a Changing Society.* Princeton, NJ: Princeton University Press.

Edwards, Bob and John D. McCarthy. 2004. "Strategy Matters: The Contingent Value of Social Capital in the Survival of Local Social Movement Organizations." *Social Forces* 83(2): 621–651.

Einwohner, Rachel. 1999. "Gender, Class, and Social Movement Outcomes: Identity and Effectiveness in Two Animal Rights Campaigns." *Gender and Society* 13(1): 56–76.

Elias, Norbert. 1978. *The Civilizing Process.* New York: Urizen Books.

Eliasoph, Nina and Paul Lichterman. 2003. "Culture in Interaction." *American Journal of Sociology* 108(4): 735–794.

Emirbayer, Mustafa. 1997. "Manifesto for a Relational Sociology." *American Journal of Sociology* 103(2): 281–317.

Emirbayer, Mustafa and Jeff Goodwin. 1994. "Network Analysis, Culture, and the Problem of Agency." *American Journal of Sociology* 99(6): 1411–1454.

Emirbayer, Mustafa and Ann Mische. 1998. "What is Agency?" *American Journal of Sociology* 103(4): 962–1023.

Ennis, James G. 1987. "Fields of Action: Structure in Movements' Tactical Repertoires." *Sociological Forum* 2(3): 520–533.

Evans, Erin M. 2015a. "Bearing Witness: How Controversial Organizations Get the Media Coverage They Want." *Social Movement Studies.* Advance online publication. doi:10.1080/14742837.2015.1060158.

Evans, Erin M. 2015b. "Stumbling Blocks or Stepping Stones? The Problems and Promises of Policy Reform Goals for the Animal Advocacy Movement." *Sociological Perspectives.* Advance online publication. doi:10.1177/0731121415593276.

Fantasia, Rick. 1988. *Cultures of Solidarity: Consciousness, Action, and Contemporary American Workers.* Berkeley: University of California Press.

Fantasia, Rick. 1995. "Fast Food in France." *Theory and Society* 24(2): 201–243.

Faunalytics. 2015. "Why Use Research?" Retrieved October 15, 2015 (https://faunalytics.org/why-use-research/).

Federal Bureau of Investigation. 2002. "The Threat of Eco-Terrorism." Retrieved September 25, 2015 (www.fbi.gov/news/testimony/the-threat-of-eco-terrorism).

Fédération Nationale des Chasseurs. 2015. "Qui sont les chasseurs?" Retrieved October 2, 2015 (www.chasseurdefrance.com/decouvrir-la-chasse-en-france/qui-sont-les-chasseurs/les-chasseurs-qui-sont-ils/).

FEDIAF. 2012. "Facts and Figures 2012." Retrieved October 10, 2015 (www.fediaf.org/facts-figures/).

Ferguson, Priscilla Parkhurst. 1998. "A Cultural Field in the Making: Gastronomy in 19th Century France." *American Journal of Sociology* 104(3): 597–641.

Fiddes, Nick. 1991. *Meat: A Natural Symbol.* London: Routledge.

Finsen, Lawrence and Susan Finsen. 1994. *The Animal Rights Movement in America: From Compassion to Respect.* New York: Twayne Publishers.

Fischler, Claude. 2001. *L'Homnivore*. Paris: Editions Odile Jacob.

Francione, Gary. 1995. *Animals, Property, and the Law*. Philadelphia, PA: Temple University Press.

Freedman, Rory and Kim Barnouin. 2005. *Skinny Bitch*. Philadelphia, PA: Running Press.

Friedland, Roger and Robert R. Alford. 1991. "Bringing Society Back In: Symbols, Practices, and Institutional Contradictions." Pp. 232–263 in *The New Institutionalism in Organizational Analysis*, edited by Walter W. Powell and Paul J. DiMaggio. Chicago: University of Chicago Press.

Gaarder, Emily. 2011. *Women and the Animal Rights Movement*. Piscataway, NJ: Rutgers University Press.

Gamson, William A. 1990. *The Strategy of Social Protest*. Homewood, IL: Dorsey Press.

Gamson, William A. and David S. Meyer. 1996. "Framing Political Opportunity." Pp.275–290 in *Comparative Perspectives on Social Movements: Political Opportunities, Mobilizing Structures, and Cultural Framings*, edited by Doug McAdam, John D. McCarthy, and Mayer N. Zald. Cambridge: Cambridge University Press.

Ganz, Marshall. 2004. "Why David Sometimes Wins: Strategic Capacity in Social Movements." Pp. 177–198 in *Rethinking Social Movements: Structure, Meaning, and Emotion*, edited by Jeff Goodwin and James M. Jasper. Lanham, MD: Rowman and Littlefield.

Giddens, Anthony. 1984. *The Constitution of Society: Outline of the Theory of Structuration*. Berkeley, CA: University of California Press.

Gitlin, Todd. 1980. *The Whole World is Watching*. Berkeley: University of California Press.

Giugni, Marco. 1998. "Was it Worth the Effort? The Outcomes and Consequences of Social Movements." *Annual Review of Sociology* 98: 371–393.

Goodwin, Jeff and James Jasper. 1999. "Caught in a Winding, Snarling Vine: The Structural Bias of Political Process Theory." *Sociological Forum* 14(1): 27–54.

Gramsci, Antonio. 1988. *A Gramsci Reader: Selected Writings*. Edited by David Forgacs. New York: Schocken Books.

Greenebaum, Jessica. 2012. "Managing Impressions: 'Face-Saving' Strategies of Vegetarians and Vegans." *Humanity & Society* 36(4): 309–325.

Greenhouse, Steven. 1988. "McDonald's Tries Paris, Again." *The New York Times*. June 12. Retrieved October 2, 2015 (www.nytimes.com/1988/06/12/business/mcdonald-s-tries-paris-again.html?pagewanted=all).

Griswold, Wendy. 1983. "The Devil's Techniques: Cultural Legitimation and Social Change." *American Sociological Review* 48(5): 668–680.

Haenfler, Ross, Brett Johnson, and Ellis Jones. 2012. "Lifestyle Movements: Exploring the Intersection of Lifestyle and Social Movements." *Social Movement Studies* 11(1): 1–20.

Haines, Herbert. 1988. *Black Radicals and the Civil Rights Mainstream, 1954–1970*. Knoxville: University of Tennessee Press.

Hall, Stuart, Charles Critcher, Tony Jefferson, John Clarke, and Brian Robert. 1978. *Policing the Crisis: Mugging, the State, and Law and Order*. London: Macmillan.

Hamilton, Robert A. 1990. "State Seeks to Reduce Population of Swans." *The New York Times*. January 14, p. CN16.

Happy Cow. 2015. Retrieved October 10, 2015 (www.happycow.net/).

Haveman, Heather A. and Hayagreeva Rao. 1997. "Structuring a Theory of Moral Sentiments: Institutional and Organizational Coevolution in the Early Thrift Industry." *American Journal of Sociology* 102: 1606–1651.

Haveman, Heather A., Hayagreeva Rao, and Srikanth Paruchuri. 2007. "The Winds of Change: The Progressive Movement and the Bureaucratization of Thrift." *American Sociological Review* 72(1): 117–142.

Hays, Sharon. 1994. "Culture and Agency and the Sticky Problem of Culture." *Sociological Theory* 12(1):57–72.

Heller, Chaia. 2007. "Techne versus Technoscience: Divergent (and Ambiguous) Notions of Food 'Quality' in the French Debate over GM Crops." American Anthropologist 109(4): 603–615.

Herzog, Hal. 1993. "'The Movement Is My Life': The Psychology of Animal Rights Activism." *Journal of Social Issues* 49(1): 103–119.

Hickson, David J. 1987. "Decision-Making at the Top of Organizations." *Annual Review of Sociology* 13: 165–192.

Hitlin, Steven and Glen H. Elder. 2007. "Time, Self, and the Curiously Abstract Concept of Agency." *Sociological Theory* 25(2): 170–191.

HSUS (Humane Society of the United States). 2015. "An HSUS Report: The Welfare of Animals in the Meat, Egg, and Dairy Industries." Retrieved September 30, 2015 (www.humanesociety.org/assets/pdfs/farm/welfare_overview.pdf).

Hulot, Nicolas. 2006. *Pour un Pacte Écologique*. Paris: Calmann-Lévy.

Hunger Report. 1993. *The Hunger Report: 1993*. Providence, RI: The Alan Shawn Feinstein World Hunger Program, Brown University.

Jasper, James. 1997. *The Art of Moral Protest: Culture, Biography, and Creativity in Social Movements*. Chicago: University of Chicago Press.

Jasper, James. 2005. "A Strategic Approach to Collective Action: Looking for Agency in Social-Movement Choices." *Mobilization* 9(1): 1–16.

Jasper, James. 2006a. *Getting Your Way: Strategic Dilemmas in the Real World*. Chicago: University of Chicago Press.

Jasper, James. 2006b. "Emotions and the Microfoundations of Politics: Rethinking Ends and Means." Pp.14–31 in *Emotions, Politics, and Society*, edited by Simon Clarke, Paul Hoggett, and Simon Thompson. London: Palgrave Macmillan.

Jasper, James. 2011. "Emotions and Social Movements: Twenty Years of Theory and Research." *Annual Review of Sociology* 37: 285–303.

Jasper, James and Dorothy Nelkin. 1992. *The Animal Rights Crusade: The Growth of a Moral Protest*. New York: The Free Press.

Jasper, James and Jane Poulsen. 1995. "Recruiting Strangers and Friends: Moral Shocks and Social Networks in Animal Rights and Anti-Nuclear Protests." *Social Problems* 42(4): 493–512.

Johnston, Laurie. 1974. "Protesters Demand the City Shut its 3 Zoos." *The New York Times*. November 18, p. 35.

Keane, Anne. 1997. "'Too Hard to Swallow?' The Palatability of Healthy Eating Advice." Pp.172–192 in *Food, Health and Identity*, edited by Pat Caplan. London: Routledge.

Kete, Kathleen. 1994. *The Beast in the Boudoir: Petkeeping in Nineteenth-Century Paris*. Berkeley: University of California Press.

Koopmans, Ruud. 2005. "The Missing Link Between Structure and Agency: Outline of an Evolutionary Approach to Social Movements." *Mobilization* 10(1): 19–33.

Lakey, George. 1992. "From Tactics to Strategy." Retrieved October 10, 2015 (www.trainingforchange.org/tools/tactics-strategy-0).

Lamont, Michèle. 1992. *Money, Morals, and Manners: The Culture of the French And American Upper-Middle Class*. Chicago: University of Chicago Press.

Lamont, Michèle. 2000. *The Dignity of Working Men: Morality and the Boundaries of Race, Class, and Immigration.* New York: Russell Sage.

Larson, Jeff. 2013. "Social Movements and Tactical Choice." *Sociology Compass* 7: 866–879.

Larson, Jeff and Omar Lizardo. 2015. "An Institutional Logics Approach to the Analysis of Social Movement Fields." *Social Currents* 2(1): 58–80.

Lawson, Carol. 1990. "New Yorkers, etc." *The New York Times.* November 19, p. 50.

Levine, Morgan E., Jorge A. Suarez, Sebastian Brandhorst, Priya Balasubramanian, Chia-Wei Cheng, Federica Madia, Luigi Fontana, Mario G. Mirisola, Jaime Guevara-Aguirre, Junxiang Wan, Giuseppe Passarino, Brian K. Kennedy, Min Wei, Pinchas Cohen, Eileen M. Crimmins, and Valter D. Longo. 2014. "Low Protein Intake Is Associated with a Major Reduction in IGF-1, Cancer, and Overall Mortality in the 65 and Younger but Not Older Population." *Cell Metabolism* 19(3): 407–417.

Libération. 2002. "L'assassin présumé de Pim Fortuyn, protecteur des animaux." *Libération.* May 11, p. 9.

Libération. 2003. "La Veggie Pride. Etre Vegan. Végétalien, végétarien. 40 millions d'escargots. Sites A lire." Retrieved January 20, 2016 (www.liberation.fr/week-end/2003/05/17/la-veggie-pride-etre-vegan-vegetalien-vegetarien-40–millions-d-escargots-sitesa-lire_434043).

Lichterman, Paul. 2006. "Social Capital or Group Style? Rescuing Tocqueville's Insights on Civic Engagement." *Theory and Society* 35: 529–563.

Lounsbury, Michael. 2005. "Institutional Variation in the Evolution of Social Movements: Competing Logics and the Spread of Recycling Advocacy Groups." Pp. 73–95 in *Social Movements and Organization Theory*, edited by Gerald F. Davis, Doug McAdam, W. Richard Scott, and Mayer N. Zald. Cambridge: Cambridge University Press.

March, James G. and Johan P. Olsen. 1989. *Rediscovering Institutions: The Organizational Basis of Politics.* New York: Free Press.

Martin, Patricia Yancey. 1990. "Rethinking Feminist Organizations." *Gender and Society* 4(2): 182–206.

Maurer, Donna. 2002. *Vegetarianism: Movement or Moment?* Philadelphia, PA: Temple University Press.

McAdam, Doug. 1983. "Tactical Innovation and the Pace of Insurgency." *American Sociological Review* 48(6): 735–754.

McAdam, Doug. 1994. "Culture and Social Movements." Pp. 36–57 in *New Social Movements: From Ideology to Identity*, edited by Enrique Laraña, Hank Johnston, and Joseph R. Gusfield. Philadelphia, PA: Temple University Press.

McAdam, Doug. 1996. "Conceptual Origins, Current Problems, Future Directions." Pp. 23–40 in *Comparative Perspectives on Social Movements: Political Opportunities, Mobilizing Structures, and Cultural Framings.* Edited by Doug McAdam, John D. McCarthy, and Mayer N. Zald. Cambridge: Cambridge University Press.

McCammon, Holly, Soma Chaudhuri, Lyndi Hewitt, Courtney Sanders Muse, Harmony Newman, Carrie Lee Smith, and Teresa Terrell. 2008. "Becoming Full Citizens: The U.S. Women's Jury Rights Campaigns, the Pace of Reform, and Strategic Adaptation." *American Journal of Sociology* 113(4): 1104–1147.

McCarthy, John D. and Meyer N. Zald. 1977. "Resource Mobilization and Social Movements: A Partial Theory." *American Journal of Sociology* 8: 1212–1241.

McCormick, Christopher. 1995. *Constructing Danger: The Mis/representation of Crime in the News.* Halifax, Nova Scotia: Fernwood Publishing.

McMahon-Howard, Jody Clay-Warner, and Linda Renzulli. 2009. "Criminalizing Spousal Rape: The Diffusion of Legal Reforms." *Sociological Perspectives* 52(4): 505–531.

Meadows, Michael. 1998. "Making Journalism: The Media as a Cultural Resource." *Australian Journalism Review* 20(2): 1–23.

Melucci, Alberto. 1995. "The Process of Collective Identity." Pp.41–63 in *Social Movements and Culture*, edited by H. Johnston and B. Klandermans. Minneapolis: University of Minnesota Press.

Méry, André. 2002. *Les Végétariens: Raisons et Sentiments.* Tressan, France: Editions La Plage.

Meyer, David S. and Joshua Gamson. 1995. "The Challenge of Cultural Elites: Celebrities and Social Movements." *Sociological Inquiry* 65(2): 181–206.

Meyer, Megan. 2004. "Organizational Identity, Political Contexts, and SMO Action: Explaining the Tactical Choices Made by Peace Organizations in Israel, Northern Ireland, and South Africa." *Social Movement Studies* 3: 167–198.

Moody, Michael and Laurent Thévenot. 2000. "Comparing Models of Strategy, Interests, and the Public Good in French and American Environmental Disputes." Pp.273–306 in *Rethinking Comparative Cultural Sociology: Repertoires of Evaluation in France and the United States*, edited by Michèle Lamont and Laurent Thévenot. Cambridge: Cambridge University Press.

Morris, Aldon. 1984. *The Origins of the Civil Rights Movement: Black Communities Organizing for Change.* New York: The Free Press.

National Beef Cattlemen's Association. 2015. "Average Annual Per Capita Consumption of Meat." Retrieved September 29, 2015 (www.beefusa.org/uDocs/averageannualper capitaconsumptionofmeat.pdf).

Ocasio, William. 1999. "Institutionalized Action and Corporate Governance: The Reliance on Rules of CEO Succession." *Administrative Science Quarterly* 44(2): 384–416.

Oliver, Christine. 1991. "Strategic Responses to Institutional Processes." *Academy of Management Review* 16(1): 145–179.

Olivier, David. 1992. "Qu'est-ce que le spécisme?" *Cahiers Antispécistes* 5.

One Voice. 2014. "L'expérimentation animale en France en 2014: un état des lieux." Retrieved September 30, 2015 (www.one-voice.fr/wp-content/uploads/2015/06/Experimentation-animale-en-France-en-2014.pdf).

Pacelle, Wayne. 2008. "Violence Hurts Us All." Retrieved September 25, 2015 (http://blog.humanesociety.org/wayne/2008/09/nonviolence.html).

Patton, Michael. 2002. *Qualitative Research and Evaluation Methods*, Third Edition. London: Sage.

Pellow, David Naguib. 2014. *Total Liberation: The Power and Promise of Animal Rights and the Radical Earth Movement.* Minneapolis: University of Minnesota Press.

PETA (People for the Ethical Treatment of Animals). 2015a. "'Running of the Bulls' Factsheet." Retrieved September 25, 2015 (www.runningofthenudes.com/bullfighting_facts.asp).

PETA (People for the Ethical Treatment of Animals). 2015b. "Ingrid Newkirk's Biography." Retrieved October 3, 2015 (www.ingridnewkirk.com/).

PETA (People for the Ethical Treatment of Animals). 2015c. "Would You Approve an Experiment That Would Sacrifice 10 Animals to Save 10,000 People?" Retrieved October 3, 2015 (www.peta.org/about-peta/faq/would-you-approve-an-experiment-that-would-sacrifice-10-animals-to-save-10000-people/).

PETA (People for the Ethical Treatment of Animals). 2015d. "Animals Used for Food." Retrieved October 3, 2015 (www.peta.org/issues/animals-used-for-food/).

PETA (People for the Ethical Treatment of Animals). 2015e. "Victory: PETA Wins Shameway Campaign!" Retrieved October 3, 2015 (www.peta.org/about-peta/learn-about-peta/success-stories/farmed-animal-campaigns/shameway/).

Pew Commission on Farm Animal Production. 2009. *Putting Meat on the Table: Industrial Farm Animal Production in America*. Baltimore, MD: The Johns Hopkins Bloomberg School of Public Health.

Pew Research Center. 2002. "The Pew Global Attitudes Project: Among Wealthy Nations, the U.S. Stands Alone in its Embrace of Religion." Retrieved October 6, 2015 (www.pewglobal.org/files/pdf/167.pdf).

Pfeffer, Jeffrey and Gerald R. Salancik. 1978. *The External Control of Organizations: A Resource Dependence Perspective*. New York: Harper and Row.

Pifer, Linda, Kinya Shimizu, and Ralph Pifer. 1994. "Public Attitudes Toward Animal Research: Some International Comparisons." *Society and Animals* 2(2): 95–113.

Polletta, Francesca. 1999. "Snarls, Quacks, and Quarrels: Culture and Structure in Political Process Theory." *Sociological Forum* 14(1): 63–70.

Polletta, Francesca. 2004. "Culture is Not Just in Your Head." Pp. 97–110 in *Rethinking Social Movements: Structure, Meaning, and Emotion*, edited by Jeff Goodwin and James Jasper. Lanham, MD: Rowman and Littlefield.

Polletta, Francesca and James Jasper. 2001. "Collective Identity and Social Movements." *Annual Review of Sociology* 27: 283–305.

Potter, Will. 2006. "Industry Group Picks Up the Pace, Hopes to Rush Through 'Eco-terrorism' Law." Retrieved September 25, 2015 (www.greenisthenewred.com/blog/nabr-ad-rollcall/104/).

Potter, Will. 2008. "Humane Society Defends Donation to Eco-Terrorism Witch Hunt." Retrieved September 25, 2015 (www.greenisthenewred.com/blog/humane-society-defends-green-scare-donation/644/).

Potter, Will. 2011. *Green is the New Red: An Insider's Account of a Social Movement Under Siege*. San Francisco: City Lights Books.

Potter, Will. 2012a. "New Grand Jury Subpoenas Related to UC-Santa Cruz Investigation." Retrieved September 25, 2015 (www.greenisthenewred.com/blog/grand-jury-uc-santa-cruz-california/6104/).

Potter, Will. 2012b. "'I plan on Exercising Every Right that I Have' to Oppose California Grand Jury, Activist Says." Retrieved September 25, 2015 (www.greenisthenewred.com/blog/california-grand-jury-animal-rights-brittany-kenville/6623/)

Potter, Will. 2013. "Breaking: Another Activist Subpoenaed to California Grand Jury." Retrieved September 25, 2015 (www.greenisthenewred.com/blog/california-grand-investigating-animal-rights-activists/6682/).

Preventative Medicine Research Institute. 2015. "Preventative Medicine Research Institute." Retrieved September 29, 2015 (www.pmri.org/).

Project Censored. 2010. "#20 Terror Act Against Animal Activists." Retrieved September 25, 2015 (www.projectcensored.org/20-terror-act-against-animal-activists/).

Quinn, Robert E. and John Rohrbaugh. 1981. "A Competing Values Approach to Organizational Effectiveness." *Public Productivity Review* 5(2): 122–140.

Ragin, Charles C. 1987. *The Comparative Method: Moving Beyond Qualitative and Quantitative Strategies*. Berkeley, CA: University of California Press.

Rao, Hayagreeva, Calvin Morrill, and Mayer N. Zald. 2000. "Power Plays: How Social Movements and Collective Action Create New Organizational Forms." *Research in Organizational Behaviour* 22:237–281.

Regan, Tom. 1975. "The Moral Basis of Vegetarianism." *Canadian Journal of Philosophy* 2: 181–214.

Regan, Tom. 1983. *The Case for Animal Rights*. Berkeley: University of California Press.

Revol, Anne-Marie. 1998. "Le Delire Terroriste des Amis des Bêtes". *Le Figaro*. December 4.

Rich, Motoko. 2007. "A Diet Book Serves Up a Side Order of Attitude." Retrieved September 29, 2015 (www.nytimes.com/2007/08/01/books/01skin.html).

Rose, Arnold. 1968. "Law and the Causation of Social Problems." *Social Problems* 16(1): 33–43.

Ruef, Martin and W. Richard Scott. 1998. "A Multidimensional Model of Organizational Legitimacy: Hospital Survival in Changing Institutional Environments." *Administrative Science Quarterly* 43: 877–904.

Saguy, Abigail. 2013. *What's Wrong with Fat?* New York: Oxford University Press.

Samuel, Henry. 2007. "France 'No Longer a Catholic Country.'" *The Telegraph*, January 10. Retrieved October 6, 2015 (www.telegraph.co.uk/news/worldnews/1539093/France-no-longer-a-Catholic-country.html).

Schlosser, Eric. 2001. *Fast Food Nation: The Dark Side of the All-American Meal*. New York: Houghton Mifflin.

Schneiberg, Marc and Sarah A. Soule. 2005. "Institutionalization as a Contested, Multilevel Process: The Case of Rate Regulation in American Fire Insurance." Pp. 122–160 in *Social Movements and Organization Theory*, edited by Gerald F. Davis, Doug McAdam, W. Richard Scott, and Mayer N. Zald. Cambridge: Cambridge University Press.

Schneiberg, Marc, Marissa King, and Thomas Smith. 2008. "Social Movements and Organizational Form: Cooperative Alternatives to Corporations in the American Insurance, Dairy, and Grain Industries." *American Sociological Review* 73(4): 635–667.

Schofer, Evan and Marion Fourcade-Gourinchas. 2001. "The Structural Contexts of Civic Engagement: Voluntary Association Membership in Comparative Perspective." *American Sociological Review* 66(6): 806–828.

Schurman, Rachel. 2004. "Fighting 'Frankenfoods': Industry Opportunity Structures and the Efficacy of the Anti-Biotech Movement in Western Europe." *Social Problems* 51(2): 243–268.

Scott, Suzanne G. and Vicki R. Lane. 2000. "A Stakeholder Approach to Organizational Identity." *The Academy of Management Review* 25(1): 43–62.

Scully, Matthew. 2002. *Dominion: The Power of Man, the Suffering of Animals, and the Call to Mercy*. New York: St. Martin's Press.

Seijts, Gerard H., Gary P. Latham, Kevin Tasa, and Brandon W. Latham. 2004. "Goal Setting and Goal Orientation: An Integration of Two Different yet Related Literatures." *Academy of Management Journal* 47: 227–239.

Selznick, Philip. 1957. *Leadership in Administration: A Sociological Interpretation*. New York: Harper and Row.

Sewell, William. 1992. "A Theory of Structure: Duality, Agency, and Transformation." *American Journal of Sociology* 98: 1–29.

Shprintzen, Adam D. 2013. *The Vegetarian Crusade: The Rise of an American Reform Movement, 1817–1921*. Chapel Hill, NC: University of North Carolina Press.

Simon, Stephanie. 2001. "THE NATION; For All of God's Creatures; Activists for Animals Are Finding a Receptive Audience in the Faith Community, Including on the Religious Right." *Los Angeles Times*, November 6, A 12.

Simons, Marlise. 2001. "Paris Journal; Gastronomes Have a Beef with a Renouncing Chef." *The New York Times*, February 9. Retrieved October 2, 2015 (www.nytimes.com/2001/02/09/world/paris-journal-gastronomes-have-a-beef-with-a-renouncing-chef.html).

Singer, Peter. 1975. *Animal Liberation*. New York: Avon Books.

Singer, Peter. 2009. *The Life You Can Save: Acting Now to End World Poverty*. New York: Random House.

Singer, Peter. 2015. *The Most Good You Can Do: How Effective Altruism is Changing Ideas about Living Ethically*. Melbourne, Australia: Text Publishing.

Smith, Jackie, John D. McCarthy, Clark McPhail, and Boguslaw Augustyn. 2001. "From Protest to Agenda Building: Description Bias in Media Coverage of Protest Events in Washington, D.C." *Social Forces* 79(4): 1397–1423.

Smithey, Lee. 2009. "Social Movement Strategy, Tactics, and Collective Identity." *Sociology Compass* 3(4): 658–671.

Snow, David, Burke Rochford, Steven Worden, and Robert Benford. 1986. "Frame Alignment Processes, Micromobilization, and Movement Participation." *American Sociological Review* 51: 464–481.

Soule, Sarah A. and Jennifer Earl. 2001. "The Enactment of State-Level Hate Crime Law in the United States: Intrastate and Interstate Factors." *Sociological Perspectives* 44(3): 281–305.

Spencer, Colin. 1995. *The Heretic's Feast: A History of Vegetarianism*. London: Fourth Estate.

Spock, Benjamin. 1998. *Baby and Child Care: A Handbook for Parents of the Developing Child from Birth Through Adolescence*. New York: Dutton.

Stallwood, Kim. 2002. "Stages." *The Animals' Agenda* March/April.

Swidler, Ann. 1986. "Culture in Action: Symbols and Strategies." *American Sociological Review* 51: 273–286.

Swidler, Ann. 2001. "What Anchors Cultural Practices." Pp.74–92 in *The Practice Turn in Contemporary Theory*, edited by Theodore R. Schatzki, Karin Knorr Cetina, and Eike von Savigny. London: Routledge.

Taylor, Verta and Nancy Whittier. 1992. "Collective Identity in Social Movement Communities: Lesbian Feminist Mobilization." Pp.104–129 in *Frontiers in Social Movement Theory*, edited by Aldon D. Morris and Carol McClurg Mueller. New Haven, CT: Yale University Press.

Thompson, James D. 1967. *Organizations in Action*. New York: McGraw-Hill.

Thornton, Patricia H. and William Ocasio. 1999. "Institutional Logics and the Historical Contingency of Power in Organizations: Executive Succession in the Higher Education Publishing Industry, 1958–1990." *American Journal of Sociology* 105: 801–843.

Thornton, Patricia H., William Ocasio, and Michael Lounsbury. 2012. *The Institutional Logics Perspective: A New Approach to Culture, Structure, and Process*. Oxford: Oxford University Press.

Tilly, Charles. 1978. *From Mobilization to Revolution*. Reading, MA: Addison-Wesley.

Tilly, Charles. 1979. "Repertoires of Contention in America and Britain, 1750–1830." Pp. 126–155 in *The Dynamics of Social Movements*, edited by Mayer N. Zald and John McCarthy. Cambridge, MA: Winthrop.

Tilly, Charles. 1986. *The Contentious French*. Cambridge, MA: Harvard University Press.

Tilly, Charles. 1995. *Popular Contention in Great Britain, 1758–1834*. Cambridge, MA: Harvard University Press.

Tilly, Charles. 2006. *Regimes and Repertoires*. Chicago: University of Chicago Press.

Touraine, Alain. 1977. *The Self-Production of Society*. Chicago: University of Chicago Press.

United States Department of Agriculture. 2002. "Profiling Food Consumption in America." Retrieved September 29, 2015 (www.usda.gov/factbook/chapter2.htm).

Unti, Bernard. 2004. *Protecting All Animals: A Fifty-Year History of The Humane Society of the United States*. Gaithersburg, MD: Humane Society Press.

U.S. Fish and Wildlife Service. 2011. "2011 National Survey of Fishing, Hunting, and Wildlife-Associated Recreation." Retrieved October 2, 2015 (www.census.gov/prod/2012pubs/fhw11–nat.pdf).

USA Today. 2005. "Animal Activist Groups Praise Santorum." June 27. Retrieved October 15, 2015 (http://usatoday30.usatoday.com/news/washington/2005-06-27-santorum-animals_x.htm).

Veggie Pride. 2015. "Foire aux questions." Retrieved October 3, 2015 (www.veggiepride.org/foire-aux-questions/).

Veggie Pride NYC. 2015. "Official Press Release: Veggie Pride Parade NYC 2015." Retrieved October 3, 2015 (www.veggieprideparade.org/dept/pr.htm).

Waldau, Paul. 2001. *The Specter of Speciesism: Buddhist and Christian Views of Animals*. Oxford: Oxford University Press.

Ward, Jane. 2000. "A New Kind of AIDS: Adapting to the Success of Protease Inhibitors in an AIDS Care Organization." *Qualitative Sociology* 23(3): 247–265.

Weber, Max. 1978. *Economy and Society*. Berkeley: University of California Press.

Welfarm. 2015. "Nos success." Retrieved September 26, 2015 (http://pmaf.org/nous-connaitre/nos-succes.html).

Williams, Rhys. 1995. "Constructing the Public Good: Social Movements and Cultural Resources." *Social Problems* 42(1): 124–144.

Williams, Rhys. 2002. "From the 'Beloved Community' to 'Family Values': Religious Language, Symbolic Repertoires, and Democratic Culture." Pp. 247–265 in *Social Movements: Identity, Culture, and the State*, edited by David Meyer, Nancy Whittier, and Belinda Robnett. Oxford: Oxford University Press.

Williams, Rhys and Timothy Kubal. 1999. "Movement Frames and the Cultural Environment: Resonance, Failure, and the Boundaries of the Legitimate." *Research in Social Movements, Conflicts, and Change* 21: 225–248.

Writers Reps. 2015. "Dominion." Retrieved October 6, 2015 (www.writersreps.com/Dominion).

Zald, Mayer N. 1996. "Culture, Ideology, and Strategic Framing." Pp. 261–274 in *Comparative Perspectives on Social Movements: Political Opportunities, Mobilizing Structures, and Cultural Framings*, edited by Doug McAdam, John D. McCarthy, and Mayer N. Zald. Cambridge: Cambridge University Press.

Zald, Mayer N. 2000. "Ideologically Structured Action: An Enlarged Agenda for Social Movement Research." *Mobilization* 5(1): 1–16.

Index

AAVS (American Anti-Vivisection Society) 13
abattoirs 12
abolitionism 13, 17, 129, 131, 134–5
ACE (Animal Charity Evaluators) 115, 118, 120
activism: analysis of 148–9; campaign-style 22; considered a cult in France 39–42, 98; and culture 7–8, 10; environmental 28; see also animal entertainment; animal rights movement; animal testing; bullfighting; cockfighting; dogfighting; farmed animals; fur; vivisection
activists: arrest and fining of 18; as extremists 90–1, 98; implications of research for 150–3; perspectives of 148–9; property destruction by 18; sacrifices and compromises made by 134; selection of tactics by 147; as terrorists 93–8
Adams, Carol J. 17
adoption centers 21
ADS see l'Armée des Douze Singes
advertising 20, 76–7, 85, 87, 119, 120
AEPA (Animal Enterprise Protection Act) 96–8
Aequalis Aniamal (Animal Equality) 22
agency: consumer 72; and culture 6, 8, 145, 150; individual 140; and strategy 8; and structure 7–8
Agulhon, Maurice 14, 15, 38
ALF see Animal Liberation Front
Alford, Robert 108
Alliance Végétarienne 22, 41; see also Association Végétarienne de France

Alliance Végétarienne (journal) 22
altruism, effective 120
American Anti-Vivisection Society (AAVS) 13
American Dietetic Association 43–4, 48, 57
American Humane Association 13–14
American Society for Prevention of Cruelty to Animals (ASPCA) 5, 13, 14
American Vegetarian Society 15
Amory, Cleveland 14
anarchism 21
Anderson, Pamela 78–80, 88
Angeli, Ève 88
animal activism see activism; activists
animal adoption 78
animal agriculture see factory farms and farming; farmed animals
Animal Charity Evaluators (ACE) 115, 118, 120
Animal Enterprise Protection Act (AEPA) 96–8
Animal Enterprise Terrorist Act (AETA) 6, 75, 96–8, 141
animal entertainment 3, 12, 152; see also bullfighting; circuses; zoos
animal equality 16, 131
animal experimentation see animal testing
Animal Fighting Prohibition Act (2007) 152
animal liberation(s) 17, 99, 135, 147, 153
Animal Liberation (Singer) 16, 17, 120, 134
Animal Liberation Front (ALF) 18, 19, 75, 77, 90, 93, 95, 98, 99; ALF Credo 18–19
animal protection movement 13, 14, 23, 145

animal research *see* animal testing
animal rights 129; objection to term 36; as
  secular ethical issue 38; and veganism
  70–1; welfare vs. abolition debate 122
animal rights activism *see* activism
animal rights activists *see* activists
Animal Rights conference 120
animal rights movement: and
  environmentalism 28–33, 56; first wave
  17–19, 145; ideological divides in
  France 129–32; second wave 3, 19–21,
  145; philosophies of 16–17; radical
  flank of 18
Animal Rights National Conference 19
animal shelters 3, 15
animal suppliers, violence against 17
animal testing 3, 5, 6, 13, 14, 17, 19,
  123; on dogs 6, 14–15, 151; federal
  guidelines on 151; federally funded
  18; in France 30; precautions against
  activists 81
Animal Welfare Act (1966) 151; 1985
  amendment 151
Animale Amnistie 9, 84, 85, 125, 128
animals: used for clothing 3; cruelty to 13,
  18, 29–30, 51; used for entertainment
  3, 12, 152; exploitation of 3, 13, 14, 17,
  18, 61, 65, 90, 115; used for food 3;
  used for fur 3; human dominion over 15,
  34–5; of 17; slaughter of 12, 14, 115; as
  "subjects of a life" 16; *see also* animal
  testing; companion animals; farmed
  animals
Animals, Property, and the Law
  (Francione) 17
anthropocentrism 31, 38, 57
anti-cult laws 40
anti-fur campaigns *see* fur; fur protests
anti-GMO movements 4, 6, 54–5
antispeciesism 17, 55, 56, 129, 130, 132,
  137–8; in France 20–1, 127; *see also*
  speciesism
Antispécistes Lyon 64, 92
antivivisectionism 15, 131–2, 145; *see also*
  vivisection
Arnal, Muriel 22
artifact analysis 10
ASPCA *see* American Society for
  Prevention of Cruelty to Animals

Association des Dieteticiens de Langue
  Française 48
Association Végétarienne de France (AVF)
  9, 16, 17, 22, 23, 37, 39–41, 50–3, 56,
  60, 66, 68, 70, 73, 85, 87, 125, 126,
  128, 136–7; *see also* Alliance
  Végétarienne
Atkins Diet 47, 48
Atkins, Robert 48
ATLAS.ti software 10
AVF *see* Association Végétarienne de
  France
AVIS *see* l'Association Végétarienne &
  Végétalienne d'InformationS

baboons, liberation of 17–18
Baby and Child Care (Spock) 44
Ball, Matt 19
Banaszak, Lee Ann 140
Bardot, Brigitte 4, 5, 22, 39, 86, 88–9
Barnouin, Kim 48
Battle Creek Sanitarium 15
Becker, Howard 30, 45
Beckham, Victoria, 48
Becoming the Change (conference) 33–4,
  76, 96, 98
Bergh, Henry 13, 14
Berman, Richard 95
Bernard, Claude 15
Bernard-Pellet, Jérôme 85
Bernsetin, Mary 6
bioethicists 151
BirdLife International 32
birds, protection of, 32; *see also* chickens
Bonnardel, Yves 20–1, 71
Bourdain, Anthony 49
Bourdieu, Pierre 7, 60
Bové, José 4
bovine spongiform encephalopathy (BSE)
  43
Brigades Vertes (Green Brigade) 17
Brillat-Savarin, Jean Anthelme 59
Britain, animal rights activism and
  awareness in 3–4, 50, 152
Brown University 28
bull-baiting 12
bullfighting 4, 12, 32, 61, 62–3, 64, 84, 86,
  92, 124–5
Burdivega 29

Cahiers Antispécistes 21, 71
Cahiers Antispécistes Lyonnais 20–1
cancer, linked to diet 43
CAP *see* Collectif Antispéciste de Paris
Carroll, William 75, 92
cart-horse drivers 12, 14
Case for Animal Rights The (Regan) 16
Cathars (religious sect) 39–40
cats: as companion animals 13, 125,
    130; used in laboratory testing 6, 151;
    protection of 32
Cavalieri, Paola 21
celebrity endorsements 10; in France 86–9;
    in the U.S. 78–80, 99
Center for Consumer Freedom (CCF) 95
Centre Nationale de la Recherche
    Scientifique (CNRS) 17–18
Chasse-Pêche-Nature-Traditions (Hunting-
    Fishing-Nature-Tradition; CPNT) 62–3
chickens 3, 20, 22, 121
chimpanzees, used in laboratory testing
    151; *see also* primates
Christian Vegetarian Association (CVA)
    34–8, 42
circuses 22, 152; *see also* animal
    entertainment
Civil Rights movement 116–17, 140
CIWF (Compassion in World Farming) 22
CLAP *see* Collectif de Libération à Paris
climate change 29
CNRS (Centre Nationale de la Recherche
    Scientifique) 17–18
cockfighting 5, 12, 62, 152
Coffe, Jean-Pierre 49
COK *see* Compassion Over Killing
Cole, Matthew 66
Collectif Antispéciste de Paris (CAP) 9,
    21, 30, 39, 55, 63, 70, 125, 130–1, 136
Collectif de Libération à Paris (CLAP) 21
college students, as target of vegetarian/
    vegan outreach 19
Comité Radicalement Anti-Corrida
    (CRAC) 62, 84, 87
Commando Lynx 17
commercials 119; *see also* advertising
companion animals 3, 4, 12–13, 22;
    affection for 125, 130; mistreatment of
    15; protection of 21–22, 130; testing on
    22, 130; *see also* cats; dogs

Compassion in World Farming (CIWF)
    22
Compassion Over Killing (COK) 19, 20,
    73, 116–139
Concentrated Animal Feeding Operations
    (CAFOs) 28
Confédération Paysanne 4
consistency: in France 140–2, 148; of
    individuals with organizational ideology
    in 127–8; of organizational ideology and
    tactics in 127–8; of personal practices
    in 124–6
corrida see bullfighting
Cox, Chris W. 95
CRAC *see* Comité Radicalement Anti-
    Corrida
Cromwell, James 78
Crozier, Michel 64
cultural resources 10, 27–8, 147;
    contextuality of 101–2; *see also*
    environment; food; health; media;
    religion; terrorism
culture: and activism 6–8, 10; and
    institutional logics 139–41; shaping
    repertoires 147; and social structure 7–8,
    108–9; as "toolkit" 27, 105, 110; *see
    also* cultural resources
CVA *see* Christian Vegetarian
    Association

dairy product consumption 16–17, 43, 44
De Soucey, Michaela 64
Demarquette, Jacques Colin 16
Deschanel, Emily 78
dietary reform 15
Dietitians of Canada 43
Dillard, Courtney 112
direct mail 118
discrimination, based on species 17, 129
dogfighting 5, 80, 151–2
dogs: and bull-baiting 12; as companion
    animals 13, 125, 130; in France 4;
    used in laboratory testing 6, 14–15,
    151; liberation of 17; protection of 32;
    sympathy toward 118
domestic animals *see* companion animals
*Dominion: The Power of Man, the
    Suffering of Animals, and the Call to
    Mercy* (Scully) 35

Downey, Dennis 123, 141
Downey, Liam 106, 109–10
Dunayer, Joan 21

E. coli 43
Earl, Jennifer 151, 152
Earth Liberation Front (ELF) 75, 96
Earthlings (film) 78
ecofeminism 17; *see also* feminism
ecoterrorism 75, 93–5, 96, 98
"Effective Advocacy: Planning for
    Success" (PETA) 120
Effective Animal Activism 120; *see also*
    Animal Charity Evaluators
effective altruism 120
effectiveness 118–22
egg production 3, 121; *see also* chickens
Einwohner, Rachel 150
Eisman, George 46
ELF *see* Earth Liberation Front
Eliasoph, Nina 140
Emirbayer 8
environmentalism 28–33, 56
ethnography 10
Evans, Erin 77, 151

factory farms and farming 14, 19, 21, 28,
    113, 145; *see also* Concentrated Animal
    Feeding Operations (CAFOs)
Fantasia, Rick 64
FARM (Farm Animal Rights Movement)
    19
farm animal advocacy 22–3
Farm Animal Rights Movement (FARM)
    19
Farm Sanctuary 78
farmed animals 3, 4, 5, 13, 20, 22, 23;
    eating of 125; as majority of animals
    killed 3, 115, 121; slaughter of 12, 14,
    22; transport of 14
fast food 64, 74
Fast Food Nation (Schlosser) 43, 46
Faunalytics 117–18, 120
Fédération des Luttes pour l'Abolition des
    Corridas (FLAC) 62
feminism 148; *see also* ecofeminism
Ferguson, Priscilla Parkhurst 58, 59, 60
Fischler, Claude 64
flyers 33, 36, 37–8, 131

foie gras production 4, 30, 61, 62–5
Fondation Brigitte Bardot 5, 22; *see also*
    Bardot, Brigitte
Fortuyn, Pim 90
Fourcade-Gourinchas, Marion 6
France: activists considered cultists in
    39–42, 98; ambivalence of military
    imagery in 98–100; animal cruelty
    in 12, 30; animal rights activism in
    3–6, 11; animal rights movement
    compared to U.S. 6–7, 10, 23; animal
    testing in 30; antispeciesism in 20–1;
    antivivisection in 15, 123; celebrity
    endorsements in 86–9; compared to
    U.S. 133–9; consistency in 140–2,
    148; consistency of individuals with
    organizational ideology in 127–8;
    consistency of organizational ideology
    and tactics in 127–8; consistency of
    personal practices in 124–6; culinary
    traditions in 61–5, 74; cultural
    opportunities and obstacles in
    53–4, 145, 147; debates over health
    arguments in 54–7; environmental
    activism in 28–29; first wave
    animal rights movement in 17–18;
    gastronomy in 58–61, 74; historical
    national repertoires in 139; ideological
    divides in 129–32; love of animals
    in 4, 125, 130; misconceptions about
    vegetarianism in 51–3; pragmatism
    in 136; second wave animal rights
    21–3; U.S. influences in 136–9;
    veganism viewed as deadly in 48–51;
    vegetarianism in 16, 22–3
Francione, Gary 17
Freedman, Rory 48
Freedom in Peril (NRA) 95
Friedland, Roger 108
Fuhrmann, Irene 22
Fund for Animals 14, 111–12
fur 17, 19, 20, 21, 111, 125, 126
fur animals 22
fur protests 82–3, 115, 118

gastronationalism 64
gastronomy 58–61, 74, 123
Gaultier, Jean-Paul 84, 89
gay rights 140

Giddens, Anthony 7
Gitlin, Todd 82, 90
Giugni, Marco 136
globalization 4, 64
"going green" 28
Goodwin, Jeff 8, 101
Gore, Al 28
government surveillance 99–100
Graham, Sylvester 15
Grammont, Jacques-Philippe Demas de 15
Grammont Law 15
grassroots organizations 114
Great American Meatout (U.S.) 19, 58
Green Party 32
Green political parties 28
"green" lifestyle choices 28
"Green Scare" 98
Greenebaum, Jessica 73
Greenpeace 75, 76, 92
Greystoke 99
Griswold, Wendy 7
group style 140

habitus, of activists 147
Haenfler, Ross 124
Hardy, Tom 78
hate crimes legislation 151, 152
Hays, Sharon 7
health arguments: in France 54–7; in the
    U.S. 46–8
Hegins protests 111–12
hens *see* chickens
hoof and mouth disease 43
Horne, Barry 90
horses 12, 14, 15
HSUS *see* Humane Society of the United
    States
Hulot, Nicolas 4, 28
Humane Methods of Slaughter Act 14
humane movement 13; *see also* animal
    protection movement; animal rights
    movement
Humane Research Council 117–18
Humane Society of the United States
    (HSUS) 5, 14, 95, 96, 111, 113, 118,
    121, 149
humanism 21, 31, 38
hunting 3, 14, 17, 19, 21, 61, 63, 111,
    124–5; of baby seals 22

identity/ies: collective 71; French national
    63–5; morally coherent 127; social
    movement 105, 107, 108, 110, 127–8;
    vegan 71, 149; welfarist 134
An Inconvenient Truth (Gore) 28
Institut Pasteur de Lille 51
institutional isomorphism 105, 107, 133,
    137
institutional logic 114, 147; and culture
    139–41
institutional theory 124
instrumentalism 16
International Campaigns 9, 125–6
internet 86
interviews, in-depth 8, 9–10

Jarboe, James F. 93
Jasper, James 8, 16, 31, 101, 107, 127

Kant, Immanuel 16
Kellogg, John Harvey 15
Kemmerer, Lisa 33–4
Kete, Kathleen 14

L214 63
La Loi Grammont 15
lab animals 22; *see also* animal testing;
    vivisection
Laboratory Animal Welfare Act 18
Lamont, Michèle 139
LaPierre, Wayne 95
l'Armée des Douze Singes ("Army of the
    Twelve Monkeys"; ADS) 37, 123, 131
l'Arpège (restaurant) 60, 61
Larson, Jeff 106, 107, 110
l'Association Végétarienne &
    Végétalienne d'InformationS (AVIS) 9,
    23, 54, 68, 88
LEA 21
leafleting 19–20, 120
leather 3, 55, 67, 78, 90, 100, 126
LeCerf, Jean-Marie 51
Le Glaive 9, 84
Les Cahiers Antispecistes 132
"Les Estivales de la Question Animale"
    21, 50, 99, 100, 148
Liberty University 35
Lichterman, Paul 140, 141
The Life You Can Save (Singer) 120

"Lifestyle Management Program" (Ornish) 44
lifestyle movements 124, 127
Ligue pour la Protection des Oiseaux (LPO) 32
Lizardo, Omar 110
lobbying 22, 53, 95, 112, 145
Lyman, Howard 46

McAdam, Douglas 6, 101, 105
McCammon, Holly 105
McCartney, Paul 79
McMahon-Howard, Jennifer 151, 152
mad cow disease 43, 53
Maison de l'Environnement 29
Mamère, Noël 32
marital rape legislation 151, 152
market research 77–8
Meadows, Michael 75
meat-borne illnesses 43
meat consumption: reduction in 51; in the U.S. 44–5; viewed as unhealthy 43
meat production 3
meat recall 43
Meatless Mondays 28
media coverage 10, 75, 152; in France 83–6, 89–91; internet 86; negative 80–3; social media 86; U.S. strategies 76–8
medicine, and vivisection 13
"Mention V" label 68, 73
Mercy for Animals 19, 73
milk production 3
Monaghan, Dominic 78
monkeys, used for research 18; *see also* primates
Moody, Michael 139–40
"The Moral Basis of Vegetarianism" (Regan) 16
Morgan, Karen 66
Morris, Aldon 116
The Most Good You Can Do (Singer) 120

National Association for Biomedical Research (NABR) 98
National Humane Society 14; *see also* Humane Society of the United States (HSUS)
National Institutes of Health (NIH) 18, 151
National Organization of Women 86

National Rifle Association 95
naturalism 21
Nelkin, Dorothy 16
neoinstitutional theory 129
néo-végétarianisme ("new vegetarianism") 51, 52–3, 66
new institutional theory 129
New Left 82, 90
Newkirk, Ingrid 18, 134
NIH *see* National Institutes of Health
Nihous, Frédéric 62
Noailles, Comtesse de 15
Noé (Noah) 22
Norris, Jack 19, 47, 72
Notin, Charles 22
NYSE Hostage 95

obesity 47, 53
Olivier, David 17, 20–1
One Voice 5, 6, 22, 123, 130
open rescues 20
Operation Greystroke 17
oppression, of women and animals 17
organizational behavior 105–7
organizational strategies 146
organizational theory 139
Ornish, Dean 44

Pacheco, Alex 18
Pacte Ecologique 28
paleo diet 48
Pariset, Étienne 14
participant observation 8, 9
Passard, Alain 5, 60, 61
patrimoine culturel 62–3, 74
Pellow, David Naguib 95
People for the Ethical Treatment of Animals (PETA) 5, 17, 18, 19, 49, 75–9, 84, 91, 96, 114, 120, 121, 127, 128, 137; philosophical stance of 134–5
PETA *see* People for the Ethical Treatment of Animals
PETA France 53, 56, 85–6, 88, 89, 136–7
petitions 123, 130
pets *see* companion animals 15
philosophies, of animal rights 16–17
Phoenix, Joachim 78
pigeon shoot protest 17, 111–12
pigs, used in laboratory testing 151

plant-based diets *see* veganism;
    vegetarianism
PMAF *see* Protection Mondiale des
    Animaux de Ferme
pollution, from CAFOs, 28
Potter, Will 95, 98
Pour l'égalite Animale 21
pragmatism 11, 112–13, 115, 135; in
    French organizations 136; in the U.S.
    140–2, 148
primates, used in laboratory testing 17–18,
    151
Prior, Karen Swallow 35
Product Launch Analytics 68–9
programme national nutrition santé
    (PNNS) 54
property destruction, by activists 18
Protection Mondiale des Animaux de
    Ferme (PMAF; Worldwide Protection
    of Animal Farms) 5, 22, 65, 86; *see also*
    Welfarm
public health 14
puppy mill legislation 121

qualitative analysis 10

racism 17, 127, 129, 131
Ratner, R. S. 75, 92
Rebato, Stephanie 49, 91
recruitment 10, 75
refuges 21
Regan, Lauren 98
Regan, Tom 16, 80–1
Reisler, Lionel 22
religion 33; as cultural challenge in
    France 37–9; cultural context of 101; as
    cultural tool in the U.S. 33–7, 152; and
    vegetarianism 33
Renaud 86–7
repertoires 146; shaped by culture 147;
    symbolic 146–7
research laboratories, sale of pound
    animals to 14
research: analysis of 10; implications for
    activists 150–3; limitations of 150;
    methods, 8–10; and policy solutions
    150–3
resource mobilization 113–16; *see also*
    cultural resources

Reus, Estiva 21
Riesler, Marie 22
The Road to Wellville (film) 15
Roberts, Peter 22
rodents, used in laboratory testing 151
Rohlinger, Deana 106, 109–10, 123, 141
Royal Society for the Prevention of
    Cruelty to Animals (RSPCA) 13
Running of the Bulls 92
Running of the Nudes 92
Ryder, Richard 17

Sacco, Patrick 99
Salomon, Yves 91
Salon de l'Environnement 29
Santorum, Rick 121
Sarkozy, Nicolas 62
Schlosser, Eric 43
Schofer, Evan 6
Scully, Matthew 35
SDS 90
Sea Shepherd Conservation Society 76,
    96
Senate Agricultural Committee (U.S.) 28
Seventh Day Adventists 37
sexism 17, 127, 129
*The Sexual Politics of Meat: A Feminist-
    Vegetarian Critical Theory* (Adams) 17
Shapiro, Paul 20
Shprintzen, Adam 15
Shrigley, Elsie 16
Sierra Club 29
Silver Spring monkeys case 18
Silverstone, Alicia 78
Singer, Peter 16, 17, 21, 120, 131
Skinny Bitch (Freedman and Barnouin) 48
slaughterhouses (abattoirs) 12
smoking 54
social media 86
social movement organizations (SMOs)
    11, 105–6, 136, 141; culture of 8,
    108–9; effectiveness of 118–22; field
    approach to 106; French 135; U.S.
    133; institutional logics of 110, 115,
    121; learning process of 117–18;
    organizational behavior of 105–7;
    strategies and tactics of 107–8; success
    of 145–6
Société Française contre la Vivisection 15

Société Protectrice des Animaux (SPA) 5, 14–15, 21
SOS *see* Speak Out for Species
SOS Animaux (TV show) 22
Soule, Sarah 151, 152
SPA *see* Société Protectrice des Animaux
Speak Out for Species (SOS) 9, 36, 37, 45–7, 81
speciesism 17, 20–1, 127; *see also* antispeciesism
Spock, Benjamin 44
Standard American Diet 47
Stop Gavage 32, 62, 63, 66, 124, 136–7
strategy: and agency 8; components of 107; and decision-making 11; meso-level approach to strategic choices 108–10; organizational 146
structure: and agency 7–8; culture as 7–8
suffering, diminishing of 16, 19, 115, 125
Summit for Animals 141
Swidler, Ann 27, 109, 146
Swit, Loretta 78

tabling events 9, 38, 39, 40, 51, 52, 54, 81, 84, 125, 131, 150
Tahin Party 21
Taub, Edward 18
theory of value–rationality 129
Thévenot, Laurent 139–40
Tilly, Charles 146–7
Touraine, Alain 109
trapping 3, 14

Un Monde Vegan 70
Union National des Végétariens (UNV) 22
United Egg Producers 20
United Kingdom *see* Britain
United States: animal cruelty in 12; animal rights activism in 3–4, 5, 6, 11; animal rights movements compared to France 6–7, 10, 23, 133–9; celebrity endorsements in 78–80; counter-movements in 95–8; culture as beneficial in 145; first wave animal rights movement in 18–19, 111; health arguments and "health crazes" in 46–8; historical national repertoires in 139; influences on French organizations 136–9; inconsistent choices in 133–6;

media strategies in 78, 152; pragmatism in 112–22, 132, 135, 140–2, 148; use of religion in 33–7, 152; second wave of animal rights activism in 19–20, 113, 117, 121; veganism seen as healthy in 43–6
University of Pennsylvania Head Injury Lab 18
Unnecessary Fuss (film) 18
utiltarianism 16, 131, 132, 134

value-rationality 129
van der Graff, Volkert 90
veal production 14, 83
Vegan Day (France) 58, 70
Vegan Outreach 114–16, 114–16, 122, 148
Vegan Society 15–16
vegan/vegetarian foods: availability of 68–70; promotion of 58; *see also* vegetarian restaurants
vegan/vegetarian outreach 19, 21, 113, 126; on college campuses 19; in France 66–70; in U.S. 66
veganism 3–4, 5, 15, 17, 19, 145, 147; and animal rights philosophy 67, 70–1; based on concern for animals 55–7; as cult 39–40, 66; in France 21; health benefits of 48; misconceptions about 51–3; promotion of in France 66–70; promotion of in the U.S. 72–4; seen as healthy in the U.S. 43–6
vegaphobia 66
vegetarian organizations 23; religious 34; in the U.S. 15
vegetarian restaurants 5, 16, 70, 114, 126
vegetarian starter kits 116–17
vegetarianism 145
vegetarianism 3, 15–16, 19, 20–1, 145; based on concern for animals 23, 31, 50, 51, 56–7, 67, 70–1; Christianity and 34–9; as cult 39–42; environmental benefits of 28–33, 56; in France 5, 21–3; health benefits of 23, 56; for reducing hunger in developing countries 56; misconceptions about 66; multiple arguments for 138; negative image of 39–40, 87; professional endorsement of 43–44; and vitamin deficiencies 49–52

vegetarians: as extremists 67;
misconceptions about 71
Végétariens Magazine 67–8
Veggie Pride 23, 37, 71, 90, 137–8
Veggie Wave 70
veggiephobia 66
Ventura, Jean-José 22
Vick, Michael 80
violence: institutionalized 12; in protests
17
vitamin deficiencies, and vegetarianism
49–52
vivisection 13, 14–15, 17, 21, 111, 123;
see also animal testing; antivisectionism

war of position 92–3
Watson, Donald 16
Watson, Paul 76, 96
Weber, Max 129
welfarism 129, 130, 131, 134, 135

Welfarm 5, 22, 63, 67
Whale Wars (television series) 76
White, Caroline Earle 13
Whites, Zara 88
wildlife protection 3, 4, 13, 21, 22, 13, 78
Williams, Rhys 27, 101, 146, 147
women, oppression of 17
women's suffrage movements 140
World Farm Animals Day 19
World Hunger Program (Brown
University) 28
World Vegetarian Day 41

Yankovic, Weird Al 78

Zald, Mayer 106
Zombie, Rob 78
zoos 3, 82, 96–7; *see also* animal
entertainment
Zuccolo, Ghislain 22, 65